Route of Conquest
(after Prescott)

N

Tlatlauquitepec
Teziutlán
Altotonga
Quiahuitzlan
Perote
COFRE DE PEROTE
Los Altos
Ayahua-lulco
Jalapa
Xico
Zempoala
Cardel
Ixhuacán
Vera Cruz
PICO DE ORIZABA

MILES
0   10   20   30

RECONQUEST OF MEXICO:

*An Amiable Journey in
Pursuit of Cortés*

Reconquest

MATTHEW J. BRUCCOLI

# of Mexico

An Amiable Journey in Pursuit of Cortés

THE VANGUARD PRESS INC.

NEW YORK

Library of Congress Catalogue Card Number: 74–76440
ISBN 0–8149–0742–3
Designer: Ernest Reichl
Manufactured in the United States
of America

To my father
who filled our home with books
And my mother
who placed no curfew on my reading

RECONQUEST OF MEXICO:

*An Amiable Journey in
Pursuit of Cortés*

1

There is, I am convinced, no more exciting adventure story than Prescott's classic *Conquest of Mexico.* I had spent pleasant winter evenings with the book, and it so whetted my interest that I proceeded to track down the historian's original sources. The letters Cortés himself wrote to his king as reports to the "home office"—*cartas-relaciones,* as they are known—proved even more fascinating than Prescott. Then I came upon that most captivating eyewitness account, *The History of the Conquest of New Spain* by Bernal Díaz del Castillo, who had himself been one of the *conquistadores* and who, as a soldier of less than exalted rank, tells the story with more human objectivity than would a high officer who may be prone to polish his own star a little brighter in history's firmament.

I discovered other chroniclers, ancient and anonymous, but I must lay to Bernal Díaz more than to any other the responsibility for my decision to retrace in person the route of the *conquistadores,* against the combined protests of malfunctioning heart, spine, and stomach. I am not the first to be moved to action by the power of the pen.

Perhaps it would be accurate to say I was misled into undertaking the project for, while Díaz describes most graphically the great battles, makes unexpectedly sophisticated comments on events—for a soldier—and discusses a remarkable variety of those elements that comprise history's grand tableau, he says rather little about the kinds of problems a tenderfoot of sedentary habits (at least in recent years) should expect to encounter. Such trifles as blisters and saddle sores were beneath the notice of a *conquistador*—who appears to have been immune to both. I got no clue from reading Díaz that a number of trivialities might loom as matters of some concern to me.

Díaz had good advice on the importance of keeping my crossbow always at the ready, but he neglected to tell me that a common safety pin might prevent the loss of important papers. He gave no warning that I might not be quite ready for some of the tidbits sold as food on the sidewalks of Tlatlauquitepec, and that I had better be equipped with appropriate remedies. The chroniclers of the period, Díaz and Cortés both included, spoke in almost Lucullan terms of the foods with which they were provided by this or that cacique—Dickens did not speak so appetizingly of Christmas puddings. Not once does Díaz complain that something upset *his* stomach.

I did file for future reference the procedure followed by Díaz and his comrades in the treatment of wounds after a battle with a company of Tlascalans. ". . . We dressed our wounds," says he, "with the fat from a stout Indian whom we had killed and cut open, for we had no oil."

Clearly, Díaz would not serve as a practical handbook, at least for a traveler with my more limited objectives. His *History* did, however, help me construct an itinerary. By careful reading I was able to identify certain principal checkpoints on a modern map, though this was not entirely without its difficulties. The old Spaniards had no less trouble with the pronunciation and orthography of Indian place names than does any tourist today. One has only to motor through a few towns in Rhode Island to understand what the *conquistadores* must have gone through in traversing the Mexico of four and a half centuries ago. Moreover, names of villages have changed as often as there have been revolutions. We might remind ourselves, when we are tempted to attribute this confusion of names to instability or

Latin caprice, that Manna-hat-tin became New Amsterdam and then New York within a comparatively short span of years.

Díaz gives only little topographical information. The breed of men of his century must have been far sturdier than ours and I received no warning that, to get from one town to another, I would more than once need to skirt a precipice or climb a mountain. The *conquistadores* would tramp their "one day's march" and, I suppose, take for granted the intervening dangers and discomforts, whereas we today are apt to be quite upset if the back of our airliner seat does not recline sufficiently for a nap on a five-hour flight.

There has not evolved in modern times any systematic, continuing body of research on the route of Cortés, and this is an added difficulty in preparing an itinerary. Some wags of my acquaintance said there would be signs on the highways proclaiming "The Cortés Trail," with arrows pointing the way; billboards hawking attractions in the "Washington-slept-here" tradition. Not so, as I would learn. Indeed, the few scholars who have any interest in the subject differ sharply as to specific segments of the route. Whether Cortés traveled to the north or to the south of the Cofre de Perote, for example, is subject to dispute. My own interpretation of the Díaz story convinces me that the *conquistadores* went to the south of the Cofre upon departing Jalapa.

To compound the difficulties, some towns mentioned by the old writers no longer exist at all. Some, like Xico, have been moved to other locations. The route is far from being clearly defined.

What I owed to Díaz, more than any practical counsel, was the inspiration to do the thing at all. To someone who had received a hint that the blood was clotting, this was a great deal.

The winter moved on at a particularly maddening pace, for my fireside thoughts became obsessive as they lingered on the subject. The more I pondered the project, the greater grew my impatience to be off. But I held firm for an October departure, since it is written that the rains of Mexico cease at precisely midnight of September 30. The wait served the purpose of simmering me down a little, and afforded me the opportunity to think out some of the realistic aspects of an adventure conceived in an armchair.

I decided I should have a companion, for an unshared pleasure is a song with no ear to hear it. To wander alone through jungles and over mountains would be a little rash for one in my effete state. This kind of thing is usually done, of course, but by exceedingly rare spirits. John Colter comes to mind, solitary trapper in the wild Rockies of the early nineteenth century, hiding from pursuing savages, stumbling, the first white man to do so, upon the incredibly eerie phenomena of Yellowstone. Another is Charles Doughty, who wandered for years, a peripatetic hermit among the nomads of Arabia Deserta, ultimately to produce his classic account of Arabian life in the quaint style that so reflected his long isolation from his own kind. Heroes of mine, yet I cannot claim quite so rare a spirit. I looked for a companion, then, among my friends and associates. The results of my search were revealing, and the reader will no doubt recognize many of his own acquaintances among the gallant residents of Suburbia whom I invited to join me.

They included the Scoffers. Oh Columbus! Who has not encountered them? These scoffed not only at the would-be adventurer, but even at the reading of books that treat of the silly subject.

There was the jaded sophisticate who had among his memories the occasion of being served by topless waitresses. Could my proposal offer a fulfillment to equal that?

Another associate declined because he had already had his brush with fearful adventure, having come terribly close to eating an oyster on the half shell. To wander on trails so remote from a Kozy Korner Hamburger Kounter was as outlandish an idea as he had heard.

There were those who would dearly have loved to join me—so they said—but their wives would never allow it. If Xanthippe had never existed, these great libertarians would surely have created her.

Some to whom I wrote must indeed have thought the idea beneath contempt; they never answered the letters.

And others . . .

We must look elsewhere than in New Suburbia for the Humboldts of tomorrow.

I would search alone, then, for the Cortés trail.

What does one pack? This is no Caribbean cruise, nor is it a two-week trip to Miami with motel in the package. Clothing? What do I know about the prescribed garb for an outing of this genre? See Díaz to learn that the followers of Cortés wore "armor" of quilted cotton and suffered horribly from the misty heat of the *tierra caliente;* and some, mostly the poor Indians whom the Spaniards had collected in the hotlands to be their bearers, died from the icy *chipi-chipi,* the drizzle that falls on the high mountain passes.

I assembled a collection of old clothes, including a moth-eaten sweater, a seedy sports jacket, some old shirts already used to being laundered in hotel bidets, and other closet oddments. For shoes the choice was critical. I selected a pair of those well-advertised, lightweight, pseudo-suede shoes called Muffle-Huggies or something like that, more comfortable for pondering than for doing.

Departure at last—and a dilemma. Should all go into a knapsack, or in standard tourist luggage? I had an awkward vision of myself, bespectacled and in business suit, trudging from village to village with a suitcase in hand, counterbalancing its weight by hanging out my tongue. Yet how out of character I should be in the other alternative, dressed like a tramp with knapsack on my back, and in this fashion checking in at a metropolitan ticket counter. I solved the problem by packing my tramp personality within my conventional one: the knapsack within the suitcase. Then, at Mexico's Buenavista railroad station, I checked my city self: suitcase; suits; return plane ticket; portfolio of credit cards; yes, even cash, except for a minimum allowance to see me through a week on the road. All the para-phernalia of my city self I checked at Buenavista, and when I boarded the train for Vera Cruz, it was as a tramp, bearing all my possessions on my back.

2

I spent several days in Vera Cruz summoning up the courage to strike for the "interior." I wandered through the city in its rattling streetcars and buses, browsed through its multiflavored markets, and supped on oysters and *huachinango* at its back-street cafés in order that I might rightfully be able to claim a fair acquaintance with the first city to be founded by Europeans on America's mainland. It was procrastination, of course.

Now it was the twelfth of October, with all the connotations of that date—a temperate, cloudless morning cooled by the steady northern breeze blowing in off the Gulf. It was hard to imagine that this had been a region of pestilence in which Europeans died as a matter of course from the *vómito*—the plague that some historians identify as malaria, others as yellow fever. It may be that October is exempt from the damp heat that once rendered the city pestilential. I found the weather delightful.

Cortés's first allies in his march to Tenochtitlán were the Cempoalans, and their town (now Zempoala) must be my own first stop on the Conqueror's trail. Today one reaches it handily by means of a country bus that, keeping generally parallel with the sea, substantially duplicates the Spaniards' route. It was my first introduction to this category of public conveyance, which bears no more kinship to the buses on which tourists usually make their dutiful inspection of exotic places than that they are provided with wheels. These venerable vehicles are invariably furnished by their drivers with ornate altars over the instrument panels and a profusion of holy relics and pictures rendering the windshields virtually opaque. Nevertheless, the solace and self-confidence offered by this sacred furniture is such that the drivers are able to negotiate some of the world's most terrifying, crumbling, cliff-hanging passes with a blithe insouciance possessed only by those of us who trust implicitly in the goodness of God, and who believe that our mortal stay on earth is a trivial thing compared with Eternity.

Against strong native competition I scrambled successfully for a seat and was promptly imprisoned there by a load of lumber that a wizened old lady dragged into the aisle. Another passenger deposited an improvised crate of turkey poults on the rack over my head so that I was treated from time to time with a shower of the debris that uneasy fowl are apt to generate when they are transported against their will. Then, when it appeared that not another standee could possibly claw his way into the bus, another did precisely that, bringing aboard a floral wreath of such proportions that it had to be warped through the door.

There are express *camiones* on these intervillage routes and there are the slower local categories. There is also a sub-class that stops not only at all local stations but at whatever wayplace the passenger may demand. It was one of these on which I rode, and was therefore able to enjoy a complete turnover of travel companions every few minutes. It must be said that one will never see better humor manifested in any comparable crush of humanity and its baggage. I was to experience many more of these *camiones* and can state that the poor of this world show far more compassion toward one another than do the rich toward their peers. An ancient Indian señora, arrived too late for a seat, squatted in mid-aisle to compound the noisy congestion. The ticket taker attempted vainly to persuade her to move. In the end, passive resistance defeated him; he patted her sympathetically—affectionately, really—on her bent shoulders and climbed over her to seek more affluent patrons. Another customer has climbed in who does not have the price of a fare. The ticket taker lectures him, is quite annoyed with him, has had enough of these goings-on—and lets the matter go because the poor fellow intends to go only a few kilometers anyway. New passengers come aboard at each jungle stop, never fail to bid a *"Buenos días"* to the passengers already on board; and it is *"Adiós"* all around when passengers disembark, some out the door, others out the windows because of the load of lumber in the aisle. I am sentimental and I find myself unable to condemn the State for such inefficient operations.

Passengers bound for Zempoala are supposed to change buses at the town of Cardel, about an hour out of Vera Cruz. This day the driver, making what appeared to me a purely unilateral decision, collected another peso from me and we continued on in the same vehicle. It was *"Adiós"* to my seat companion and her turkey poults, which had long since exhausted themselves in their crate over my head; but her seat was taken by a young Indian lass whose black braids reached down to her waist in the fashion that has not altered since her ancestors migrated across the Asian land bridge these many millenia past. She had in her lap a pamphlet, the title page of which caught my eye. *"Despertad!"* it warned. *"Se Acerca el Fin de las Iglesias?"* (Is the end of the Church at hand?) After four and a half centuries, the missionary zeal of Hernán Cortés was meeting a counterforce. She was an official "agent" of Jehovah's Witnesses, she explained to me, for my interest in her pamphlet had not escaped her. Was I not concerned that man's mean sojourn on earth was drawing to a close? Did I read my Bible? She demanded answers.

"But . . . but, señorita," I stammered, "I have too small Spanish to engage in these profundities."

Did I not know that the Bible was available in the language of my choice? Could I do better with my time than to prepare myself for glory? Read verse such and such! Study chapter so and so! How she went at me, that Indian maid! But could I rightly complain, considering with what fervor and presumption our ancestors have bedeviled hers and continue to do? She had my head awhirl by the time she gathered up her basket of

17

tracts, said her *adiós* with appropriate warnings as to my future conduct, and disappeared into one of those nameless waystops in the jungle. It was a lesson to me not to assume that Indians carried only tortillas in their hampers.

3

The doom of which my bronzed and braided young evangelist had tried to warn me seemed indeed to strike when I stepped off the *camión*, a lonely gringo in the dusty village of Zempoala. But loneliness was the least of it compared with my desolation when I found to my horror that I had lost my documents. My passport was gone; my medical certificate that recorded a long series of disagreeable inoculations, each of which I would have to suffer all over again in the event of future travel, vanished with it; and—the ultimate horror, that imperative of travel south of the Border—my Mexican tourist card was gone! In heart-sinking disbelief I kept returning to empty pockets as if I could somehow re-create the papers by force of will or by spontaneous generation.

The townspeople appeared at their doors to stare at me, a pale stranger—ashen, really—slapping vainly at pockets as I stood in the center of the little square where the bus had deposited me. I was an outlaw in an isolated Mexican village. I must somehow, furtively, escape the country. We *read* of people escaping from countries—but how many of us are ever confronted with the fact? Worst of all, I must give up a project over which I had spent a long winter's—and an equally interminable summer's—excited contemplation, and at the very threshold of its undertaking.

But . . . hold! What would a more seasoned *aventurero* do? What would the wise criminal do? He would think out all his alternatives. But I could think of few. And as I considered my next course, behold! across the square and headed toward me came a dark young fellow in the uniform of the village constable. There! It is precisely this that one does, thought I, as if I had cleverly determined the ploy for myself—one turns himself over to the police.

I will always think fondly of *Agente* Agustín. When I stammered my plight to him he proceeded, first of all, to commandeer a *coche*—an automobile—in which we sped as in a film pursuit after the bus on which I had been traveling, on the chance that we might find the precious documents fallen beneath the seat I had shared with the Jehovah's Witness and the loose-boweled turkey poults. What a wild pursuit it was! The *camión* that had made stops beyond numbering within the twenty miles from Vera Cruz to Zempoala had now turned into a streaking comet. We sped along the coastal road for an hour before, at last, we came upon it and waved it down. The driver was sympathetic, and some scores of Indians who all remembered me well searched every cranny of the bus with me. No documents.

"*Adiós*," they all bade me, "*Vaya con Dios*," as Agustín and I turned back toward Zempoala. We drove along the craggy coast where the lavender waters of the Gulf broke into frothy lace along the shore; past Villa Rica, one of the earlier sites of Vera Cruz; and Quiahuitzlan, the town that had seemed to Cortés to be a fortified port—now an archeological dig on the sheer face of a mountain—but I had no heart for the wonderful historicity or the wild beauty of the scene.

"But it is not finished, señor. We will advertise your lost papers." Agustín's encouragement carried no conviction.

The "advertisement" had in fact taken place on its own momentum, for, when we arrived in Zempoala, it was clear that the entire town already knew it harbored an outlaw. Agustín invited me to make his little constabulary *mi casa*—my home —while he made an inspection of the several streets of the town. The wind might have blown the papers about, he said. A gesture, of course. We now had a consultation with a cluster of elderly gentlemen within a ring of interested villagers on the walk before the constabulary door. They knew before long that I had come to follow the trail of the *conquistadores*.

"But—alone?" one of the elders reproved me gently. "You cannot do a thing like this alone, señor. One needs companions. One gets tired. One may lose more than papers. In all the world there are *sinvergüenzas*—scoundrels."

Another sidewalk advisor suggested to Agustín that I be taken to the *presidente* himself, for it was he alone who had the power —possibly—to authorize preparation of an "Act." Only so could it be explained officially that I had once been the possessor of papers. The "Act," be it understood, would not itself be a legal replacement for the necessary tourist card, but *might* permit my continued presence in Mexico at the discretion of whatever Authority into whose hands I might fall as I continued my way through the villages and sierras that lay before me.

We drove to the *Municipio,* a sort of county seat where the affairs of Zempoala and surrounding towns were administered. The *presidente* was not at his office. If the matter was one of extreme urgency, we were told, he might admit us to his presence at his domicile. Agustín paled a little. In the year 1519, caciques had similarly paled at the Spaniards' insistence upon being taken into the presence of Moctezuma. Despair gave me courage, so I, too, insisted, and off we went, accompanied by a lesser cacique, to seek out the *presidente* at his home.

We drove some miles through thick jungle, blue-black pigs giving way with most swinish reluctance on dirt roads that were little more than footpaths. We passed a few *jacales*—cane huts, whose protective coloration, as it were, made them scarcely visible in the surrounding tangle of growth. The house of the *presidente* was a *jacal* that had, by accretion through the years, evolved into a substantial bungalow, easily recognized for what it was, the dwelling of a person of importance. We found that person in profound slumber on a canvas cot in the shade of a cluster of blue-blossomed trumpets, bamboos, and banana trees.

The broad leaves of the bananas produced a gentle clacking sound in the slightest of breezes, which was most conducive to repose.

Read Bernal Díaz to recognize the *presidente:* "He was so fat," said Díaz, speaking of that *presidente* of four and a half centuries ago, ". . . that I must call him the Fat Cacique." It was the Fat Cacique, in ample flesh, who was sleeping here under the bananas!

The problem of awakening this Presence now faced us. Who was to beard the lion? All I could contribute was a subdued throat-clearing, affected as I was by the obvious awe in which the *presidente* was held by my two escorts. It fell, in the end, to Agustín to touch the shoulder of Caesar—gently. A moment's breathless wait. Another diffident touch . . . and the Fat Cacique stirred. His eyelids flickered slightly, then opened almost all the way when he saw me, an alien of a strange tribe. He rose, puffing from the suddenness with which his position had been altered from horizontal to vertical—as a diver is affected by the bends if he surfaces too quickly.

Agustín and the lesser cacique narrated the tale of the lost documents, and the *presidente* listened, looking with heavy lids from one rude visitor to the other. If he had not been so sleepy, the balance would have been weighed against me. Instead: "The *Presidencia* will prepare an 'Act,'" he ordered, when he was satisfied that my potential for subversion was minimal; and sank back to his cot—but not before he had nudged it a few inches deeper into the shade, for the sun had begun to leak its golden beams upon it through the leafy branches of the banana tree.

We returned to the *Municipio,* where other caciques prepared a most impressive document—an "Act"—on onionskin so transparent as to render it almost impossible to read but imposingly signed and sealed.

My heart was lighter as new life was granted—for the time being, at least—to my great project, thanks to the "Act" of the Fat Cacique. We returned, Agustín and I, to Zempoala.

4

Cempoala, the "great town" of Bernal Díaz, so white and glistening that upon the *conquistadores'* first seeing it they took its buildings to be of solid silver, was first in this New World to welcome the Spaniards. Zempoala, more dusty than silvery and no longer that great Totonac metropolis it had been in 1519 —Zempoala did as much for me. The town adopted me, commiserated with me on the matter of the documents, laughed with me, and fed me. The latter entertainment was initially provided the Spaniards by twelve Indians who, upon instructions from their fat prince, brought to the hungry visitors "fowls and maize cakes." Cortés "thanked them and made much of them," according to their chronicler—and I herewith must do the same for the *familia Marqués*. The charm and grace of this mestizo family!

I was well known to the inhabitants by this time, if for no other cause than that I had not been out of the company of the police since I set foot in the town. When Agustín and I reappeared in Zempoala with my treasured *laissez-passer,* word was awaiting me that I would have dinner, at my convenience, at the *casa de los Marqués* a few doors down the street from my headquarters at the *Comisariat de la Justicia.* The Marqués family had in its number seven daughters, upon one of whom, at least, Agustín looked with something more than passing interest. Thanks to this tender circumstance and their proximity to the police station, I had my first opportunity to share in the homely life of a village family.

Travelers looking from the windows of air-conditioned buses see in passing many of the houses in which the "natives" live and, in the surface tourist judgment, they seem indeed quite squalid. The Marqués dwelling was like that, the usual one-story affair attached to a dozen others, with an unglazed window giving out on the cobbled street. What need for glass windows in *tierra caliente* where the sun brightly gilds the earth in every season. Years of the weather's warm attention had baked the painted calsomine of the structure into the pastel tint so typical of the plastered, multicolored houses in hot places.

I entered directly off the street into the "living" room. It was the principal room of the house, but where very little living was actually done. Another door opened onto a courtyard that was surrounded by the rooms where the various functions of life took place, none more animated, naturally, than the kitchen. This was a "city" house and had no stable off the patio. Instead, the courtyard was ringed with the family's sleeping quarters, the beds sheltered by an awninglike roof but otherwise quite out in the open. Most of the posts supporting the roof were decorated with reed cages for the small birds that are as common an ornament in Mexican village homes as is philodendron in a New York apartment—but, needless to say, considerably livelier and certainly offering a more varied display of color. Toilet facilities were provided in a niche that also faced the patio, with such privacy as a carelessly hung swinging door could afford. Maintaining aplomb was a trial whenever I had occasion to use this rustic "powder room," as my legs could be seen to the knee by the entire family bustling about in the courtyard. I could have spared myself any unease; it is only in the salons of our more polished—yes, uneasy—society that any note is taken of these proceedings, and aplomb has nothing to do with it.

A more attractive, a cheerier family than the Marqués one is not likely to encounter. Its wants so few, its needs obtainable at little cost: one must ask again the eternal question whether they who have an excess of material things are really more content. Two girls of the seven were still to be married. One,

Marta of the waist-length braids, lived at home with mother
à ménage. I suspected it was she who was most likely to alter
Agustín's way of life, and soon. Her older sister—by minutes,
in my judgment as an anthropologist of some hours' standing—
was Graciela—Chela to her friends; she was studying to be a
nurse and stayed with a married sister in Vera Cruz, but happened
to be visiting at home when I arrived in Zempoala. Marta
laughed always; Chela laughed only when the humor of a
situation was unequivocal. Perhaps in this the Totonac genes
dominated the Spanish. Yet Chela, the solemn one, wore her
hair in a short, boyish style. What *is* an anthropologist to do
with such contradictions?

I sat at table in the living room, a lonely stranger, "cynosure
of neighboring eyes" that stared at me through the open window
as I puffed my pipe (this alone will label the alien in Mexico),
while Marta, Graciela, and señora their mother fussed about in
the courtyard and kitchen, generating the odors of something
unknown and presumably edible. Graciela stayed at her culinary
duties while Marta came out from time to time to exchange
a pleasantry, as a hostess will whose guest is left too long alone.
Most charming was the utter absence of shyness on the part of
these pretty, bronze fawns. When my pipe went out, Marta took
the matches from my hand and tried unsuccessfully, and with
pealing laughter, to relight it for me. A pipe smoker has his
own way of cupping his match over the bowl, which I did;
whereupon Marta conjured up the precise look of admiration—
no, adoration—as I enwreathed myself in smoke, as much as to
say I was marvelously clever. A bright female may grow as a
wildflower in her jungle, but will know without a tutor how
to make a man feel he is the Caliph of Baghdad and Commander
of the Faithful. "Did you see how he did that?" she cried to the
onlookers at the window, as if she could scarcely believe her eyes.

Dinner took some time to prepare. No one is more gracious
than the Mexican housewife who is called upon without warning
to prepare food for the passing stranger, which she will set
about to do patiently and even cheerfully, without benefit of

thermostatically controlled ovens or electric mixers. She will say, "*Sí señor,* you are in your house," and set to it immediately. Her prompt acceptance of the commission will bear no relation to the actual time of serving, and the visitor will soon learn that it is considered quite boorish of him to hurry the cook. Let him inquire as to how dinner is proceeding, to be sure, in order that he may conduct interim business while he is waiting. "The *comida* will be ready when you return," he will be assured—but he had best not return too soon. Señora has no stock of canned foods, and will likely need to visit the hen rather than the refrigerator for the eggs. Furthermore, in the villages tortillas do not come (please God they never will!) in sanitary, waxed-paper wrapping, ready to "heat-and-serve."

So I sat, *en grand seigneur* awaiting dinner, sipping from a large tumbler Marta had brought out to me. It was a pleasant concoction of their own, prepared by mixing *caña* (sugar cane); *buro,* an herb that can be identified in the Aztec pharmacopeia; and spirits. Rose-colored, its effect upon the humor of this lonely wayfarer was also rosy. It functioned well as apéritif, so that when the first course, an innocent-looking salad, was placed before me, I lost no time in sampling a forkful. Brimstone and fire! I gasped, and my eyes poured tears.

"Marta! Graciela!" I cried to the girls.

"*Mande*—you wish . . . ?"

"*Estoy muriendo*—I am dying!"

Muffled laughter in the kitchen. Graciela came out with a glass of water. I asked her, with croaking voice and genuine curiosity, "Can you and Marta eat this? Then you are mightier than I and all *my* tribe."

Graciela, the one who seldom smiled, smiled. "*Dice que nosotros somos más fuerte que él,*" she relayed happily to Mama and sister, who were busy in the kitchen with the next lethal course. It is natural that the Totonac is pleased to be told that he (or she) has powers superior to those of the foreign invader. In support of this thesis, out came little brother Isidro, six years old and three feet tall, who drew up a chair beside me, reached for a tortilla (a stack of them, hot off the fire, had been placed on the table—the very "maize cakes" of old) and with that antique utensil—the tortilla is as much a utensil as it is a food-stuff—proceeded to scoop up and consume every bit of the fiery salad. He never blinked and, moreover, eschewed with a soprano snort my offer of the water Chela had served me in my extremity.

Eggs *ranchero* came next. Throughout all my subsequent wanderings I found eggs available, usually *ranchero,* which means on a bed of whatever saucy herbs may be traditional with the particular family serving them. The dish therefore may vary from community to community, but will always have the common denominator of chopped *chiles,* the peppers that give Mexican cuisine its atomic character. The salad had so de-nerved my throat and palate that I was able to manage the eggs with relative ease, as well as the frijoles accompanying them, Isidro polishing off whatever I left on my plates, to the delight of his mother and sisters.

Mexican cooking in the sierras and the interior villages must be little changed from that of pre-Columbian times, and the archeologist makes as authentic an inquiry into the everyday ways of the ancient Indians when he eats this cuisine as he does by digging up their potsherds.

A pleasant after-dinner stroll down a street or two, around a corner and then another, through a rich, green thicket of tropical vegetation where twinkled bright blossoms of oleander and orange, and lo! rising out of the jungle, the pyramids that figured with such drama in the history of the Conquest. Pearl gray against the backdrop of forest and sky, the *teocallis*—the houses of god—stood there, slumbering in a grassy clearing. (*Teo* is god; and *calli,* house. So mind-boggling a similarity between the Nahuatl *teo* and the Greek *theos!*)

I waded through deep grass, my ankles stung by burrs that drew blood; and stood before the hoary monuments envisaging the scenes that must have been when this was the great ceremonial center, barbarous and splendid, for fifty thousand Totonacs from fifty neighboring villages. Men and women, priests and princes once thronged this haunted plaza in obeisance to Quetzalcoatl and his pantheon of gods.

Three principal pyramids stand today, the characteristic pre-Columbian, stepped pyramid forms constructed in Time's mists of round river stones and a mortar of crushed seashells. After the Conquest, the Spaniards permitted the jungle to swallow the temples, for they were pragmatists, busying themselves with the business of colonization, gold mining, and other matters of more immediate concern than the preservation of heathen relics. By the end of the nineteenth century, trees had sprouted from the crevices between the stones of the Great Pyramid and the Temple of the Chimneys.

The site of the great ceremonial center is now cleared, in the main, of wild growth. The pyramids, except for their sylvan surroundings and the abrasions of time and weather, must have looked much as they do now on that day when Cortés ordered the idols toppled from their summits and replaced with Christian altars.

No other action more graphically describes the character of the man. He had found friends in a world as remote and hostile as the moon. Keeping these Totonacs as friends, propitiating them, could mean survival to the Spaniards, possible success in an impossible venture, their very lives. But, no! He would not countenance the idols to which his hosts sacrificed.

The caciques of Cempoala, just recently subjugated by the Aztecs, were smarting from the demands of Moctezuma's tax collectors—there was a delegation of them in town at the very moment of the Spaniard's visit—who would take young men and maidens for sacrifice if onerous tribute was not paid. So the Cempoalans offered to ally themselves with the Spaniards against the tyrant of Tenochtitlán. What good fortune for the undermanned *conquistadores*. In their wild innocence, the Cempoalans offered their guests eight Indian girls to cement friendship,

". . . all daughters of chiefs," says Díaz, great gossip as well as historian. ". . . These are for your captains, and this one [the niece of the Fat Cacique himself] is for you, milord Cortés. She is the mistress of towns and vassals." A tempting offer, though another chronicler has noted that the royal niece had more money than good looks; but the single-minded Don Hernando replied that before the Spaniards could accept the ladies they would have to abandon their idols: ". . . The girls must become Christians and the people must give up sodomy." (We are told by Bernal Díaz that ". . . they had boys dressed as women who practiced that accursed vice for profit." Díaz was as honest a soldier as any, but possibly not above painting the potential enemy in his blackest colors.) Give up your idols, change your nasty habits, and we will accept your princesses and your allegiance, says Cortés. This took a bit of brass, considering that the handful of Spaniards had the sea at their backs and uncounted hosts of barbarians at their fore.

"Take the girls, gentlemen, but let our gods be," the Cempoalan chieftains said in darkening mood, and gathered their warriors to defend the pyramids.

Cortés turned to his men. "If we do not pay God so much honor as to stop them from sacrificing to these damned stones, how can we ever accomplish anything worth while? Knock them down!" Díaz, the participant, describes the ensuing scene: ". . . Some fifty of us soldiers [note his characteristic choice of pronoun], clambered up and overturned the idols, which rolled down the steps and were smashed to pieces. . . . When they saw their idols shattered, the caciques and the *papas* [priests] . . . wept and covered their eyes, and they prayed to their gods for pardon . . . saying that they were not to blame, that it was the *teules* [the foreign devils] who had overthrown them."

Cortés, gambling, had read the situation well. Since calamity did not immediately descend upon the Cempoalans when the idols fell, the caciques decided the old gods had been false—or at least had not the mustard of their reputation after all; and the Cempoalans were won over to the Spaniards. Because the ploy succeeded, Cortés gets credit as a wise man, as well as a brave one. If the outraged Indians had let fly their ready arrows, history, if it remembered Don Hernando at all, would say he had been a quixotic fool.

A final, troubling thought: did the toppling of the idols really prove their falseness? With the violation of their gods, the Cempoalans did in fact see the Totonac civilization die.

5

Who can contemplate a relic of antiquity and not have the urge to reach out and touch it? Who can stand before a pyramid and not feel compelled to climb it?

I made my way up the front face, as processions of Totonac priests had done centuries past. These ancient American pyramids, unlike those of Egypt, were essentially platforms atop which were located the temples proper—to be exact the *teocalli* of which we have spoken—where various rites of an extraordinarily bloody kind were performed. Prescott tells us that the walls of the temple that had been on the pyramid where I now stood ". . . were black with human gore," and the priests who had custody of this temple had wildly disheveled hair so matted with blood it could not be combed.

It was in the company of their ghosts that I now sat, on a fragment of crenellated wall—and imagined how this place must once have shrilled with the screams of sacrificial victims. All silent now. Below me, bounded on three sides by the now empty ceremonial court, the great pyramidal forms. A family of Indians appeared from somewhere threading its way, Indian file, through the brush that covered the plaza, past the pyramid atop which I sat; and disappeared into the high corn in a *milpa* off to the east. They had delivered canastas of grain to market at Zempoala and were returning to reload their baskets in the field: father, mother, and a son who might have been five or six years old but bore more than his fair share of the family's burden of living.

I resumed my lonely ruminations. An episode of the Conquest, as swashbuckling as any in fiction, had occurred here, where I sat. Velásquez, the governor of Cuba who had sent Cortés on this voyage of discovery in the first place, realized that Cortés was the last man in the world he should have selected if he, Velásquez, was to gain any profit or glory for himself. Cortés stood to get *all* the profit and *all* the glory from the venture. So the governor, spluttering with vexation, dispatched Pánfilo Narváez to relieve Cortés of his command. But if Cortés had been too big to be Velásquez's man, Narváez was not big enough.

Cortés was busy relieving the great Moctezuma of an empire when he received word of the arrival from Cuba of his replacement. Leaving Moctezuma in Tenochtitlán, in the hands of his trusted captain, Pedro de Alvarado, Cortés returned to Cempoala to take care of Narváez in person. It is said that the confrontation took place precisely here, on the pyramid on which I now sat. On a dark, wet night the doughty Captain-General made a surprise attack on his rival, who had thought he had found for himself and his men a stronghold among these proud pyramids. Poor Narváez was no match for Cortés, however, who not only defeated and captured the governor's man in the battle but gained his opponent's men for his own side. What swordplay had taken place on the steps at my feet! What clanging of steel! What cries and Spanish oaths! And now, solitude—absolute stillness.

But no, the stillness was not absolute. I thought I heard a faint, melancholy whistling. Do lizards whistle? for they were my only companions on this haunted pile, scuttering among the stones. The whistling became louder and was now identifiable as a lugubrious tune of some sort. In my ghost-ridden humor the tune would have sounded mournful if it had been "Yankee Doodle." It seemed to rise out of the stones of the pyramid, and set my spine atingle. Then it came from the broken wall beside me, as if some spirit were actually perched at my elbow. A hand appeared, reaching over the wall. Quetzalcoatl! Now followed a young fellow in straw sombrero, who coolly bade me *"Hola!"*

as if we two had had a date of long-time standing to meet thus on the Great Pyramid. A stocky chap, he was rather lighter-skinned than usual in *tierra caliente.* He was beardless, but sported the longest sideburns in Mexico. Perhaps in no other setting would he have appeared so satanic.

"*Buenos días,*" I responded, uncertain whether my position in the company of a flesh-and-blood Totonac was more secure than if it had been the unsubstantial spirit of one of his ancestors in this eerie solitude.

We chatted for a half hour, and I never completely lost my uneasiness, although, in fact, a more gentle person one could not deserve to find in the circumstances. It was only—I thought nervously—it was only that this fellow might be just the one who had gotten it into his head to avenge his ancestors. The conditions were so right: utter solitude; the two of us atop the very pyramid from which Cortés had toppled the gods of his forefathers; a glistening camera slung from my shoulder to place unfair temptation in his way and compound existing incentives to foul play.

I told him I had come to his country in order to "discover" the trail of the Spaniards.

"*Vaya!* Have you come alone to do this, señor?"

"No," I said quickly (for I have read suspense novels). "*Hay compañeros*—friends who are about to join me." I scanned the horizon, like Bluebeard's anxious wife.

"You are wise," he said. The Zempoalan elders had said, precisely on that subject, that I had *not* been wise.

Though at the moment I could not tell, my new companion was in fact a most amiable young *chamaco,* lonelier than I and glad of the opportunity to *platicar*—to chat with what was to him an exotic stranger who was slightly mad to be wandering about on forgotten byways just for fun.

We talked of many things.

"*Nueva York?* It is so far away. *Tan lejos.*"

"No, not far," I said. "A flight of but five hours."

"*De verdad? No me diga*—you don't say! Then *la ciudad de México* is more distant than your country?"

I explained that the airplane on which I had flown down from New York flies at some six hundred miles per hour. Since it was evident to the *chamaco* that one who had flown at such speed could not be an ordinary human being, it followed easily that he should equate me with those *indios,* the *voladores,* who climb the pole at the time of the *fiesta* (there stood such a pole in the ceremonial area below us) and fly from its summit suspended by their heels. They too are a special class, hereditary practitioners of the black magic. They smoke a certain demonic *yerba,* perhaps the same weed the señor was puffing in his pipe.

I had thought the *voladores* were just high-spirited young fellows such as those who climb greased poles at our own fairs and carnivals. But no. The *voladores* are a different breed of men, like dervishes—feared a little, or held in that subtle contempt with which ordinary men look upon those who have direct communication with supernatural forces.

Ah, he would like to travel to faraway places as I was doing— perhaps as far as Mexico—*la Capital*—someday.

"*Fumando yerba como yo y los voladores?* Smoking the magic grass as I and the *voladores* do?" I asked.

"*No, por Dios!*" he said, shrinking at the idea, for he was not a *mágico*—no offense—like me and my fellow weed-smokers.

I would learn quite early in my wanderings not to be surprised at the familiarity with certain particulars of history exhibited along the trail by the *campesinos* and villagers. They will tell of things almost as matters of family experience that we must go to the books to learn. I asked him, *platicando,* who was this Cuauhtémoc whose name I saw even on the labels of beer bottles.

"Cuauhtémoc was the last prince of the *indios,* whose feet the Spaniards burned so he would say where the treasure was hid but he never told."

"A terrible thing for those Spaniards to do!" I hastened to say. "These pyramids," I asked, to change the subject, "who were the builders?"

"Ah, señor, the ancients—long ago. Before I was born," he said, and added, to emphasize the immeasurable antiquity of the monuments, "—before you were born, *aun.*"

"And what became of them?" I was leading him—prying—to see what a *campesino* would have to say about his people's cultural past.

"Murieron—they died." The reply had a simple honesty.

While we chatted, the two young sisters Marqués arrived, having completed their household chores and come to be my guides among the ruins. They, too, displayed a respectable knowledge, though charmingly contradictory, of their history.

"Marta," I asked the laughing one, "would you sacrifice *me* on these altars?"

"Pues—no-o," she said, hesitating slyly, "not *today.*" Thus she reserved a little latitude for herself in the event of a change in the balance of power tomorrow.

Graciela, the serious sister, did not see this as a laughing matter. To begin with, in her view my knowledge of history was faulty. A lecture followed, in a tone quite severe but nonetheless agreeable to hear, coming from a pretty lass in the soft language of sixteenth-century Spain (no affected Castilian lisping for the Mexicans!) Toltec . . . Totonac . . . Zapotec . . . Mixtec . . . Aztec . . . Chichimec . . . she straightened me out on the respective virtues and failings of all these nations. It was a musical litany from Miss Sobersides as she clarified history for me in most competent fashion, completely exonerating the Totonacs of Cempoala, *her* forebears, whose culture, she asserted, was *most* advanced and pacifistic, and whose ritual offerings had been limited to flowers, fruits, and fowl! I had my choice of accepting *her* authority, or that of Bernal Díaz and Cortés himself, who reported that they had seen with their own eyes the ghastly evidence of human sacrifice in Cempoala. I reserve my decision.

6

It was not easy to part from my new-found family in Zempoala. This is one of the difficulties of solo wayfaring. A coincidence, a stroke of good luck (or of bad) may bring one into the life of hospitable friends in some byway, as happened to me on this occasion; and one must summon up all his singleness of purpose to take up gear and say farewell, hardly daring to hope to encounter similar cordiality at the next strange station on the way.

I would happily have lingered a while longer in Zempoala, but no sooner had we returned from our visit at the sleeping altars than a tropical storm burst suddenly on the village, as tropical storms do. Within minutes Zempoala had become a little Venice. As I stood in the doorway of the *casa Marqués* watching the downpour, a bus pulled up into the town plaza and I was informed that this *camión* would be leaving for Jalapa within the hour. This was curious, because there was no regular service directly to Jalapa from Zempoala. One needed to return first to Cardel—or so I had been told. This was my second experience with the ambivalent schedules of the local buses.

The sudden turn of weather seemed to have drawn down the curtain on my day in this village; so, impetuously, and in order not to prolong the little ache of parting, I took up my knapsack, bade *adiós* to all, and boarded the *camión*, once again having the good luck to secure a seat.

One of the great pleasures of life, to counterweight its sorrows, is the knowledge that one has friends in far-off places; and it was no small gratification to me to be able, now, to count friends in the Zempoala where the *conquistadores* had formed their first alliance on the march upon Moctezuma; where Cortés and I had both negotiated with fat caciques, each in our way, in order that we might pursue our march. I departed, a document of sorts in my pocket and my pack upon my back. Cortés, more potent negotiator, departed, according to his chronicler, with forty Totonac chieftains to serve as guides and two hundred *tamanes,* or porters. Prescott speaks of thirteen hundred warriors and a thousand *tamanes.* Take your choice. One of the fascinations of exploring the Cortés trail is that information is not cut and dried. In any case, the little army of adventurers now had some allies in the New World—and somebody else to carry the baggage.

Among the characteristics distinguishing the fairly complex culture of the pre-Columbian Mexicans from that of any Old World civilization of comparable, relatively advanced development, the most distinctive is that, having no domestic beasts and, incredibly, having never stumbled upon the concept of the wheel, the Mexicans were a load-bearing race. The cargo of the splendid, if barbarous, indigenes was borne as a matter of course on human backs. The *tamanes* comprised, therefore, a significant and indispensable percentage of the Indian labor force. This load-bearing propensity is manifest to this day, and one never ceases to marvel at the burdens carried by men, women, and children in the sierras and the cities as well. I frequently observed women among my fellow passengers in the intervillage buses who, upon reaching their stations, would take up formidable cargoes by means of a strap of some sort that fitted across their chests. A supreme effort would get their canastas off the ground, the weight causing the poor creatures to stagger backward. They recovered by leaning well forward, then tottering ahead for a few steps. Thus, forward and backward they would stagger and reel until they found a tenuous balance, setting off for market, or for miles to some distant, thatch-roofed *jacal* that was home, laughing and chattering like birds all the way.

The *camión* was furnished predictably with its elaborate shrine of saints and angels, and the driver was another of that mad confraternity of dashing desperadoes who use their vehicles as their *charro* predecessors once used spirited horses. He plunged the bus unhesitatingly through the torrents the storm had unleashed in the streets, and within minutes we had left the town and commenced our ascent from the tropic lowland of the coastal region. Night fell abruptly as we rattled and jounced on, but not before we had seen coconut palms and banana trees give way to geometric patterns of maguey, plantings of coffee, and fields of sugar cane and corn.

To gain Jalapa, the *camión* literally gnashed its teeth as it ground out altitude in an endless series of loops. We *norteamericanos* do not realize how wild and rugged is our neighbor south of the border, and it is impossible to appreciate fully the stamina and perseverance of those sixteenth-century adventurers unless one covers the ground for himself. Flashes of lightning blinded me and possibly the driver too, and made black night blacker as the bus hugged the sheer faces of deep *barrancas,* moving from tier to tier of craggy sierras. We stopped at a few villages—generally nothing more than collections of *jacales*—to deposit or board a passenger or two—in all cases Indians bearing sacks and canastas of papayas, guavas, and other exotic produce. The windows of the huts toward which they headed or from which they came glimmered with the feeble yellow light of oil lamps. The scene could have been little different four centuries ago. To be sure, the road's fragmenting macadam had not been here then, and the Spaniards had needed to hack their way along Indian trails that had never seen the traffic of horsemen or cannon. A grueling anabasis it must have been. The *conquistadores* must have grumbled and groused, I suppose, like soldiers everywhere and in all times, and whispered behind their hands that their Captain had lost his mind. They made their jokes—grim ones probably, for the chance of becoming the entree at a cannibal feast must have been constantly on their minds. No idle fear, either, for more than one soldier met that fate before the adventure was done.

I had spent a winter with my history books, but only now, as we climbed to Jalapa on a stormy, gloomy night, did I begin to understand the history of the Conquest in human terms.

7

Jalapa is a beautiful little city whose principal streets all run uphill—never down. It spills off its shelf in the foothills of the Sierra Madre Oriental like caramel on a pudding. At an elevation of some 4,500 feet, the town has fled the shifting dunes of the coast and the tropic heat of the lowlands. Here, instead, are the more temperate airs to which those who could afford it in the olden days used to escape during the vaporous season of the *vómito*. It was a right respectable town even when the *conquistadores* first came upon it, a city of canals, according to its name's meaning, though there is no trace of a canal now that I could see. Altogether a lovely place it must have been.

It is a measure of the Spaniards' pertinacity and stamina that all Bernal Díaz deemed it necessary to record about their difficult ascent is the terse statement: ". . . We left Cempoala in the middle of August 1519, marching in good order, with scouts and some of our swiftest soldiers in advance; and the first day's march took us to a town called Xalapa. . . ." (Cortés himself says *two* days' march—and I say three. They could not have been *that* swift.) And that is all the mention of Jalapa.

Ah, the reader is catching us up on our capricious spelling. Jalapa . . . Xalapa. . . . But what is a conscientious chronicler to do? The name is spelled one way or the other at will. On one map it is "Jalapa" and on another "Xalapa," though the same printer publish them both. On the front of the town's buses it is "Jalapa"; but "Xalapa" is lettered along the sides. It is "Xalapa" on page one of an official document, and upon my word, "Jalapa" on page two!

Well, whichever it is—let us settle for Jalapa because we will have a superabundance of X's before we reach Tenochtitlán—the city deserves a little more attention from us than was paid it by good Bernal. There are a number of points of interest here, not the least of them being the pretty girls, for this is a college town and its co-eds are as bright-eyed and long-stemmed as any to be found in Old Stateside U. They are the daughters of the well-to-do, whose mothers probably—whose grandmothers certainly—wore tall combs and lace mantillas, studied music and the domestic arts in the seclusion of their own patios, and were not available for an anthropologist the likes of me to ogle. These pert creatures contrast provocatively with the Indian girls. In the great covered market these sad little creatures may be seen weaving a thousand species of flowers into colorful garlands and bouquets.

Indian artistry with flowers is truly extraordinary. But where, one asks, can enough buyers be found for such vast quantities of floral displays as one sees in the shops and markets everywhere in Mexico? In fact, the Mexicans of all strata of society have the same love of flowers as had their remotest ancestors. I often saw Indians whose stock of pesos must have been slim indeed, staggering under the cruel loads I have mentioned, but carrying withal a colorful and delicate arrangement of blossoms to their poor hovels. It is humbling to discover sensibilities in those we hold humble.

Such as these were the Indian girls whom the Spaniards saw when they reached Jalapa. They found them exotic—beautiful, even—and so did I, though it was evident by observing their mothers that they withered fast, like the flowers they wove. They added much, we may be sure, to the attractions of this new world for the lusty and lonely young warriors (that bearded centaur, Cortés himself, was only thirty-four) as they came upon these unknown cities, wondrous in their unexpectedness, and marveled at the variety of products offered at the *tianguis*—the market; and eyed the girls who sold them.

Jalapa was my gateway into the sierras, the last "civilized" town I would see before I disappeared into the mountains, and I was once again, as I had been in Vera Cruz, timid to commit myself. I needed to invent no pretext, however, to delay my journey. Here I awoke to the awful realization that the "Act" of the fat cacique of Zempoala would not serve me beyond that fair town's limits. Jalapa's banks would sell me no pesos in spite of the most abject pleading and complex reiteration of my story. If I had this problem here, what must become of me in the villages of the interior? I had no choice but to present myself before the *Municipio* of Jalapa and again make public declaration of the lost documents.

The reaction of the municipal nabobs seemed to be kind. They listened to my story with sympathetic *tsk's* and a *"Qué barbaridad!"* here and a *"No me diga!"* there, appearing to view the matter as difficult but not altogether beyond solution. Another "Act" must be executed to supplement—no, *supplant* the one of Zempoala. This must have the seal of their own *Procuraduría General de Justicia* for, while it could not be denied that Zempoala was a place of doubtless archeological importance, neither must I be allowed to forget that it was Jalapa that was the capital of the State. José Antonio Cerbera was assigned to accompany me to the *Jefatura*. In this suave fashion was I turned over to the police!

The *Jefatura* is an ancient building from the colonial times, with dimly lighted rooms from whose low-vaulted ceilings the calcimine flakes and settles as dust on the floor and furniture. *Tosca's* Mario Cavaradossi could have sung his aria here on the eve of execution, and an audience would have applauded the authenticity of the setting. It was about ten o'clock in the morning when I entered this grim precinct; it would be dusk before I emerged.

José Antonio guided me through a series of introductions to functionaries of successively mounting importance, narrating my story to each and in no case omitting to explain that the señor had come to follow in the footsteps of Hernán Cortés. The reader should know that Cortés is by no means a revered hero in contemporary Mexico. Indeed, why should he be? It is not the birthday of Lord Cornwallis that is celebrated in our own country. The colonial period lasted three hundred years in Mexico, a time of *encomiendas* that gave to the colonists the Indian's land and control of the Indian's destiny. It was a time that saw the conquered people degenerate at Spanish hands, and their considerable civilization liquidated. It must be said that the maltreatment of the Indians was strongly opposed by enlightened clerics—Las Casas, among others. We will return to this sad subject. The annihilation of a major, complex, if barbaric, civilization was virtually complete within the lifetime of the Captain-General, and his name will be associated forever with the worst features of the Age of Discovery, at least in the view of the conquered.

It is possible to make extenuating arguments. That delightful aristocrat, Madame Calderón de la Barca who, genteel Victorian lady though she was, rode and tramped through the wild, primitive Mexico of the 1840's with a verve to put my own timid venturings to shame, had this to say of Hernán Cortés as she recollected the sacrificial victims of the Aztecs: ". . . twenty to fifty thousand human victims annually! . . . Let the memory of Cortés be sacred, who, with the cross, stopped the shedding of innocent blood, founded the cathedral [of Mexico] on the ruins of the temple which had too often resounded with human groans. . . ."

So there we are. The fact is that one does not win friends automatically by identifying with Don Hernán—and my escort, José Antonio, *did* keep bringing the matter up when I would have preferred to stress other virtues in my confrontations with Mexican authorities.

The *jefe* himself was a handsome young man with a pencil-line mustache and a color tint that clearly identified him with Moctezuma and not Cortés. I have considered—and dismissed—

the possibility that he kept me in a chamber adjacent to his courtroom in deference to my position as a visiting *norteamericano* while he devoted himself to redressing the grievances and disputes of countless lesser wretches. The surroundings, which I was given more than ample time to meditate upon, were not conducive to peace of mind. The décor of my oubliette included a couple of the most rickety of chairs; an antique table on which sat an equally venerable typewriter; and a sofa that bristled with broken springs, spewing out its stuffing as if it had become quite intolerable. What other forgotten Cuauhtémoc had sat there while his tormentors deliberated fresh tortures? A stack of vintage rifles stood unguarded in a corner.

But the undoubted attraction—the point of interest that drew my eye irresistibly—was a large "Wanted" poster on the wall. There simply never has been a more grizzly trio than the three desperadoes it advertised. A reward of ten thousand pesos was offered for their capture.

"Señor," said Don José, observing my interest in the poster, "these cutthroats are hiding in the sierra through which you will be passing, and you will have the opportunity to make your fortune."

In time my turn came to stand before the *jefe,* who smiled rather tightly, I thought, as José inevitably prefaced the account of my missing papers with an explanation of my infatuation with the despot who had conquered the land of the proud official's fathers.

"But my interest is historical," said I weakly.

The *jefe* summoned a deputy, with whom he pondered the case at some length. The deputy was then dispatched to the *Municipio* on an errand I did not at first comprehend. José explained that the execution of a new "Act" was one of supercession, involving concurrence by several branches of government. The procedure took time, time that I had little choice but to employ in the contemplation of the *bandidos* who stared at me relentlessly from the wall.

At last the deputy returned and sat himself before the typewriter to prepare the "Act." He was no typist, and the document, in quintuplet at the very least, was prodigiously long, its preparation made even longer by the deputy's many halts to wind back the typewriter ribbon. This required that the reel be twirled with his finger. When the "Act" was at last completed, it was discovered that the carbons had been inserted backwards, so the whole dreary thing had to be done over! The *jefe,* when he had disposed of several more aboriginal causes, signed the document with a singularly undecipherable scrawl appropriate to a person of high station; then, unsmiling, he shook my hand, wished me *buena suerte,* and released me to whatever fate lay lurking in the sierra.

8

Xico was my next objective. I had no idea how to reach it, or what to expect if I did—and this was to be very much my normal form whenever the time came to leave one place and set off for another. It is not true that twentieth-century sophistication necessarily gave me the advantage over Cortés. He had his Cempoalan guides who knew the lay of the land, who gave him sober counsel, advance information on what accommodations might be available, and similar basic tour data. The information I would gather was rather more haphazard, and not always of the hard-nosed variety.

After my release by the Jalapan police, I returned to my hotel to advise the desk clerk I would be checking out on the following morning. I was moving on to Xico, I told him.

"Xico, señor? You cannot wish to go to Xico."

If the response nonplused me momentarily, it was not because I thought he was being rude—the clerk was a most pleasant fellow. But even a more experienced Mexico hand could be put off by a discouraging word from a native. For all I knew, there might be a plague in Xico. "I am a student of your country," I said. "Is it forbidden to visit Xico?"

"*Por Dios,* no," he said. "I did not say it was forbidden, but that the señor would not wish to go there."

"Why should I not wish it?" I asked.

"It is the place of the *brujas*—the witches."

He was having fun with a stranger, surely—"putting on" a dude in the old tradition of the West—and he expected me to laugh, I thought. So I did. *"Entiendo*—I see you are telling me a joke."

"No, señor. I am telling you the truth. It is not something of which I would speak lightly."

"You mean," I said, "that *la gente*—the people in the country —tell stories about witches to the children?"

"These are not stories for children," he said. "It is well known that they of Xico, and the vicinity, are able to turn people into beasts. They have had this power since the ancient times."

There was not a clue in his tone or manner to suggest he was not in dead earnest. And, more dismal still, he added particulars. If anyone in Jalapa had a score to settle, he could have it done cheaply by paying a *bruja* in Xico. It happened every day. There were hundreds of people in Jalapa with one or more atrophied limbs, as the señor had surely observed. This was all the work of Xico witchcraft.

I would have found this information less startling if my informant had been an unschooled *indio* of the sierra. But this was a literate chap whom I had interrupted at his reading about *el boxing* in the daily paper. A city man, he was—in a business suit. And he was earnestly warning me of people who might take it upon themselves to transform my head into that of a chicken. It was unsettling.

That last evening in Jalapa I had dinner in an odd combination of fruitstall and restaurant in which several rough, wooden tables were placed between mountains of vegetables, fruits, sacks of corn meal and *caña,* and other staples. How limited our choices become in the Hunky Dory Super Markets of our Suburbia when one has seen chayotes and papayas, tamarinds and guavas, quelites and ejotes in the least of village *tiendas.* Great cauldrons of wondrous-smelling things steamed in the kitchen of the establishment, and the grocer-chef persuaded me that the *caldo marisco* bubbling in one of them would give me pleasure.

He ladled out a pot of the shellfish stew and a *muchacha* served it, together with the inevitable stack of hot tortillas and a saucerful of halved *limones*. The *limón* is a kind of green lemon—no, a sort of lemony lime—no, it is only itself, a tart *limón,* and is as standard an accouterment of the southern Mexican cuisine as is the tortilla. I attacked the stew awkwardly, for the crustaceans were whole and their armor impregnable to knife or fork. A merciful little gentleman at my table—he was a barber with a shop down the street—explained that one squeezes the *limón* over everything (*muy sabroso, señor!*), then breaks the shellfish apart with one's fingers, and sops up the soup with the tortillas. This I did, and found the dish superb. We chatted, and soon I had told him how I was pursuing the trail of the *conquistadores.* He declared the project astonishing.

"Who does such a thing?" he cried. But he was kind to me, much as the devout Moslem is kind to an idiot who, touched in the head by Allah, must therefore be treated reverently and helped along his way.

My guide to the etiquette of a *caldo marisco* instructed me as to my route to Xico. To my delight, it would involve others of those mad little rural *camiones.* As for the town's reputation for being hag-ridden, he reacted with a somewhat subdued laugh that could better be described as sheepish than happy. He said it was an old story; but I believe it would have been difficult to extract a sworn declaration from him that it was not a true one. Some of his best friends were from Xico, he seemed to say. And, indeed, his associate in the barbershop was one of them. This was my good fortune, for his fellow *peluquero* would know where I might get horses for the journey beyond. Now, this was heady stuff; I had not touched a live horse since my school days! Yet it was something I must consider, for, beyond Xico, the route was impassable by any but four-legged transport. I agreed to stop by the barbershop later to consult with his associate; and my new friend, having finished his dinner, left me to finish mine.

When I had eaten, the *muchacha* brought me my accounting, which by my decoding of it, amounted to about a dollar—very little indeed for a dinner that had been truly splendid. I paid it and left to seek out the barber, and I was in his shop having myself a Jalapan haircut on condition that the barber not touch my incipient beard, when in came the *muchacha* from the restaurant. The girl had been sent in search of me (since I had been seen conversing with the barber at dinner, they had a clue as to my whereabouts) to explain that I had misread the dinner bill and had *over*paid by a half-dollar, which she refunded me! So much for those who cry that all the world is bent upon cheating them.

Barber number two, dark, younger than his partner, said he would meet me at my hostel early next morning and accompany me to Xico to help arrange for "beasts." He insisted, against my protests, that the barbering business could spare him. When morning came, he never appeared. It may be that he had second thoughts about being seen with me. Having discontinued shaving at the outset of my journey, I may have begun to look too fearsome for his taste. Nor did he show up for duty at the *peluquería,* to the mortification of Barber number one, who had recommended him. I absolved him of blame, but once again found myself, knapsack on my back, venturing alone into the unknown.

Bernal Díaz says that from Jalapa—*he* writes it Xalapa—". . . we went to Socochima, a fortified place with a difficult approach. . . ." Most authorities identify the present-day Xico, or rather Xico Viejo (its original site) as the Socochima of the *conquistadores'* route. Perhaps the best verification of this is the fact that the approach to Xico Viejo is indeed difficult, as I would shortly discover.

Today, the highway and railroad, upon leaving Jalapa, proceed to the north of the Cofre de Perote, en route westward to Mexico City—and offer comfortable transport thereto, whether by train, bus, or motorcar. The bulk of scholarship, however, holds almost perversely that the Spaniards traveled southward when they left Jalapa, to follow trails along the southern shoulders of the Cofre, the box-shaped mountain known to the *indios* as Naucampantepetl. Local opinion supports this view and the inhabitants assert *sin duda alguna*—positively—that the *conquistadores* passed their way in 1519. One will find some who say they remember the occasion very well.

My own choice, then, was clearly this one, for would the ghosts of Cortés and company elect to eat the dust of the highway to the north when the hills were fresh and green to the south? It seemed to me I would have a better chance of encountering them on the wild southern shoulders of Naucampantepetl.

A *camión* whose final disintegration was postponed only by grace of a particularly vivid shrine of the Virgin of Guadalupe that the driver had erected alongside the gearshift lever took me to Coatepec—Snake Hill, if you please. There I dismounted with a gaggle of cargo-bearing aborigines of both sexes, whom I joined in scrambling down a steep embankment to another road where we would await a second *camión,* one that, hopefully, enjoyed grace for survival equal to the first. This would carry me to Xico. The wait was pleasant. A thousand feet below the level of Jalapa, this is a region of oranges and coffee, fragrant with the perfume of both, and innocent of any but the most occasional gasoline vehicle. My companions squatted by the roadside, those who were equipped to do so immediately proceeding to nurse the babies whose heads had been bobbing loosely about in their mothers' rebozos, demonstrating the extraordinary resiliency of infant necks.

A half hour later our *camión* appeared, rattling up out of the valley, and we were aboard and again on our way, slowly, for we were now regaining altitude with every winding mile that we advanced upon Xico. Our companions on the road were mainly pedestrians who, together with their burros, bore the overflowing cornucopia of the region.

The roads, as one advances into the interior, are not good under normal conditions, and were considerably worse during my visit due to the heavy rains of the previous spring. Our stops were as numerous, naturally, as were the passengers who, dismounting, were swallowed forthwith by the thick greenery that was turning more to scrub oak and pine as the altitude became less congenial to broad-leafed, tropical vegetation. The newer *autopistas* of Mexico run straight for considerable distances, particularly on the approaches to the capital, but no country road goes anywhere without tacking laterally in order to progress forward like a ship clawing to windward. Scale on a map of this wild and beautiful land is virtually useless for purposes of estimating surface distances. A village may come well into view, but the apparent proximity may be deceptive. Intervening *barrancas* will need to be circumnavigated, craggy hills surmounted, and one soon learns that a village appearing to be within hailing distance may be a respectable march away. In these hills it is said with justification that one does not draw up a chair to dinner until he has first planted his foot in the plaza.

I have had tiring walks and drives in this country, but never tiresome ones. The route over which the Cempoalan guides took the Spaniards is one of savage beauty that the centuries since have done little to alter; and it was affecting for me to see a landscape as those long-gone adventurers had seen it; to see even slight details through their eyes. When the modern, daydreaming wanderer stubs his toe against a stone on the trail, there is a good chance that a *conquistador* of long ago, his mind for the moment on mother or sweetheart whom he had little chance of ever seeing again, had stubbed *his* toe against the same stone. Relays of tireless runners delivered *huachinango*—the red snapper of the Gulf—fresh daily, it is said, for the great Moctezuma's table via these very trails. One can become exhausted following in their footsteps, but never bored. And if the traveler finds a segment of the route that now provides the convenience of a "modern" *camión,* why, his fellow passengers are the Totonacs and the Aztecs themselves, in the flesh, seeing poor times, perhaps, but carrying the blood of some of history's most intriguing peoples. Tiresome? Not if one has any interest at all in what people were, are, or will become!

Such thoughts occupied me constantly, and I was brooding thus when the rattling vehicle deposited me in Xico, in the middle of a cobbled street that seemed to run straight on to the foot of a misty mountain. The street was lined on each side with the plain faces of single-storied dwelling places, their original reds or blues baked by time and the sun to chalky hues. No hotel could I see; no restaurant; no bus station where I might seek advice, exchange a sympathetic glance with a fellow wanderer, make conversation or at least eavesdrop on the conversation of others to somehow mitigate my loneliness. An Indian woman emerged from one door and disappeared into another like a mouse running along the wainscot. That was the extent of the traffic. No children playing; no cluster of idlers standing at the street corners, of whom I might make an inquiry. I could see the twin bell towers of the colonial church farther down the street, looking unaccountably grand, at least from a distance, but dust seemed to have settled upon Xico, smothering all mortal sound. Where, in this ghostly town, would I sleep this night?

Then, as I stood there trying to figure my next move against a very real sense of hopelessness, a rotund, bespectacled gentleman in sombrero and tight trousers that gave him a Pickwickian air looked out from a doorway, stared a moment or two, then approached me and announced: *"Soy el Juez."* My first encounter in Xico was with the town's judge and, as it would develop, a more unlikely rascal a lonely wayfarer could not hope to meet.

9

Don Manuel invited me to stow my knapsack in his judicial quarters (one of those anonymous doors that lined the *calle* opened to this seedy little cell) but we stood out on the street to visit together. This did not mean the judge was deficient in hospitality. The tiny office could not have contained half the number of gentlemen of the town whose eyes apparently had been at their windows and who soon came around to see the stranger. Xico does not see many.

The townsmen, in straw sombreros all, proved to be an amiable lot, all cronies of Don Manuel's—and very soon to be cronies of mine. My desire to be accepted into the community, as well as a wish to be inconspicuous in these hills, dictated that I should wear similar headgear, so with great good humor on the part of the entire company I tried on each of their hats to determine size; but the cephalic indices in the mountains of Mexico differ distinctly from those of our evidently fatter northern heads. Of mine, at any rate. I found no hat that would fit me, either on the heads of my new friends or in the shop around the corner where abided a vendor of vegetables and sombreros.

Xico, I learned, is prouder of its association with the march of the Spaniards upon Tenochtitlán than official Mexico's usual wont toward the subject. At least those Xicotecas with whom I fell in seemed to be. Don Manuel, for one, was not loath to proclaim that the Spaniards certainly had passed this way, and he spoke of Xico Viejo, whose population had been decimated by the plague. He thought it had been in the early eighteenth century, *más o menos,* that the plague had struck, driving the survivors down from the hill to settle the Xico of today.

Bernal Díaz says that the people of Socochima (i.e., Xico-chimalco; i.e., Xico; i.e., Xico Viejo) did not pay tribute to Moctezuma, were well disposed toward the strangers who were marching against the tyrant, and gave them food. Even such distant memories persist, and it can be observed that the descendants of those people who found in the Spaniards of 1519 allies against the demanding Aztecs, while they do not always revere the memory of the conquerors in view of the latters' conduct after Mexico fell, do tend to identify themselves with the winning side in the epic that was the Conquest. Attribute this leaning to the simple fact that in the earliest times of the colonial era there were practical advantages to being on good terms with the party in power. The Tlaxcalans were a case in point. After their initial resistance to the intrusion of the Spaniards into their independent territory in one of the most gallant, if bloody, episodes of the Conquest, the people of Tlaxcala joined with the intruders and participated with even greater ferocity than had the Spaniards themselves in the destruction of the hated Aztec empire. The Tlaxcalans were a formidable ally in Spain's subjugation and colonization of Mexico. As a result they thereafter were granted privileges not generally enjoyed by the rest of the indigenous peoples. Such opportunism is not exclusively an Indian trait. (It should be added here that this advantage did not survive into modern times, and the Indians of Tlaxcala are today not especially distinguishable from the descendants of the less cooperative tribes.)

Well . . . the people of Xico became *my* allies. Don Manuel, in answer to my question regarding the accessibility of Xico Viejo, pointed toward an area on the dark face of a distant mountain, a foothill of Naucampantepetl. *"Sí señor,* you can reach it in a couple of hours, *nada más*—no more," he assured me. The cronies debated how best a gringo of unproven strength might climb to Xico Viejo, the majority holding that it would be an easy walk, though too dangerous for beasts! But I should be accompanied, they said, by someone who knew the turnings of the trail. While they speculated on which local boy might be drafted to my service, a sturdy young chap strode by, his sombrero shading the sullen face of brooding King Ahuizotl himself. His trousers tapered tightly to his ankles, the style by which the Indians of the sierra can usually be identified and favored by them almost since pants (along with Christianity) were introduced to the New World by the Spaniards. It was obvious he would choose to discard one of his legs rather than walk abroad without the machete that swung at his hip.

"Honorio," the *juez* called to him. "The señor will give you five pesos [forty cents!] if you will show him up to Xico Viejo."

"When I have eaten," said Honorio, closing the deal with no further conditions or codicils.

A half hour later Honorio presented himself before me— he did not often so hurry his meals, as I would learn—and we set off, I succeeding only for the first few minutes in matching the stride of my taciturn *compañero*. We traversed the few streets of the town, looked in on a couple of other grocers in vain for a sombrero that might fit me, and were soon at the foot of the mountain, on an unseen escarpment of which had once perched the Socochima of old.

The path by which we began our ascent was paved in a rather pretty pattern with cobbles—evidence that the stones had been laid by Spanish colonists centuries before; and passed along cool groves of orange trees with foliage more blue than green, their fruit hanging like lanterns of patined bronze. A pair of Indian women, mother and daughter they may have been, were coming down the path, laughing as usual under ghastly burdens of firewood. " *'Diós,*" they bade me gently. The Indian woman's is that kind of Madonna-like beauty that renders her such a perfect, if unwilling, subject for a camera, whether she is in repose—how seldom one sees her so—staggering under her eternal cargo, or washing at some brookside. And from her, always, that shy smile and soft " *'Diós.*"

Within a very few paces the colonial pavement came to an end, a short section to reappear later on and again disappear. Over the entire route of the conquerors' trail one finds this to be so. And yet one sees few stone walls, fewer cobblestone structures, to indicate that the inhabitants have used the ancient road as a quarry. But perhaps the stones have been carried off to build some rich man's *rancho* beyond the view of the trail on which I passed. A mystery, nevertheless, how bits of ancient pavement would appear unexpectedly in secluded byways. The dirt trails in between would stretch on for miles, deeply rutted, veritable *barrancas* washed out of them during seasons of ravaging rain —ditches often so deep that climbing out of them to negotiate a bit of pavement again was like scaling a wall. It was because of this rough character of the trail that my friends had advised against making the ascent on horseback. It would be, as they said, "unsafe for beasts." And yet, as we mounted upward and the trail became steeper so that the stones loosened by my scrambling feet rattled down the hill behind me, lo! *arrieros* appeared, leading burros bearing loads of maize and firewood and lumber in the form of planks new-sawn up above where timber might yet be found—planks so long that the lumber rather than the beasts carrying it seemed to be fitted with tiny hoofs, for one must look hard to see the animals themselves. These little caravans were on their way down to deliver their cargo to Xico. "*'Diós,*" of course, from all parties, with kindly, almost courtly doffing of sombreros by the *arrieros.*

We struggled (certainly *I* struggled) to gain a rise, only to have the path drop precipitously down again into a dell, twist around a turn or two at the rocky bottom, and start again to climb. False summits all, for when I thought I had reached a peak, down again we headed, my calf muscles knotting from the strain of holding back. But the next climb gained a little on the last; and after an hour, and then another, the air had become perceptibly rarer and I found I was swallowing mightily, but with little effect, as if at a carpenter's rasp that had lodged in my chest.

What had I done! It was such little time since that coronary occlusion had felled me and I had been the subject of sober conferences decreeing grimly that I would be better advised thereafter to find surface modes of travel to and from my office —the subway steps would be too steep! Now I was climbing a wild Mexican mountain, panting, aching, delaying until it seemed my lungs would collapse—no, *had* collapsed, before I reined Honorio in and advised him to pause and rest for a bit under an oak. I am nothing if not considerate of others!

Why do we do such things? Is it that we must strive for unattainable heights because only so can we satisfy a longing for untouched beauty? Or must a man test himself, even secretly, and strive to achieve small victories?

For several hours we dipped and rose. Sometimes our path was notched into the steep side of a valley into whose depths I must stare with almost unwilling fascination, asking myself always, "What am I doing here?" and answering invariably, "How *good* it is to be here!"

There are different solitudes. The solitude of the mountains affects the spirit differently than does that of sea or desert. These still sierras have a quality of their own, lonely but not desolate; noiseless yet not voiceless. It is tranquil here, serene. Background music is provided by hidden brooklets that play for us a rippling obligato. Behind hummocks and hills, hidden by copses and high corn, these cool mountain streams chortle and giggle as they rush over the black lava stone of the sierra. Their laughter grows louder when we approach them. How mischievous they are when we must ford them by jumping from stone to wet, polished stone. The sound of their laughter proclaims their names. This crystalline rivulet is Huehueyapam; another is Xoloupan. Petlacalapa, the pretty one, murmurs; Tlanyahualapan, the giddy one, chatters. They frolic among the rocks, repose for an instant in saucerlike craters, then forfeit tranquillity by cascading in aquatic joy to the rocks below, there to plash and prance a multicolored ballet.

It happened! I lost my footing when I thought I had survived

one of the last impossible rises, flayed my arms futilely to re-
cover my balance, to keep from rolling down the hill with the
tumbling stones. I learned now, and dearly, that Muffle-Guppies
are no substitute for sturdy hiking boots when one is indeed
following the Cortés trail and not just reading about it. My toes
wedged between some stones—it was good fortune or bad—
keeping me from losing my hard-won altitude, but the tendons
were wrenched cruelly.

Honorio, stone-faced always, rushed to help me to my feet, then
turned and disappeared into the reeds and bamboo. Hish, hish,
I heard his machete cut, and out he came with a tall staff for
me to lean on. It was sturdy, aromatic, and supported me, limping, up to Xico Viejo and down again. I would limp into
Tenochtitlán and, months later, would be limping still through
New York streets. The wayfarer may be as insouciant as he
pleases about his traveling habits, but let him be correctly shod
when he seeks the legendary kingdom of Prester John!

Consider this, then, to appreciate the calamity. I am on top
of a mountain. The threshold of my march in pursuit of whatever it is I pursue has scarcely been passed and two hundred
miles still roll out before me. My foot dangles limply and
when I touch it to the ground it must be done gingerly. I
must grip my staff tightly to lighten each step, and soon a blister
blooms on the palm of my hand. Other blisters have already
burst on the soles of my carelessly shod feet. What am I to do?
My limited options allow but one answer. Push on, say I,
making a virtue of necessity.

Honorio looks at me curiously. It is apparent that he, who
has so far spoken to me only in Nahuatl "ughs," has something
he must say. "I ask your pardon, señor," he begins . . . but
falters. Then, grimly determined, *"Qué es su edad?"* I answer that
I will be glad to tell my age, but he must first tell me his.
"Veinte y cinco, señor." When he was born, say I, my twenty-
fifth birthday had been long gone. "Ugh," he says, or rather,
"Xugh."

It is easy to see that I am a mystery to him, for I have been clambering up the mountain with a will, if without grace or agility, even though I have no maize to collect nor kin to visit when I reach the top. The sun has been beating down on my gray head (for so he sees me) and the mountain is taking its toll. I must pause from time to time to wipe the perspiration from my spectacles so that I will not go blindly toppling down to be swallowed by a bosky *barranca*. All this, so that I may see some stones in the place where Xico had been when the Spaniards first came? I believe it is now that Honorio decides to be kind to me; and the five pesos I am to give him are only a secondary motivation. He is perceiving the fact that I am come to call on his ancestors, and am taking considerable pains to do so. I am close to being a friend.

A few stone mounds are all that can be seen of Xico Viejo. But there is also a trace of life, for a half dozen Indian huts are nearby and a few more are hidden from my view behind the various tiers of hills. One rough wood hut is slightly longer than the others, about the size of a garage, and of similar architecture. It is a schoolhouse, the most remote and isolated institution of learning I have ever seen. The faculty has spotted me, and children trot out, a dozen or so, to pipe a shy *"'Diós"* to me. The faculty, which consists of a single young man in something like a business suit to give him dignity before the student body, greets me and bids me *bienvenido*. He comes from Xico down below, as I had done today, but he, *every* day. He does not understand why I should marvel at this. *"Pues, señor,"* he tells me, "the *arrieros* and *cargadores* make the round trip twice a day to bring down the crops." It is so, Honorio informs me. This epic ascent that I had achieved in some three agonizing hours, a feat that had bruised me, wracked my lungs, knotted my every muscle, crippled my foot, perhaps forever—this ascent is made twice daily by the men who gather and deliver the corn—and often by their women, too!

Now, as if this astonishing information must be illustrated for me, I hear a rhythmic "Hoop, hoop, hoop, hoop" from down the trail beyond the schoolhouse. The chant grows louder and a cloud of dust rises behind a hill. A troop of *cargadores* appears, their rapid, shuffling gait the cause of the dust cloud. Each man is short, gnarled, of indeterminable age, wears a dusty serape, and carries an enormous sack of maize. A tumpline— a strap across his brow—helps support the weight (one sees his picture to the life in the ancient Aztec codices), and he must lean well forward and keep his hoop-hoop-hoop pace brisk, else gravity will lay him on his back. I must step aside quickly to let this troop huff by. A hundred yards more and they stop before a particular hut. The act of stopping causes their loads to drop to the ground with a great thud. From this dusty depot the incredible bearers take over, those who must carry the loads down my man-killing mountain. This is how it has been done since the days when relays of *tamanes* delivered trade goods and tribute from the Gulf to Moctezuma's warehouses, and for a thousand years before.

Wretched people, who must bear these burdens hoop-hoop-hoop until their terminal fall from the weight of that final load? Are they so wretched? I know they were laughing as they shuffled past me. I know no expense-account luncheon could ever taste as good to me as their pulque and frijoles taste to them after a tour of duty of *this* order. I, for one, have never looked with particular envy upon the doddering "civilized" pensioner who never did what he had dreamed of doing when his juices were running, and now, too late, can only dream. If he can do that. No, I am not certain that the one is more wretched than the other.

Our descent from Xico Viejo was, if anything, slower and more fatiguing than our ascent. My own opinion is that it is harder to go down a mountain than to go up. Going down is regression; going up is aspiration. . . .

We still seemed to climb up as often as we scrambled down, for such is the nature of this wild terrain. Once or twice we had to step aside to make way for the brisker-paced *cargador* and his little old mother who were making their last trip for the day; and at last, five hours after we had set off on this expedition, and in deepening dusk, we were on that bit of pavement that passed through the orange grove. This time, aching, desiccated, I eyed the fruit in the trees with something more than my earlier aesthetic interest. This was observed by Honorio, who gestured to me to wait while he entered the grove. I have respectable Spanish, but Honorio always communicated with me by grunts and signs, as though it were against nature to address a gringo in normal tones.

He emerged from the grove with several fine-looking oranges, green on the outside but moist gold within, and I proceeded to claw off the rind with my thumbnail. Honorio held up a hand, indicating that I desist. Taking the orange from me, he danced it around on the palm of his hand while his machete whooshed and flicked at it—and handed me a perfectly peeled fruit! Never, never have I tasted so exquisite an orange. Nor did it detract from its flavor to know, as I had learned in the course of our ascent, that Honorio was by profession *matante de puercos*—a slaughterer of pigs—and that his machete was a tool of his trade!

10

The judge had locked up his "chambers" for the day by the time we returned, but a neighbor was keeping a patient vigil and had a message for me from the good Don Manuel. It directed me to go to his home, where he had taken my gear, and where, if I would do him the honor, I was to pass the evening with him. Honorio guided me to the judge's domicile, an adobe dwelling like all the others in a cobbled side street. I knew by now that behind the doors and shutters of these unpretentious habitations one stood a good chance of finding quarters that were something more than merely functional—primitive, perhaps, but with an air for which one pays arty decorators substantial fees to simulate. So it proved to be with Don Manuel's place.

He greeted me at the door and led me through the main *sala,* a combination of parlor and bedroom, into the kitchen, where I found the cronies seated around an uncovered deal table. A bare light bulb hung from a roof beam, the house boasting no ceiling other than the roof itself, which sloped, as is customary, downward toward the inner courtyard. The sun had fairly set by now, and the small light revealed only dimly the several sombreroed figures who sat in obeisance to a bottle of rum. One could imagine Rembrandt's "Syndics"— a wild version. One of the gentlemen present I had not yet met, and I was presented to him by my host. It was the *ex- presidente* of Xico, Don Adalberto Andrés, voted out of office not long since and in consequence, as he shortly revealed, of a distinctly cynical turn toward the world's vagaries. He was tall and thin, in contrast with Don Manuel's squat pudginess, and sported a sombrero that must have cost twice as much as the ordinary utilitarian headgear worn by the others—probably as much as a dollar. We shook hands and he apologized for the sad condition in which I found the village—things were going downhill under the new administration. But what was one to expect from politicos without ideals? Heaven forbid that he should speak thus only because his chair in the *Municipio* was now occupied by another! The gentlemen present would attest that, in other days. . . . "True . . . true," murmured the cronies.

"*Qué importa!*—What does it matter!" said the *ex-presidente*, filling a glass for me. I toasted Mexico with a sip. Don Adalberto held the bottle out to top off my glass—or so I thought. No, he would not pour until I emptied it. I did, and he refilled it, and his own. I sipped again, and again he held out the bottle. "Just a drop," I begged, for my glass was quite full. "No, señor," said the *ex-presidente*. "A question of honor. You must empty the glass or I cannot pour." I tossed off the rum and he refilled. And so the evening started.

The rest of the company drank on a similar schedule, inhibitions fled, and conversation ran a broad gamut. They spoke with some vehemence on the subject of a locally unpopular measure then being taken by the United States to control the flow of marijuana across the border; but my new friends graciously deemed me personally unaccountable and, in my honor, toasted my country. Other toasts followed, and another bottle. My pursuit of the Spaniards' route of conquest naturally came under discussion, and I was complimented on the depth of my research and the attention I was paying to detail to ensure the authenticity of my project.

"But señores," I babbled, for the rum was thickening my tongue, "I am missing a critical element in my march. I travel without the company of a Doña Marina." (Doña Marina is an important figure of the Conquest, and we will discuss her more fully in her proper place.)

"*Ni yo tampoco*—nor do I!" quoth the judge. "*Es mejor así*— it is better to travel without the nuisance of women." It came out that he was at the time having domestic difficulties, a condition to which all the present company was privy. The cronies nodded their agreement with the judge's misogynism of the moment.

At this point I was completely unconscious of blisters and sprained tendons, but the same potions that had anaesthetized me from pain sharpened my awareness of the absence of women in this party. The rural Mexicans are a strongly male-oriented society, of course. This does not mean, however, that the female sex is not discussed and female properties defined. "*Si lo hacen, no lo dicen,*" said the judge, which called for a toast to the secretive nature of Xico's womanhood.

If, earlier, I had worried about where I might find food and lodging in this mountain village when I landed here so utter a stranger, I now knew a solution to the problem must be in the hands (or claws) of Quetzalcoatl, God of Life and creator of men. Of this much I am certain: that if, back home in Suburbia, some caprice should seize me and I were to go deliberately past my regular station stop to seek adventure at the end of the line, there would be a good chance I would be arrested for vagrancy. Here, in the Mexican sierra, I was deep in my cups with the caciques of the village.

A woman now came in from the patio with a basketful of fresh-baked tortillas. Ah! Food at last, thanks be to the Feathered Serpent! Chilli of the judge's own making had been heating on the oil stove and was presently served us in earthen dishes. We scooped up the stuff with the tortillas—I with the deftness born of drink. How good the lethal concoction was! The *ex-presidente* demanded that I empty my glass so he might honorably refill it. I did, and he did.

"A toast to the Judge for the excellence of his cuisine!"

"To hell with women!" cried Don Manuel, and announced he would recite a poem.

"*Viva el Juez!*" we cried, and he recited the verses that I here offer in translation. I guarantee the burden, though I have changed the lady's name, being unable to find a rhyme for Ortencia:

> Do not weep, my dear Amparo
> 'though you've let me sip your honey.
> I would marry you tomorrow
> But I do not have the money. . . .

Further toasts were obviously in order, and proposed. I asked if it would be possible to hear some music; and a noisy consultation ensued as to where some evidence of folkloric art might be found to please their gringo *compañero*. There is, as we have said, no cabaret, no theater, no restaurant, no hotel in Xico—but one of the gentlemen thought it might be possible to assemble some amateur *mariachis*. Honorio, who had sat, unsmiling, apart from his betters through all this evening's sipping and supping, was dispatched somewhere, and returned—how much later it is hard to say, for the *ex-presidente* continued to test my honor and time had become for me a great, amorphous cloud. Honorio had succeeded in locating a group of *muchachos*—fellow members of the pig-sticking confraternity, for all I knew—who would serenade me at the house of Señora Ramirez y Castro.

Off we went: the judge, the *ex-presidente,* the cronies, and I, through the streets of Xico, whooping and yodeling, the night illumined only by the spirits we had imbibed so freely. At the señora's—she was a particular *amiga* of the judge—a new bottle of rum awaited sacrifice, which rite we dutifully performed while the slaughterers of pigs thumped out *mariachi* and *ranchero* airs. Remarkably good musicians they were, unless the rum deceived me.

The factors that distinguish the Mexican culture-style from that of old Spain make an interesting study. Being no musicologist, though I am most fond of the art, my own conclusions may be overly reactive and romantic, but I believe, with William Weber Johnson, that there is the beat of the Aztec drum—the *huehuetl*—in the thumping *guitarrons*. The *chirimia*, a clay flute of pre-Hispanic times, is recalled by the peculiar falsetto with which the singers reach their impassioned high notes. This falsetto is a musical mannerism I never heard in Spain. Something vaguely like it is found in the ululation of the Arabs, and one is tempted to imagine a link with Moorish Spain—but in fact the sound is more closely related to the spirited whooping associated with the red man of America, North or South. At any rate, the firewater with which we plied ourselves (I must not lay all the blame on the *ex-presidente*) helped stir up emotions such as the *conquistadores* must have felt when they preceded me on this path and were regaled with equivalent entertainment by the very ancestors, perhaps, of these copper-skinned *chamacos*.

It was not easy during this bacchanalia to keep my mind on the problem of tomorrow's stage of my journey; and only by the exercise of a considerable force of will—which I was surprised to discover I possessed at all—could I turn the conversation from time to time to this important matter. Happily, the boisterous company had entered into the spirit of my expedition and much advice was offered—between toasts. The advice was rather confusing, as may be imagined under the circumstances. It gave me insight, not found in formal history, into the human problems faced by the *conquistadores,* who must have been as susceptible as I to these digressions. But out of the alternatives proposed by my fellow celebrants, I was able to distill a plan. If I was to remain faithful to my purpose of following the footsteps of Hernando Cortés, I would need a horse for the trail beyond Ixhuacán de los Reyes, where the mountain pass would begin to approach an elevation of ten thousand feet. The *mal país*—the bad country, this segment of the route was termed by the old Spaniards when they traversed it four and a half centuries before.

The judge and the *ex-presidente* put their heads together and determined that I should call on the president in Ixhuacán, who might help in procuring a suitable mount. So, while the tenor sang, sobbing:

> "See how sad I am!
> Where are you? Where did you go?
> Why have you abandoned me
> To wander through the sierra? Ay yeeee! . . ."

Don Manuel commanded a sheet of paper from Señora Ramirez and prepared for me a letter of introduction to the *presidente* of the Commune of Ixhuacán, Don Agustín Díaz, so replete with honorifics that it was a wonder to behold, considering the condition of the author.

I had compared an ancient map (as reproduced in my edition of Bernal Díaz) with a modern one, and had decided that the high sierra town of Perote must be the point at which I should issue from the mountain if I wished to stay on the conquerors' route and, at the same time, remain within a day's march (or horseback ride) of a civilized town. My friends agreed this would be a good plan, and assured me that the *presidente* of Ixhuacán would help me achieve that goal.

The drinking continued and we contributed our own spirited *"ay yeeee's"* to the singing. Now Honorio, his facial expression softening from sullen to merely surly, leaned toward me and whispered, *"Cuidado, señor,* this night may despoil you of *mucho dinero. . . ."* A surprisingly touching gesture of concern for a stranger's welfare on the part of this crusty *chamaco.* I was less than carefree about the prospect of a transit through the "bad land," on horseback and alone. Why not a stalwart young fellow like Honorio, I thought, to accompany me over the Pass and tote my gear as far as Perote? Did not Cortés have his *tamanes?* I made the proposal.

"De acuerdo," Honorio agreed, and, assuring him I would watch my pesos during the current carousing, we established early morning—which was fast approaching—for our departure together on the next leg of the *ruta de Cortés.*

First we must survive this night, which was proceeding with

gaiety unabated. The judge continued to recall verses on the theme that was obviously obsessing him at the time.

> We have done it, but don't sorrow,
> For I vow, sweet Isabel,
> That we'll wed in church tomorrow
> And in City Hall as well. . . .

The Aztecs continued to chant and Don Adalberto continued to pour. The subject of my fruitless search for a sombrero came up, and the *ex-presidente* clapped his own upon my head, declaring the search ended. It fitted me perfectly. He forbade my saying a single word when I protested his generosity, so we drank a toast to my newly adorned head and another to his bare one; and by now the forces of oblivion began to reconnoiter about me. It was perhaps the last opportunity I would have to make a conscious tender of payment to the *mariachis* for their music and to the lady of the house for her rum before I collapsed and they should feel obliged to go through my pockets. Hands under the table, I showed the judge a five-dollar bill, U.S. currency, with the view of determining if our entertainers would accept American money. The judge clapped his hand over the note and pocketed it, whispering that he would take care of everything—and perhaps he did, for there was no subsequent demand on me. Soon after, we were weaving our way through the dark streets of sleeping Xico; the judge, the *ex-presidente,* the cronies, and I, supported by the grim-faced Honorio. All drifted their respective ways until the judge and I were left before His Honor's door. *"Su casa,"* he said, "This is your house," and, letting me in, he left me to collapse on his bed while he went to spend the night at "his other house." I was in no condition to trouble myself with what he meant, or why he grinned as he said it.

11

Long before I fully wakened in the cold dark of predawn, I was praying for death. What was this black place? My foot throbbed, but not so exquisitely as my head. In between, I was nothing but a network of pain, for long-idle muscles had been too sorely tried on the ascent of Socochima. This was surely how those poor wretches had suffered when their hearts were torn out on the altars of the Aztecs' monster gods. I had the father of all hangovers.

And who was the jolly Buddha in Boy-Scout-style sombrero entering this purgatory with such a bright and cheery *"Hola! Buenos. . . .!"*—as if Don Manuel had not met me quaff for quaff just short hours past!

Groaning, I gave him what I could of a morning's greeting and staggered, teeth a-chatter, into the courtyard to find a cold, unlighted adobe outhouse furnished, *mirabile dictu,* with a flushing fixture (though seatless). To one side of the patio was an open cistern whose icy water I splashed on my face with a shudder. While so doing, in semiconsciousness, I was greeted with a singsong *"Buenos días, señor"* by the woman who had made our tortillas the night before. It was a Biblical tableau: the lady filling her bucket at the cistern—and I in my underwear! I fled back into the house.

While I dressed, Don Manuel set a pot of water to boil and asked if I would drink tea. I would, indeed, and my host poured. The warmth of it was good, and to my fund of learning was now added the lore that tea is not necessarily brewed with tea leaves. The judge used another herb from that Aztec pharmacopeia. *"Muy bueno para el hígado,"* he cheerfully assured me, insisting that it was certainly "tea" and promising that my liver would benefit.

I declined any other breakfast—there is little doubt it would have consisted of the chilli left over from the previous feast—and assembled my gear so I might set off at sunrise for Ixhuacán on the first *camión*—hopefully to die en route. The cold mountain air was an effective restorative, however, and by the time the judge had escorted me to the yet-deserted plaza to meet Honorio and await the *camión* my head was fairly clear, though the aching muscles and bruised foot made it difficult to carry myself with anything like the swagger of a conqueror.

It was some time before Honorio appeared—time enough for the judge to cheer me with other verses.

> I am like a ripe berry that bursts
> sweetly in the mouth.
> The *mujer* who experiences me
> dies or goes *loca*
> And wanders distracted through her house,
> desire watering her *boca* [mouth]. . . .

The *camión* and Honorio arrived at the plaza simultaneously. He silently adjusted my pack to his own sturdy frame, and it was farewell, again, to new-made friends in a remote mountain village. I will forever wonder how sober must be the justice meted out to the citizens of Xico by that rascal, Don Manuel.

It had been a relief to learn there was a *camión* to take me from Xico to Ixhuacán. All the maps I had studied showed a prominent fat line that denotes a fair road slimming alarmingly as it penetrated the sierra, to become a mere hairline from Xico to Ixhuacán, with footnotes warning of dubious passability in the event of rain. Beyond Ixhuacán, the maps showed no lines at all. Nothing. Passage through that segment would be as it had been four and a half centuries ago.

For us who see buildings, even cities, rise, grow old, and fall within the space of a generation or two—some of the ghost towns of our West, for example—it is beyond understanding that a route so significant in the discovery and development of our great New World should, nearly half a millennium later, remain as it had been a hundred years before the landing of the Pilgrims at Plymouth. Why, *we* would have properly improved it— motels and snack shoppes all along the way.

The information about the *camión* to Ixhuacán was naturally a snare and a delusion. It is true that we left Xico on the little bus, but not a half hour later, when we had reached Coatepec, Land of the Snake People and depository of coffee beans and oranges, we learned that we must disembark. The bus continued on back to Jalapa, had no intention of going to Ixhuacán at all, and never had had. I love Mexico. I love its mountain towns. The villagers have full possession of my heart. So patient they are, and so kind to strangers; there is no question they are destined for heaven. But while they are here on earth, I will never, never delude myself that a *camión* that they tell me will take me from point A to point B will, in fact, do so. That bus will drop me off somewhere along the way, but it will not be so crassly predictable as to deliver me *to* B. It may exceed my expectations and take me *beyond* B, but it will do so only if I have it on firm, local authority that B is its absolute terminus!

I will not be told that my proficiency in the language is at fault, and that I misunderstand directions. This time Honorio was with me, and he had not only Spanish, but Nahuatl as well. No, it is simply the case that the good people want to please you; and if they think you are made happy by the information that such-and-such a bus will take you to such-and-such a place, why, that is what they will tell you. Whether or not it is true is less important than the pleasure their misinformation temporarily gives you.

So we disembarked at the crossroads that was already familiar to me. But this time I knew the luxury of having my knapsack on Honorio's back while I kept my hands in my pockets, as a latter-day *conquistador* is expected to do.

The Indians were there, squatting on the roadbanks as proliferous as the wildflowers; and, as usual, they were eating, the very youngest ones from their maternal sources of supply, the older ones from their canastas, which never fail to bring forth a *taco* folded around some beans, at the very least.

Mexicans in the rural areas do not eat much. It would be cruel to quip that they do, for in material things they are the poorest of the poor. But they nibble often. A bus or train rarely stops for a moment without a throng instantly converging upon it, hawking *tacos* and *quesillos,* jellies and fruits, ices and *refrescos,* edibles in wonderful variety. The windows of the cars bristle with arms reaching down to the vendors, as if the travelers had just arrived from a trying journey through the Donner Pass. Yet these vehicles had stopped not fifteen minutes since, at another station, where the identical frantic commerce in snacks had taken place.

The demand never quite comes up to the supply, and when the bus or train departs, back go the vendors—women, mostly —to wherever it is they lurk, to make necessary adjustments in the arrangement of their trays and await the next arrival.

Some of these aboriginal caterers do things on a fairly elaborate scale. Their trays are arranged as symmetrical pyramids, unconsciously recalling, it is said, the architectural propensities of their ancestors. Others, poor little old women, will hold out a single, lone enchilada or a stuffed *chile* laid on a cold tortilla. As often as I have observed them, they have never demonstrated any great disappointment when they failed to find a buyer. Throughout their history, things have never gone their way— so the unsold articles become their own supper, and business, poor or worse, is never a total loss. It takes only an occasional sale, I suppose, to keep them on the right side of the law of diminishing returns.

I inquired of an ancient purveyor of oranges which fork of the road would take me to Ixhuacán and accepted his advice, since it seemed to accord with my map. I could not resist the temptation to ask him if that was the way the Spaniards went.

"*De verdad, señor,*" he said, anxious to oblige. "They did. Only last week."

Free of the weight of my gear, I relished the prospect of a hike to Ixhuacán. The sun now shone down pleasantly on my head, which was protected nicely by the sombrero of the *ex-presidente;* and the mountain air was delightful to breathe, now that the horror of my first awakening had somewhat dissipated. The exercise should benefit those aching muscles, I thought, and, God willing, callous the soles of my feet.

"*Vámonos,*" I commanded my army, and off we marched, my *tamane* and I.

12

The road, unpaved but comfortable for strolling once the ooze was pressed out of yesterday's blisters, lay straight before us, and level, too, for a while. If a *camión* should come along, we could flag it down. In the meantime it was a walk to enjoy.

Once we had left the crossroads of the Snake People behind, only an occasional cabin broke the solitude. Indian women, timid and curious, nodded, their lips silently bidding us *" 'Diós"* from their unglazed windows. Before the shanty doorways, turkeys paced with solemn air. But shall I perpetuate that misnomer? Let the bird himself tell his true name. We practice the ancient tongue by repeating his gobble after him. *"Guajalotl,"* he says in Aztec (and in colloquial Mexican, too). On the basis of onomatopoeia, if no other, the name has a greater justification than the Spanish *pavo. Pavo,* indeed. Not Honorio or any of his townsmen ever heard the word. It is a *guajalotl* to them. As for "turkey"—that country never saw the bird.

A mile or two, and now even Indian shanties were seen no more; the solitude became a thing of awesome majesty. The roadbank on our left fell away and rapidly deepened into a wooded abyss, while on our right rose the mountain—the Cofre de Perote that we were circling on its southern side. The Cofre— Naucampantepetl—is a dark, forbidding eminence when one looks up at it from a path worming about its foothills. But the gloom is brightened by the flowers that grow even in the shade of the conifers and oaks now dominating the wild mountain- scape. Prescott has observed, and one can observe it easily for

himself, that flowers grow spontaneously here as "noxious plants"
—weeds—grow in other countries. The heady mountain air
itself was a delight. Filtered through the tight tangle of the
forest, perfumed by the myriad flowers, completely innocent of
machine-produced pollutants, to breathe it was a completely new
experience (I speak as a city fellow) that freshened the spirit.
It seemed not to matter that my bones ached. As for the lamed
foot, its hurting abated as long as it was kept in service, though
the pain quickened whenever it was in repose. It was Quetzalcoatl's prod to keep me moving.

During the next two hours of the march not another soul
shared the road to Ixhuacán with us—at least none we could
see, for it was into some dark recess of this unpeopled region
that those three *ladrones* had fled whose eyes had stared me out
of countenance from the *jefatura* wall in Jalapa. Eventually we
came upon an old house built into a niche that some ancient
tremor had riven in the sheer rock. It was shabby, unpainted, of
uncertain geometry, and sat well above the level of the road
so that one must scramble up the bank some dozen feet to reach
its door. On a porch post was nailed a weatherworn sign an-
nouncing that here one would find Moctezuma—Moctezuma
beer.

A black-braided Indian girl was drawing water from a well
alongside, amid such a profusion of flowers as one would expect
to see only in some botanical hothouse designed to display the
exotic flora of a rain forest. Azalea surrounded her and bougainvillea hung over her head. The trees around her were heavy
with crimson, orchidlike blooms. I needed to see a sacrificial
maiden, of course, and here she was, in the very process of
immolation, with bright red lilies like tongues of flame licking
at her feet.

She was a veritable engine, hauling up the bucket with a
constant, unceasing rhythm. She threw the free rope into a
faultless coil as the bucket came up, the coil running off as she
sent the bucket back down again immediately it had been
emptied into a cistern; and again she hauled it up, not in-

terrupting the cadence of her labor even as she gave a quick swipe of her hand to her dripping forehead.

We lingered at this place for a half hour, drinking warm beer from dusty bottles. An old woman conducted a general store of sorts in the house, indicating that somewhere within the forest must be a community of Indian huts from which came occasional patronage. She took my visit quite in stride and offered no apologies for the dust on the bottles.

I now observed a little ritual Honorio followed faithfully during all the time we traveled together. Whenever we had occasion to purchase bottled drinks he would, the instant the bottle had been uncapped, scrape off a bit of the label with his thumbnail and, with the *glue* side of the scrap, wipe around the mouth of the bottle. This he never failed to do, whether the beverage was beer or *refresco*—soda pop. He followed this procedure in tumbledown Indian outposts and in "respectable" city dining rooms as well. He was not so fastidious when the drink was pulque served in unwashed earthenware *jarritos,* which, in his apparent view, had nothing of the sinister potential lurking beneath those crinkled bottle caps. With difficulty he suppressed his irritation when the bottle sometimes proved to have a silk-screened label that resisted his thumbnail. When I asked him to explain this practice, he shrugged and grunted, which said with more eloquence than words that some things were beyond the understanding of gringos.

The señora, widowed long ago, had lived fifty years in this place. It cannot be said she had witnessed great changes. Not only had there been no physical alterations in the panorama over which we looked as we sipped our *cerveza:* the dirt road; the deep ravine across the way; the Pico de Orizaba, Mexico's loftiest peak, to the south, its snow-covered cone seemingly airborne, and pink as it caught the sun's light in the misty distance; Naucampantepetl looming darkly over our heads—not only had there been no changes in all this during the fifty years of her residence here, but none that any eye could have seen in the four and a half centuries since Cortés came this way. I asked the lady my eternal question.

"*Por supuesto*—of course." She pointed toward a hog-back ridge that ran parallel with, and above our path. "The *Paso de Cortés.* There you see it," she said. There certainly was unanimity of local opinion on the authenticity of our route.

We rested long enough to awaken the throbbing in my foot and said "*Adiós.*" Not for an instant during our little visit did the Indian girl cease hauling water. She was at it as we marched down the road, and is no doubt at it still.

Soon the road began more perceptibly to slope upward and to make a turn this way and that, valleys deepening on either side as we rose to the ridge.

In this kind of mountain rambling there is the problem of determining how far distant each successive objective is. Maps do not tell you—at least the kinds of maps we who use old books as guides employ. From Xico to Ixhuacán is but a quarter of an inch on the map that illustrates my edition of Díaz, but it gives no hint of the twistings and turnings we must expect; the hugging of mountainsides while we watch the *papilotes*—the scavenger birds—wheeling below us. Neither Díaz nor Cortés himself deign to say much more than that from here they went to there, with rarely a comment on the exertions in between.

One tries to calculate from previous experiences how much time to allow for each leg of a journey. But whose experience? My own accustomed journey is two blocks to the subway. It is recorded that in Moctezuma's time that potentate's *tamanes* traveled fifteen miles a day, carrying loads of sixty pounds. I carried no such burden; but neither did I have the incentives of Moctezuma's porters, whose hearts were either in their work or on the sacrificial altars of Huitzilopochtli.

Following the windings of this crude road, it seemed improbable that a *camión* could manage it. I do not say *impossible.* If the bus were sufficiently broken in spirit by past abuse, fragile with age, with the unkempt shagginess of a mountain goat and amply furnished with its holy pictures and shrine to Guadalupe —it just might do it.

But no *camión* came. Then, at last, trailed by a plume of dust, appeared a battered jeep, the first creature we had seen on the road since leaving the Snake People refreshing themselves at Coatepec. I must by now have looked a most unsavory pilgrim, with my beard at that particularly unpleasant stage that invites arrest by the police rather than deference. My companion was a grim-looking savage to whom any discreet traveler in these lonely parts should give the widest berth. Nevertheless, I turned toward the approaching vehicle and gave the universal thumb signal, straining my face into its most benign expression. If the jeep had scurried past, its driver would have had my fullest understanding. It stopped.

The front seats held the owner, who was apparently a farmer of means, and his driver. In the covered van behind, seated "charabanc" on one of the wheel wells, was a gentleman in city dress, wearing, of course, the national headgear. Several blitz cans of fuel occupied most of the floor. The remaining wheel well was at our disposal and we climbed aboard.

The gentlemen were amused by the nature of my mission. Cortés had come this way—certainly—*sin duda alguna,* they assured me. *Americano, eh?* No one of my stripe was ever seen in *these* parts. No, I would find no *restorán,* no *coq teles* in Ixhuacán.

I quite emphatically stated that not only did I seek no cocktails, but adhered firmly to the principle of eating and drinking in my hosts' own fashion. This I do to the point of eccentricity, and possibly have my colitis to show for it. If Cortés was served *empanadas* when he preceded me through these sierras, well, I will eat *empanadas* too and share his stomachache if I must, so that I will know what life was like for a *conquistador.*

The gentleman with whom we bounced about in the van was a buyer of *ahuacotl*—avocados. I had not thought avocados were products of so high a mountain region, but this is Mexico, where orchids grow in the company of scrub oaks. I would find horses in Ayahualulco, he said, and, as that town of challenging pronunciation was his own destination, he would be happy to have my company. Again I was finding, as had Bernal and his mates, ". . . inhabitants well-disposed toward us." The *ahuacotl* buyer—the Aztecs called these wide-ranging merchants *pochtecas* —would need an hour, for he had business in Ixhuacán; then we would proceed together to Ayahualulco.

So we lurched and joggled on. What torrential rains must have fallen during the summer past, although they were hard to imagine, so dry and dusty was the road now. They must have been deluges to have carved the surface so deeply, and if our jeep succeeded in avoiding one ditch, its wheels were immediately captured by another. We were rattled about like dice in a cup, and the blitz cans played a violent tattoo on my knees. The driver now slowed the beast down to a near-halt in order to gnash in the four-wheel drive, for the trail was climbing steeply and making sharp turns upon itself. An hour or so of this exercise— walking would truly have been less strenuous—and the trail became a road again, taking us into Ixhuacán.

13

Ixhuacán appeared much like any other Mexican town that has not been dusted off to attract foreign tourists. It has its plaza—not the last we shall see—and its old church—two churches, in fact. The street by which we entered the town dipped down a few yards ahead so that whatever buildings were on it disappeared from view as abruptly as boys holding their noses and jumping into a creek; but I could see the tops of a second set of bell towers, tall enough to remain in sight. What indefatigable builders of churches those Spaniards were—with the help, to be sure, of their Indians' labor. In the remotest of villages one finds churches that, ingenuous baroque or no, would, were they located in Milwaukee, be pointed out as matchless cathedrals by the local Chamber of Commerce. The population of Ixhuacán must have been greater, in years gone by, to support two such substantial edifices.

The plaza was quite spacious, paved with stone and crisscrossed by walks. Along the length of either side were porticoes, beneath the shade of which slumbered what the imaginative viewer might construe as shops. Every shutter was closed, for it was midday. At the plaza's far end was the *Palacio de Gobierno* —the municipal building, striving mightily and succeeding only modestly to look more dignified than its neighbors. The *presidente,* for whom I carried the judge's note, was away on some business or other, a disappointment I bore easily now that I had the guidance of our congenial *pochteca* friend.

No life stirred in the plaza or under the *portales* until our presence in the town had been detected from behind some door or shutter, when an old gentleman came out, then another. Soon there were a half dozen who, when I had waved them a hello, joined me at one of the plaza's stone benches. One brought out a granddaughter who seemed terribly alone in our superannuated company.

Yes, certainly the *conquistadores* had come here, *en eso no hay duda ninguna,* although the town had not been *así grande* (so grand!) then. Ixhuacán, together with its Indian work force, had become a *repartimiento* soon after the Conquest—a grant to some Spanish don who was in favor with the Government back home; who had migrated to New Spain to help colonize the country; and who had an inclination to do a bit of personal nest-feathering. So Ixhuacán became Ixhuacán de los Reyes, a property held in the name of the Spanish kings.

This the old gentlemen told me, one remembering Don So-and-So as the name of the grandee whose "wards" the original population had become; another asserting with spirit that it had not been Don So-and-So at all, but Don Such-and-Such.

It must have been an attractive and lively place when candles lighted the shops and *haciendas*—livelier, surely, than it is now, even with the electricity that reaches Ixhuacán, albeit in small quantities. The cobblestone streets must have echoed merrily the rattle of carriage wheels—more merrily than now, when one can reach the town in jeep or *camión.* (I am not qualified to give testimony regarding the latter, for no *camión* arrived during my visit.)

There must have been entertainment then, the gay laughter of young hidalgos—sons of *somebody;* and the genteel tittering of chaperoned señoritas—else what incentive in the "good old days" (good for proud *gachupinos,* if not for the dispossessed natives) to induce young blood to come to Ixhuacán and stay, and build for Spain? But precious little young blood has come since lo, these many years, and so my companions in the plaza were all old men with only memories, good or bad depending upon how much they had drunk with their dinner.

About a month before my arrival the bishop had visited Ixhuacán and the other mountain towns of this rugged diocese, and an effort was made to decorate the streets and the church façade with ribbons. The town seemed reluctant to relinquish the small gaiety the visit by his excellency the *obispo* had engendered—the decorations were still hanging. They were poor tatters now, looking more forlorn than festive. One had to marvel at the good bishop's fortitude and dedication in making his tour. A momentous event it must have been. Having made the trip myself, take my personal affidavit that he cannot do it often.

I strolled about the town and in no time at all had visited most of its streets. They radiated from the plaza, as is almost always the case, and, with their cobblestone pavement graded to a shallow vee, must be like sluices carrying "white-water" torrents in the rainy season. Not a citizen did I see except those who had come out to greet me in the plaza. Not a woman, not a child, not a burro or a dog in the silent streets.

Ixhuacán and its bucolic environs are set in a vast bowl formed by a spectacular ring of mountains. Brown in the distance, the faces of the hills are draped with green and gold tapestries according to the maturity of the corn in the *milpas*. We had entered the town through a pass—a crack in this great bowl. To exit it, we must climb to the brim westward, in which direction lay Ayahualulco. How far to that mellifluous-sounding place—which took all of Honorio's forbearance and resignation to teach me to pronounce? *Quién sabe?* My friend the *pochteca* planned to walk. It was not worth the trouble or expense of getting horses here, he said, and it would be no more than an hour's walk. Well, I had come to follow in the footsteps of Cortés, and how better to follow footsteps than on foot?

But first we must wait for the *pochteca* to finish his business, and while we waited, some refreshment seemed to be in order. My last had been the judge's chilli and tortillas the night before, but thanks to the dissolute nature of that affair I still had no great longing for food. Honorio had not joined me this morning without first fueling, and he agreed that we would wait until we reached Ayahualulco to dine. Coffee would do no harm, however, while we waited for our buyer of avocados. The old gentlemen recommended a small shop whose door now opened.

The young woman there had never served a stranger, and set about in a fluster to make coffee. Poor stuff it was, consisting of warm milk with only a suggestion of coffee to change its color, though barely its flavor. I was uneasy in this place whose paucity of merchandise—some cordage, a few sacks of feed, votive candles, little else—bespoke an exceedingly small commerce. We asked for *pan dulce*. The "sweet" rolls were kept on a shelf theoretically above the reach of four-legged vermin, and were enclosed in screening whose mesh was fine enough to keep out dogs, but nothing smaller. The señorita placed several rolls before us beside our tumblers of coffee, and I picked one up from the counter—but another adhered to it. Pulling the two rolls apart disturbed the larvae of some insects nesting within. I did not wish to upset the lady so, acting as if this was nothing out of the ordinary, I broke off a crumb from the edge farthest distant from the torn cocoon, dunked it in the yellow "coffee," and swallowed it with little joy.

Even now I did not forget my responsibility toward the bearer of my gear who had left home and mother to be my *compañero*, so I slid the infested *pan dulce* over to Honorio. *"Tu eres más joven que yo,"* I said kindly. He, being younger than I, needed greater sustenance, and had already consumed his own rolls. As a matter of delicacy I said nothing about the hidden nest, rationalizing that he must surely have seen me abruptly clap my rolls together when I discovered their inhabitants. Honorio ate the *pan dulce* with gusto—as a sandwich, you might say. My good deed done, we returned to the plaza to await the *pochteca*.

Ixhuacán de los Reyes had depressed me unreasonably. Physically, it was a pretty place, in as grand a setting as can be found anywhere. Alpine villages are not more nobly situated. But the dust seemed to lie with an oppressive weight upon everything. Ixhuacán was like a jilted Miss Havisham who, decaying with the passing years, sat brooding while all her once pretty bridal things decayed about her.

Of course, I was not being fair to the village. If I had lingered a while; if I had waited for the absent *presidente* or had taken steps to seek him out, it is completely possible—I will say likely —that new and delightful characters would have been added to my roster of Mexican friends. Dunking that miniature zoological garden in the señorita's imperfect coffee had proved poor therapy for a man in my condition.

The story is told of the cacique who had enjoyed overmuch of meat and drink and, becoming terribly flatulent, lost his self-control in the presence of the fairest of maidens, to his unspeakable mortification. Thereafter, and for as long as he lived, he could never again abide that woman. So it was with me and Ixhuacán. My coolness toward the village was my fault, not hers.

14

We parted from Ixhuacán with handshakes at the bench in the plaza and a pat on the head for the little granddaughter who would grow old in this sad little village thinking it was the center of the universe, a delusion from which few of us are free, whatever our nation.

The merchant knew each turning in Ixhuacán, and we arrived quickly at a road that headed westward. It was a long, straight road until it reached the shadow of the hills, and we strode along it at a brisk pace, listening to the cornfields chattering as the breeze rustled the dry stalks. Far ahead, the road seemed to be paved in red and gold. When we came up to the colored pavement we found a carpet of corn grains spread out on the roadside to dry, their varieties of different colors kept separate, so producing the effect of a mosaic, gold and blood red in the sunlight. A laborer stooped low over the corn, combing through it and spreading it with a short-handled implement so the grain would dry uniformly. In this way the corn—maize—will keep indefinitely until it is ground at the mill or, in the smaller villages, will be soaked in lime and water, ground into a moist dough on a stone *metatl,* and patted into tortillas by some patient, tireless, ever-tired woman.

Travel where one will in Mexico, he is rarely out of sight of maize, or the *milpas,* the fields where it is grown. In some regions the spread of the cities has forced its cultivation on the mountains' steep sides, resulting in severe problems of erosion. But the corn must be grown. It is the *sine qua non* of Mexican life. The smell of corn, either being milled so that its dust is in the air or in some culinary process—tortillas baking, tamales steaming—the smell of corn is a characteristic of the atmosphere in Mexican towns and villages.

Ancient Mexico owed its birth, its rise to power, and its death to corn. It was corn that stopped the primitive tribes' wanderings, at least four thousand years ago. Where they saw that the corn would grow, there they laid the first foundations of their ancient civilization, the Mayas in Guatemala and the Yucatan, the Toltecs on the tableland farther to the north. Then they decided that the corn crop was under supernatural control—under the influence of the sun and the rain; and so the earliest Mexicans recognized their first gods. How to propitiate these gods upon whose good will survival depended? The Aztecs, among others who succeeded the Toltecs in this region through which I was meandering, considered that nothing was too good for such potent deities, and so the rites of human sacrifice were conceived, giving that extraordinary coloration of bloody ferocity to their culture. Yet it must be said there was more to the character of the people than "bloody ferocity." Their motive was not one of blood lust. If, among the ingredients of cruelty, are included malice and mischief, it cannot be said the Aztecs were cruel. Nor did they kill out of hatred for the sacrificial victim. What they did, they did to please their gods.

The motive was impeccable but led ultimately to their downfall, as good motives have led others and will continue to do. The appetite of the gods proved insatiable, and the Mexican forays upon their neighbors to secure the needed numbers of sacrificial victims cost them friends, as can be readily believed —and won allies for the Spaniards. And so the end came for the Aztec civilization.

It is most sobering to contemplate a tortilla!

The last man-made structure we came upon, at about the point where the street ceased to be a street and began to be a grassy path, was a small shanty that the merchant said was a *pulquería*. Part of the definition of a *pulquería* is that it be disreputable.

86

I acquired a passing acquaintance with *pulquerías* and never did encounter one that would be tolerated by any zoning board of conscience. This one was a ramshackle old outhouse that could be recognized as a source of refreshment only if one had an indigene along to tell him that is what it was.

The *pulquería* was situated on the outer limits of the town, where the lowly *cargador* or *arriero* might fortify himself after the soul had been drained out of him by the tyranny of some mountain maize field. It was around midday when we reached it, and all was quiet—but I could imagine the walls of the rickety place shuddering with the wild howls of exhausted men seeking forgetfulness.

There was no painted sign to say what the place was; the sole advertisement was its odor. It was a sour smell, the universal smell of fermentation, which would not have been especially disagreeable if the establishment had been anything but a place for refreshment. And yet, why should we single out the *pulquería* for criticism on this count? We rhapsodize over the bouquet of certain cheeses; we associate the stench of cabbage with the blessings of the family hearth; we surround ourselves ecstatically with the organic aura of ripe cigars. Sportsmen must let venison putrify a bit to bring out the good of it; partridge is not at its best, the gourmets say, unless it has a definite stench to it when served. I am condemning none of these delights as I enumerate them, and am personally partial to them all—or almost all. Rather, I join the reader in speculating on the human perversity that often makes a "bad" smell one of the conditions of perfection. This being so, I proposed that we have a glass of pulque to toast Ixhuacán a proper farewell. The *pochteca* agreed gladly, and Honorio did not say no (or anything else), so we entered.

The place had a rough wooden counter under which the proprietor kept some partially filled demijohns of the milky liquid. On the walls hung several bloated pigskins, the containers in which the pulque is generally transported on burros. I often saw these pigskins on the road, looking all the more grotesque for the hopeless reaching of their vestigial limbs. The center of the room beyond the counter was occupied mainly by a large, uncovered vat where a great quantity of new pulque lay fermenting. It seemed to do so inertly, for there was no perceptible bubbling in the vat, but the air was pungent with evidence of the process.

On the train from Mexico to Vera Cruz I had seen people drinking pulque, usually straight from bottles purchased from station vendors. I saw Indian girls hold up for sale earthenware *jarritos* brimful of it. In the bottle, a liter cost a peso—eight cents. In the earthenware jar the price was two pesos, the buyer keeping the *jarrito* for subsequent household use. Some say modern Mexico is forsaking pulque, the *octli* of the Aztecs, for a more fashionable beverage; and it is true that wherever I went I could always find a bottle of beer—excellent, too, as good as any Teutonic brew. But I believe pulque will survive as the countryman's drink as long as the maguey plant has room to grow, which will certainly be the case in the calculable future. The sheer simplicity of its production should assure its survival: the sweetish syrup exuded by the maguey is drawn as one draws soda through a straw, the "straw" in this case being an elongated gourd. A small quantity of old pulque (the *madre*) is added to the new to induce the process, it is set aside to ferment, and that is all.

One other factor remains in determining if pulque has a future, and that is whether it is good to drink. I proceeded with an empirical inquiry of the matter. We ordered glasses, which the *pulquero* filled from one of the demijohns, and my companions drank theirs with audible relish, proclaiming its quality excellent. I brought my glass nearly to my lips and stopped it there for an instant—in panic. The liquid that looked like innocent milk had the smell of something dead. It was a critical moment. If I followed my natural impulse, I would return the glass hastily to the counter, flee the premises, and never know the satisfaction of having shared this taste experience with Moctezuma. Instead, I sipped the stuff and found that, while its flavor was not altogether unlike its odor, there was a hint of nature's latent goodness in it, such as wine has—and the cheese, cabbage, and rotted venison already mentioned. I swallowed some more and had the feeling that in time I could conquer my impulse for flight—but that I would need more time than was presently available for the cause. I paid the few centavos I owed—it might have been a penny a glass, or less—and turned to depart, followed by my *compañeros*. At the door an impulse seized me. I returned to the counter and swallowed what was left in the glass—a sacrament of communion with the Aztec spirits.

This initial experience with pulque has had notable precedents. Over a century ago, Prescott wrote, ". . . it requires time to reconcile Europeans to the peculiar flavour of this liqueur, on the merits of which they are consequently much divided." That remarkable Madame Calderón, Scottish-born wife of a Spanish ambassador and accustomed to the finer things of life, found the stuff unspeakable when she first tried it. Within a few months she was drinking it with her breakfast, noting that ". . . for the first time I conceived the possibility of not disliking pulque . . . [I] found it rather refreshing, with a sweet taste and a creamy froth upon it. . . ." A matter of weeks later, we find her complimenting a hostess who served pulque fermented with pineapple juice, ". . . which is very good," quoth Madame Calderón de la Barca.

An hour after resuming our walk, the trail had lost its definition and became an open meadow. I was stretched out on the grass, my jacket rolled up as a pillow. Marigolds were scattered all about—satellites of the sun that was bathing my face pleasantly, taking the edge off the cool mountain air.

Honorio had disappeared temporarily into the conifers on private business and the *pochteca* lounged on the ground beside me, fanning his face with his sombrero, for the climb had been steep.

". . . *Un poco más,*" he was assuring me. It was an assurance he had already offered several times. Just a little more, and we would be in Ayahualulco—but I saw no sign that any village was near. I should have known that the promise of an hour's walk had been made just so I might enjoy the anticipation of it. Now the trail had disappeared—from my view, though not the merchant's—and we had come upon this glade through which a mountain stream tumbled on its way down to Ixhuacán. That community surely does not lack for water. Too seductive to resist, I bathed my feet in the rushing stream that churned itself into foam on the black, rocky river bed. Then I must lie down again for a moment or two, a little weary, perhaps, but yielding to another more powerful and more subtle urge.

More than languor—though it was that, too—to lie flat on my back on the cool ground was a sensual pleasure of a quality we have forgotten even to remember on our stuffy beds and chairs. That is routine repose, without the effect upon one's spirit produced by a capricious abandoning of oneself to earth. To lie upon the ground . . . is it a forgotten need to do just so uninhibited, so prankish, so trivial a thing that moves us to seek out wild and lonely places? Is there within us a too-long-suppressed disposition to lie flat on maternal earth, out of uxorious clutches, beyond the view of neighbors in whose eyes one is a fool to so disport himself? It is a right, we know, allowed small boys, who will fling themselves upon the ground—concede them first a loose-limbed cartwheel or two—throw their arms out wide to embrace the universe, and sigh, "A-ah!" But do only small boys need to heed this call to be at one with nature?

And so I forgave the *pochteca* his kindly fib as I stretched out and sighed "A-ah!" and assessed with a twig the sensitivities of a gigantic caterpillar that strayed slowly into range. It was a full ten inches of plump iridescence—a splendid creature.

"*Cuidado,*" warned my friend. "It is poisonous." I suppose it was; it was that beautiful.

The air should have been raw. Was this not the *mal país* that caused great suffering even to the sturdy *conquistadores?* Instead it was intoxicating, a time of pure delight despite my poor foot. It was curiously satisfying to travel between towns not linked by rails or roads. Even this was a rejection of restraint. All our lives we must stay on the road in order to get to where we are going. If we step off the road, we trespass. No Parking. Do Not Stop. Do Not Enter. No Exit. Members Only. Keep Off The Grass . . . Ho, for the sierras!

But what is a garden of delight for the visitor may be something else for the gardener. We gave up sole possession of our hilltop glade when an Indian appeared, his head bound up in a dirty rag that he held close against his right eye to stanch the flow of blood from an ugly wound. He was followed by his wife—the tiniest of creatures, pretty, too, like a wild bird (anyone who would propose that a wild bird be washed must be a —a Clerk!), but terribly worn and sad. As the poor couple came toward us, we rose, exchanged our *"'Diós,"* and asked, *"Qué le pasó?—*What happened?"

He had been struck in the eye by his pickax, he said. It had somehow slipped from a rock he had been laboring to dislodge. I raised the bandage to examine the wound and found it to be terribly deep, exposing much of the underside of his eyeball. The little wife, who could not have been sixteen, stood by, frightened and silent, while the *pochteca* gave them a careful explanation of what they must do and to whom they must apply for help when they reached Ixhuacán. They must not entrust this *herida* —this hurt—to a *curandero,* who might have the power to assuage some wound of the spirit by means of encantation and the ancient herbs, but not this bloody cut.

The Indian seemed to be not so much in physical pain—though who could tell?—as sorrowful, for a man must work if he and his family are to eat, and this was the worst of calamities. The little girl nodded her awareness of this stark fact poignantly, helplessly, and the *pochteca,* warning them emphatically to report to the responsible authority whom he named and not to the *curandero,* put his arm gently, for a fleeting instant, around the young wife's shoulder to comfort her.

"Vayan con Dios," we said, and they resumed their way down the hill to that poor Ixhuacán that had so depressed me, but which

to these sad people was a great *población,* a city of whose wonderful science they might borrow in their misery.

Honorio returned, and we continued through the field of marigolds to find the path that would lead us to Ayahualulco. The way grew steep again, but soon we came to groves of trees bearing fruit that I first took to be plums. Honorio picked one for me. *"Ahuacotl,"* he said with a little pantomime, including a turning of his eyes toward heaven to indicate how good it was for eating. I took a bite, whereupon its stone flew out like a projectile from the slight pressure it took for my fingers to hold the fruit. It was one of the plum-sized varieties of avocado our merchant friend had come to buy for the city markets. A half mile farther on and around a bend rose the bell towers of a village church. Ayahualulco.

15

The first building we came upon as we entered the town was a tumble-down *mesón,* a horse stable attached to a large shed that was the dwelling of the family operating the establishment. The merchant introduced me and explained my need for horses —and our desire for dinner. The availability of horses depended, we were told, upon the work being done in the fields, and it would be necessary to wait until the *trabajadores*—the laborers —returned in the evening before we could know if I might have horses the next morning. As for dinner, they would set to it immediately, and I was free to relax until it was ready.

"Es cosa de pocos minutos," said the lady of the house. *"El señor está en su casa."* Since it was a matter of minutes and I should make myself at home, I took the occasion to make a survey of Ayahualulco.

I did not expect much of the town—particularly since the wounded Indian had found it necessary to bypass it and walk, bleeding, a trek of several hours to the likes of Ixhuacán for help. And, in truth, there was even less to this place than there had been to that one.

The empty church was of imposing size, proving that here also there had been greater communal activity in former times. The inevitable plaza was larger than that of Ixhuacán—larger, in fact, than that of any village through which I had so far passed; but it was unpaved, overgrown with weeds, and utterly neglected. An ancient bandstand occupied its center, but the town seemed so forsaken that it was impossible to imagine any concourse of citizenry gathering there to attend a concert. The town's single street was lined, on one side only, with a row of attached houses, one or two of which were, surprisingly, of two stories and balconied. A few had windows grilled in the Spanish—or Moorish—fashion.

I saw a single "general store"—actually nothing more than a stall, which offered corn, harness, the ubiquitous votive candles, *refrescos,* and *aspirina* across a counter nailed to the lower half of a split door. A purchase of aspirin enabled me to gain this idea of its inventory.

But the greatest marvel—an anomaly, indeed, in this seemingly deserted town, was a newly built, single-storied schoolhouse of concrete and tile and glass in an architectural style that would have been quite acceptable in any new housing development back home. The school was evidence of a rural education program at that time under way—a crash program, really—to combat the traditional illiteracy of these regions. The Federal Government contributes about double the funds the rural community is able to generate on its own, and so it can erect a standardized building such as this quite speedily. Such schools are springing up throughout Mexico, though this was the first I had seen on the trail of the *conquistadores.*

I returned from my stroll seeing no more than a couple of Indian women in the lone street of the town, and sat on a veranda of the *mesón.* Let us call it a veranda. It was nothing more than a wooden stoop sheltered by the broad, overhanging eaves of the rustic place. There I passed a pleasant while before dinner, chewing the sweet seed of what appeared to be a tamarind pod. These were strewn on the ground wherever we walked, and were a favorite childrens' tidbit. Honorio told me the seeds were better than chicle, so I chewed them. I have paid more for sweets and received less pleasure.

Credit is due to my patient *tamane* for introducing me to homely matters such as this. I should also mention that he had become enthralled by a booklet I carried, quite nicely illustrated in color, depicting the flora and fauna of Mexico. It was my practice to ask him to identify the vegetation that attracted my eye as we rambled by having him point out the species, as nearly as he could identify it, from the book's illustrations. Soon he had taken permanent possession of the little volume, constantly riffling through its pages as we walked, with the intensity of a scholar though he could not read a word of it. He and the book, between them, were my guide to the fruits and flowers that so lushly festooned the trail.

If anything could possibly happen to enchant me more with these remote hills and with the people who inhabit them, it happened now. As I sat there waiting for dinner, the familiar sounds of school-let-out filled, briefly and explosively, the emptiness of the weedy plaza, and a small flock of children, momentarily disoriented by unexpected liberation, came by to inspect me before setting out for their homes. Many of these were miles distant from the town, the school serving all the little Indian communities—some consisting of no more than two or three huts—within a wide radius of Ayahualulco.

The children presently gave way to a gentleman, the schoolmaster, who approached my throne (I was seated on an empty crate at that moment, but a couple of chairs were quickly brought out), offered his hand, and addressed me in English, while the children at the veranda step and my hosts of the horse stable all looked on and listened with hushed attention.

"You are very grateful to have a visit to our very small city . . ." he began, each word distinct and evenly spaced. I started to reply, "It is my . . ."

". . . and we are very pleasure," he continued, "to welcome a visitor who does very honor for our city to see the stranger. . ."

"I thank you," said I, thinking he had paused so I might answer. "The pleasure is mine and . . ."

". . . I am the Professor Joachim Benevides Trujillo in the school. I study much your language. . ."

"You speak very well," I said. "I wish my Spanish was as . . ."

". . . I study much your language," he repeated. I was interrupting the forward progress of his address and he must back up a little in order to regain the lost momentum, ". . . and we are exultant you make honor to us and very much welcome."

Exultant! May Quetzalcoatl bless him! The fact was that the good gentleman understood scarcely a word of English. He had hastily, and with the most kindly deference toward a visitor, rehearsed a little speech of welcome. His performance was being viewed by his pupils and fellow townspeople, and to pull the thing off well he needed to speak it all of a piece, as one does when delivering something committed to memory. I was not making it easy for him with my interruptions—but neither did he let me derail him!

He went on in this fashion for some minutes and, when he finished, I did finally manage to complete a response that I meant most sincerely, for I was genuinely moved by the schoolmaster's kindness. We then reverted to Spanish (giving him the occasion, should he thereafter recount our dialogue to his friends, to ridicule my linguistic efforts in *his* language.)

He presented me with a plastic ball-point pen that he hoped would help me, when I had returned to my country, to remember his little town and the gladness with which its people had received me. Indeed I always shall. I invited him to join us at dinner, thereby delaying that event even further while my hosts sent out to find another egg.

The vocation of the teacher in rural Mexico is put to a rigorous test. The physical hardship of doing his job, of which we saw a hint on our climb to Xico Viejo, is only one. These young people—and some not so young—are representative of a Mexico determined to accomplish what she has so far failed to do despite a long succession of violent revolutions against historically negativistic administrations—that is, to enlighten the poor and bring them out of attitudes remarkably little changed since long before Columbus signed his crews aboard at Palos.

In pre-Hispanic times, the Aztecs educated only their priests and nobles. In the Spaniard's turn there was little practical change. The view prevailed that a subject people was best kept unlettered to minimize the discontent that comes with literacy.

96

The *norteamericano* disposed toward humility will recall this same brave strategy in our own ante-bellum restrictions upon the education of black slaves. In both cases, it was rationalized that this order of things was functional, profitable, and as God intended. Those troublesome idealists—the "oddballs" and social misfits of their day—who felt uneasy about placing the responsibility for such a philosophy in the Deity's heavily burdened lap found themselves most unpopular with the establishments of their respective times. One sees interesting and disquieting parallels. The humanitarian Bishop of Chiapas, Frey Bartolomé de las Casas, and other clergy of conscience were thorns in the sides of the *conquistadores* and their heirs and successors when they attempted to promote the notion that Indians were human and must be so treated. Our Abolitionists were guilty of an identical eccentricity regarding the blacks. To the degree that these liberal spirits did not succeed in challenging their eras, to that degree does society face uneasy turmoil in after generations.

And so today Mexico must send her Joaquims into these mountains to help undo the injustices of the past. The task is not easy. Large numbers of rural Mexicans do not even speak Spanish, but speak instead the ancient tongue. Many have never been to school; more have never gone beyond primary grade—and their short attendance even there has been haphazard.

Primary schooling is now legally compulsory in Mexico. But one would need truant officers with the tenacity of the Royal Mounties to find and "capture" the children of these hills. Nor is the older generation terribly impressed with the virtues of book-learning. An old country saying has it that too much reading hurts the head. But hold: I have heard a suave New Yorker argue that it is more normal for a boy to throw a ball through a hoop than to let his fancy wander in the public library. Burros live in the city as well as on the mountain.

For the Mexican hill folk, it should be said that at least the children are important cogs in the family's economic apparatus, which is why the schoolmaster does not find it easy to persuade *mamacita*, toiling at the *metatl*, that she must send a ten-year-old to school when the tortillas must be carried to father at work in the *milpa*.

But what bodes well for Mexico is the extraordinary fact that she has, today, three times as many teachers as she has soldiers; and fourteen per cent of the national budget goes to education, compared with 2.5 per cent to the military! If only for this, Mexico is greatly to be admired—and envied.

Señora came out to say that the *comida* was now ready, and we entered the kitchen, a spacious lean-to built against the rear wall of the dwelling. The sloping roof seemed proof against the elements, but the three outer walls were carelessly (or carefully) planked so that the sunlight poured in as if through latticework, while the fumes from the stoves readily found their way out, a chimney being therefore unnecessary. A large number of earthenware vessels of every size and shape, and properly blackened by honest usage, were hung with spontaneous artistry on the inner wall. The wooden table was set in the middle of the hard-packed dirt floor that no pavement could match for cleanliness. Atop a stone counter at one end of the room were two stoves, one burning oil, on which the main courses—eggs, *chiles,* rice, and beans were in their last stages of preparation; the other a *cumal* (the Aztec *comalli*), which burned charcoal. On its circular surface the tortillas were being baked, as has been done through all the recorded history of this land. But these were tortillas such as I had not seen before—plump and tasty, rather than flat and papery as tortillas are expected to be. Altogether, it was a kitchen that could have graced some feudal baron's castle.

It was arranged that I should preside at table, the schoolmaster at my right and Honorio on the other side, while three women of ages ascending from sixteen to sixty scurried to our service. Since I was an *extranjero,* bottled beer, cool with the modest coolness of some shaded cupboard, was served instead of pulque. While Honorio tore off his bit of label and performed his mystic rite, hot earthen casseroles were placed before us, together with enormous tin spoons—another concession to a gringo, for a tortilla would be the natural utensil. My dish contained two eggs, among the other fiery condiments, while Honorio's had only one. Remembering with remorse my dubious generosity in the affair of the animated *pan dulce* of Ixhuacán, I asked that he be given the two eggs, being *más joven*. This the señora agreed to do only upon my sworn declaration that I was forbidden by doctors to eat eggs in excess. That the *muchacho* should have more than the señor was curiously taken, as if such an aberration would cause scandal if word of it were to leak beyond the walls of the *mesón*. Honorio, however, ate the second egg without hesitation—in complete cold blood, one might say, fearless in the face of whatever curse might befall him for his impudence.

The *dueña* of the tortillas was a delightful old lady, taller and thinner than a *tortillera* is supposed to be, with a frank and unaffected manner and a laugh in her voice. Such grace to encounter in untraveled mountains! She called to my mind Cornelia Otis Skinner who, I would wish to advise, has been hereby paid a high compliment.

"*Gorditas*," she said, pleased with my pleasure when I commented on the unusual plumpness of the tortillas she kept replenishing as fast as we consumed them. "*Son gorditas, señor.*" Her soprano voice as she told me that these were fat ones would be the envy of a duchess—and so would her manners. I observed that the tortillas—or *gorditas*—seemed to be particularly good for having been baked over charcoal. This evoked her delighted agreement and an explanation that not only must tortillas always be prepared over charcoal, but that the charcoal must be of a certain aromatic species of wood, the name of which I have forgotten despite my incessant note-taking.

A bowl of the miniature avocados was now placed on the table. On a Mexican table all courses are apt to come to the table together, and if you lack the sophistication to determine what may be soup and what may be dessert, you had better follow your neighbor. Though we were still at our eggs, Schoolmaster showed me by his example that one could eat the *ahuacotl* as an accompaniment to the other courses, which I proceeded to do, promptly firing an avocado stone in a high trajectory across the table and effectively, though unintentionally, diminishing my great dignity *de señor* by half.

It was altogether a most pleasant *comida* in an enchanting setting. The rustic kitchen, despite its proximity to the stables, enjoyed breezes fragrantly conditioned by the mountain pines, the air cooling rapidly as the sun began to touch the lunarlike edges of the horizon.

Our *pochteca* friend, his business done, came by to bid us go with God on the morrow, while he now returned to Ixhuacán, thence to Jalapa. Schoolmaster sat a while longer with us on the veranda, anxious that I should know his country better; that I should know, in spite of all, that the *Universidad* at Mexico had been teaching medicine and the humanities nearly a century before the landing at Plymouth; and that the first printing press and the first printed book in the New World could still be examined in the capital.

Strange . . . I had spent this goodly time with the people of the *mesón,* had enjoyed their modest table, would shortly test their overnight accommodations—and I had not asked the question: "Did Cortés pass this way?" It was answered in a most unexpected, most romantic, and most unlikely fashion. The señora's youngest child was hypnotizing me with her great black eyes as I sat discussing with the family the matter of the horses for the next day. The youngster, not yet two, was as beautiful as her face was dirty, and I insisted on photographing her as she was, to her mother's horror. When I had taken the picture, *mamacita* swept her off into the house and returned moments later with the baby glowing like dark gold from an abrasive scrubbing, wearing a crisp little frock, and her hair done up in a proper ribbon. Of course I took an "after" picture and promised I would send a print (if it was conceivable that a postman could ever reach this mountain aerie). I therefore took down the child's name, which was, to my delight, Carmelita Cortés Fuente!

Let the archeologists grub for their dry stones and the historians plod through musty manuscripts to confirm the route of the *conquistadores*. I had discovered Carmelita Cortés on the very trail!

Sometimes a village has the appearance of being godforsaken only because much of its population is off at work in distant fields. With the setting of the sun and the return of the men from their day's travail, a plaza may spring back to life; loungers will gather at the benches; strollers take their *paseo* along flowered walks. Not so in Ayahualulco. There were no more souls in the plaza when the sun had dropped behind the dead volcano peaks than there had been at the time of our arrival. I regretted we had not chanced to come this way on the day of some barbaric *fiesta*. But there is no record that the Captain-General had found a feast in progress either. On the contrary, this had been the area of a most dismal passage—the *mal país*—though for us it had been a splendid day.

Since my lodging was not a hotel, I had no choice but to turn in when the family did. A bed had been made up for me in a storeroom from which the horses were equipped. No box mattress here, but cords stretched tautly across a wood frame, and upon that, a pad that did not prevent the cords from embossing their pattern on my skin. But a double dose of sleeping capsules did the work the rum had done for me when I slept on the judge's bed in Xico. (How long ago that seemed!) I lay back and thought of my predecessors of those centuries past who had huddled around campfires listening fearfully for snapping twigs, their crossbows at the ready.

I never learned precisely where Honorio passed the night—in the stable, I surmise. When I saw him the next morning he was in the company of a diminutive bundle of knotted sinew named Martín, the stable boy whom I would come to regard with awe in the course of this new day.

We breakfasted on *gorditas,* and coffee—the *café con leche* that gringos are accustomed unjustly to lament, and a few avocados. I knew the trick now, but I fired an avocado stone at

Honorio anyway so I could say I had shot an Indian. He almost smiled but caught himself in time.

The matter of the horses troubled me. In the first place, there seemed to be no great ferment to produce them, though Señor Cortés Fuente assured me the matter was being handled. It was still a question of determining what hauling needed to be done in the fields; whether *trabajadores* had cut more, or less, than the *cargadores* could carry, so that animals might be, or might not be, released for a day's extracurricular labor to carry a gringo over the pass.

I was also troubled (secretly) by the prospect of mounting the beast if I should succeed in getting one. And more worrisome still were my doubts as to my ability to *steer* it on the kind of trail I had been so far navigating on foot. I had looked down into too many dark ravines to view complacently this equestrian test.

Señor Cortés Fuente had spoken of a place called Los Altos. It appeared on no map of mine. There, he said with transcendent vagueness, we might make a connection for Perote. I could get no precise information on where Los Altos was, or what the nature of the connection would be. We were not having a language problem—it was simply that one did not sit at a desk in Ayahualulco and tick off routings and firm schedules with a transportation clerk. Moreover, it just would not do to demand city-style services from people who were offering not the service of an entrepreneur to a customer, but help to a wayfarer. Consider that, for the preparation of the dinner for three, at which three good ladies set themselves spiritedly to work with no more forewarning than Columbus had given the startled Arawaks, señora shyly asked eight pesos—sixty-four cents. For the night's lodging beneath skies under which had once slept the first conquerors of the New World, señora asked no money. (I pressed ten pesos more upon her, *con su permiso.* Try that at the Holiday Inn!) No, I will not hear smug arguments of inferior living standards and the mighty majesty of a gringo's gold. These were kind friends helping a stranger on his way.

I spent the morning with my notes, an exercise that fascinated Honorio—when he was not thumbing through the pages of my Naturalist's Guide. Encountering the color representations on paper of objects with which he was completely familiar affected him as a person is affected when he opens a newspaper and unexpectedly sees an old friend's picture.

A little drizzle began to fall around midday—more like a wet mist, as if some great, gray hen of a cloud had sat down upon our mountain.

"*Chipi-chipi?*" I asked Honorio.

"*Chipi-chipi,*" he said. "*No es nada.*"

He seemed to be right. It was nothing, and soon passed.

16

Now the moment. Martín has led a horse out of the stable and stands beside it at the veranda step, *a mi disposición.* So beautiful a beast I have not seen on the trail. He looks for all the world as though he has been groomed for San Antonio's Day, when the animals receive the curate's blessing. This is because the *mozo* has spent the morning brushing and currying, and the extraordinary grooming has given a modest mountain pony the silken, silver air of a show Arab. Nor has Martín neglected the saddle, whose leathers shine as if I am to be the very first bold *vaquero* to sit it.

Regretfully, Cortés Fuente advised me, it was the only horse that could be spared, and he would take but twenty pesos for its hire to mitigate my disappointment. But what of the *muchacho* —Honorio? Would this not mean that my journey to Perote must be aborted? I had no intention of abandoning my companion. This not only because my gear fitted his sturdy shoulders exceedingly well—far better than it did mine—but because of the understanding that had grown between us. This manifested itself in small gestures. When some rare fruit caught my eye, Honorio would sense my interest and be instantly through the tangle with hissing machete to procure one for me to sample, without a word spoken by me. If my bad foot caused me to stumble, as it did with increasing frequency, he would be quickly beside me, extending no helping hand—that would demean me —but providing his bulk for me to fall fortuitously against. When a series of earth mounds attracted my attention as we strode along the wooded trail, he thumbed through the nature guide and, grunting for my attention, stabbed his finger at the picture of the agouti whose trace they were.

As a rule silent, some subjects had for him a special relevance deserving of complete sentences, as when we were drinking Cuauhtémoc beer and I tried him with my ritual question: who was this Cuauhtémoc, etc. . . .

"Fué un gran rey indio," he said. *"El a quien los Españoles le quemaron los pies"*—the identical reply the *chamaco* of the Cempoalan pyramid had given, and in the same tone of soft reproach. The razing to the ground of all Tenochtitlán does not burn in the Indian memory so vividly as does that cruel treatment of the gallant Aztec chieftain who had continued to resist the Spaniards after Moctezuma, his uncle, had capitulated and died.

Honorio, then, was capable of more than aboriginal grunts when necessary, and I had grown to know him as a good *compañero* who went where he was pointed, would not have known the meaning of deceit in any language, delivered no pretentious lectures on his nation's past glories, or whined about her (or his) misfortunes. What better mate to have on a carefree journey of exploration than this rugged aborigine who did not know the way either!

Only one horse?

Honorio spoke up promptly to put my mind at ease. *"No se moleste, señor*—I have legs for walking."

Martín joined in. *"Es nada*—a short *paseo."*

Well, it must be so, for Martín was to accompany me to Los Altos in order that he might return the horse when I had done with it, and *he* was walking. History assuaged my tender sensibilities. There had been 509 original *conquistadores,* and but sixteen horses; and one does not gamble against heavy odds if he wagers the Captain-General rode one of them!

So, handshakes of farewell once again with good *amigos* in another place even farther away. The family Cortés Fuente arrayed itself on the veranda to give me a proper send-off—

señor and his señora; Carmelita and the sundry other progeny of Cortés; and Cornelia Otis Skinner.

With fine instinct, Honorio turned the horse as I approached it so I would have no choice but to mount on the proper side, a detail on which I had a mental block. I found the stirrup straps too short, so that my knees spread out at right angles to the direction of travel, but I did not know, for the moment at least, the degree of discomfort this posture was to cause me on the trail. Though I looked more like Quixote than Lochinvar, it seemed appropriate to say something to my audience to delude them into thinking I had been born to the saddle, so I tipped my sombrero and cried out, "*Yo soy soldado de Pancho Villa!*" With that bold declaration, I attempted clucking noises to signal my mount forward, but the "clucks" emerged too feeble to stir him. Then Martín gave him a smart clap on the rump and we sallied forth at a discreet mountain pony's pace, little suspecting that before this day was done I would have such an acquaintance with purgatory as to earn me remission of all my past sins.

The first hour put Ayahualulco well behind us—no, *below* us, for still we climbed, mounting the hills that hung over the town. I managed to establish some modicum of authority over my horse after Martín had cut me a switch, and began to think myself a horseman. In the beginning the saddle seemed not uncomfortable, though the shortness of the stirrup straps put a greater strain than proper on the muscles of my calves and thighs as I strove to find the posting rhythm.

We proceeded upward until we came to a division in the trail, at which point stood one of those weathered crosses, flowers moldering at its foot, that one comes upon so frequently in the hills.

Cortés ordered crosses raised in this region to mark the arrival of his holy mission, but these we now see tell a different story. It is possible that a cross may be erected on the spot where some spent *cargador* falls, carrying the last of his lifetime's countless cargoes. But it is likelier the tale has a more violent theme. A liter too many of pulque releases the passion that always lies just beneath the Indian's placid surface. The machete flashes—and Juan's mother has fresh cause to mourn. Honorio, when asked the significance of these lonely crosses, told a story of this kind, tersely, reluctant to give too many details of his countrymen's frailties to a foreigner.

Similar crosses are seen at irregular but frequent intervals along heavily trafficked highways in Puerto Rico. These have a related motive, but the crosses commemorate the presence of a civilizing influence, marking the spot where pedestrians are struck down by automobiles! No such traffic in Mexico's sierras; instead, an older, more passionate drama.

We were at seven thousand feet, perhaps, and climbing still, on a rough path that seemed to have been plowed lengthwise by some enraged giant of a plowman. When my horse had carried me to the top of one hill, and then another, stumbling on a surface that rapidly disintegrated into great holes, deep ruts, and loose rocks to do so, I thought he should be allowed to rest.

"No-o-o, señor," Martín would say in his singsong Indian way when I suggested this. He was surprised and amused that I should think so little of a beast's stamina, and shamed me into putting greater demands on my mount than, as a city fellow, I would otherwise have dared to do.

Up and down the rough path went. We clambered up to the head of a hill, to find it falling steeply down on the other side, forcing me to lie back, my head nearly on the horse's rump to keep from tumbling over his head as he tripped and slid down into a rocky declivity. Then up another steep hill, my cheek now close to the pony's mane, my hands clutching the pommel lest I slide off his tail.

Occasionally, when the surroundings looked as if we must have been the first humans ever to pass this way, an Indian or two would appear, headed down to Ayahualulco with the everlasting load of corn or kindling. These encounters grew less frequent as we mounted and as the hours passed. Once we met a drove of burros, heavily laden, coming down toward us. I was unable to hold my horse against the bank of the path to let them pass; instead, I charged full into the thick of them, scattering the startled animals so that the *arrieros* must scurry about to retrieve them and gather them back into procession. Patiently, the sad-looking men touched their sombreros to me when they had succeeded in calming and realigning the excited beasts, and bade me *"Vaya con Dios."* Go with God, indeed! In our great cultural capitals men are told each day to go to the devil for the slowness of their reflexes.

Something else was occurring to which I had given no thought until now. I found that I was coughing and sniffling as if I had caught a head cold. But my handkerchief showed persistent blood, and the flow increased as we continued on. Then, when we reached another summit and I could not bear another moment on a saddle that by some devilish magic had exchanged its texture of smooth leather to that of a gnarled log, I insisted I must dismount to rest the horse and limber my legs. I soon discovered I could not manage a dozen yards on foot and must be helped back onto the horse. We were moving from eight thousand to nine thousand feet, and the altitude had set my nose to bleeding.

The air became quite chill now, and a mist began to settle upon us. We were in a cloud, a clammy thing—not the puff of fleece one sees from below. The path was narrow and winding; by degrees it grew steeper and steeper and seemed to lead to the very top of the mountain. When we reached it, we found another overhanging hill, and when we reached it, another hill overhung *that.*

Then the trail took a turn and, to my horror, became almost perpendicular as it dropped abruptly into a valley where I could see a surprisingly wide river racing along its rocky course. Down flew my horse, right down the descent, bracing himself with stiffened forelegs, slipping and sliding, almost falling but never quite, while Honorio and Martín clambered over the rocks behind me.

I successfully reached the bottom, upholding the chivalric spirit of dauntless knighthood—and proving the invincibility of ignorance. A bridge had been thrown across the river for the service of the *arrieros,* and my two *chamacos* proceeded toward it. I guided my mount instead toward the river's edge. The poor creature, glistening with sweat, his mouth lathering, now looked more like the trail ponies I had seen and less like the smartly groomed show horse on which I had started, and, though Martín still laughed *"No-o-o, señor"* when I asked if the beast should rest, I insisted he should at least drink.

The boys stood on the bridge and watched while I rode the horse down to the water where I faced the classic problem. I know from my reading of great books that you cannot *make* a horse drink. What I did not know was how to communicate to him that he might drink if he *wanted* to. We stood there, the water boiling about his forehoofs, while I sat on him helplessly, waiting for him to put his frothy muzzle to the rushing river; but he would not. Then Honorio made some kind of gesture to me from atop the bridge, a sign that either I misinterpreted or that was misinterpreted by the horse when I relayed it to him. I held the bridle well forward, supposing the horse would know by this relaxation that he was free to bend his neck down. Instead, he took off across the racing current, stumbling on the slippery stones of the riverbed while I hung on to the pommel with death's own grip, clamping my jaws tight to keep from biting off my tongue. It was the animal's fastest lap, at a suddenly shifted gait that had me bouncing wildly up when the saddle was down, and down hard when the saddle came up.

The boys raced across the bridge and prepared, I suppose, to salvage my watch and camera in view of my inevitable demise. But we struggled up the opposite bank successfully—and miraculously; and Honorio declared I had performed with consummate skill.

Regaining the trail, we continued on through the unbroken solitude. The mist grew thicker, colder. Looking back to see the country I had passed, I found that the mist had swallowed it. We heard the crash of falling water and could see, through a screen of pines, the great plume of a cascade falling from above to reform into the churning, boiling river I had so cleverly forded in the ravine below.

The view from these summits must have been glorious, had the sopping mist not chosen to squat so hatefully upon us.

> "Moist blanket dripping misery down,
> Loathed alike by land and town. . . ."

But I had not yet been tested. The mist now turned to frigid rain.

"*Chipi-chipi?*" I asked Honorio.

"*Sí, señor, chipi-chipi,*" he said. He half smiled, as if something hurt but he wished to hide the pain. From under his shirt he drew a plastic poncho, or something that served him as a poncho. Martín already had one about him, reaching so nearly to the ground that only his feet were visible. If it was truly nothing more than the *chipi-chipi*, it would cease when we topped the mountain. It is hardly necessary to say that I received frequent assurances from both Honorio and Martín that this blessed dénouement was imminent.

The mountain flora still twinkled, but indistinctly now—little star-shaped blossoms in the dripping woods, yellow, blue, pink. Wet, tangled shrubs clutched at my face. The chill now reached my bones, and I signaled the boys that I must dismount but would need help to do so. The spinal disk, ruptured in a far more prosaic exercise not long before, had begun to send forth its unhappy signals, adding a new ingredient to the disintegrating circumstances.

It took all the strength of these two indefatigable marvels to support me as I fell off the horse. I dug into the knapsack for the jacket and waterproof coat that would have served me so well had I not waited until now to don them. My teeth chattered and my hands shook as, with Honorio's help, I got into the clothing —too late, for the icy chill was deep inside me. I tried to walk a little. It would help to calm my trembling if I could—but I could not. The altitude, ten thousand feet now, at least; the deep chill; the blood clotting in my nostrils and beard; the agony in my spine that communicated a feebleness, a helplessness, to arms and legs as well—all these combined to remind me that one may wait for just so long before he climbs his mountain—but no longer.

This is how one dies. I am convinced I am about to die. My heart attack had come while I was lounging in a commuter train. Here I am, standing beside my pony, and it is impossible for me to mount him. I cannot walk; my limbs will not obey my will. When I have regained the saddle, it is only because my two *chamacos* have put me there.

The *tierra caliente*—what a distant memory it is! There, in tropical Vera Cruz, one idles in shirt sleeves in the plaza, listening to rippling marimbas. There, in Zempoala, the fat cacique lies dozing in the shade of the banana trees, warmly, blissfully. There, in Jalapa, one sips a sweet, iced frappé in the old monastery garden and lets the rainbowed mist of the fountain carelessly cool his sun-baked face. It is all a dimming memory—like a light dimming to darkness.

And *home!* As for that, it has not even the reality of a memory. It is a foolish fancy. It is a dream I could not really have lived. A vain fantasy to hope it will ever become an actuality. I have no hope I shall escape these wilds.

I am crumpled ignobly on this saddle, unable to straighten my spine though I command myself to do so. My nerve ends seek out, and find, new atoms of pain. It hurts the palms of my hands to grasp the maguey-rope reins. The touch of the broad surface of the pommel is painful as I slump forward to rest my forearms on it. I try to keep my eyes closed, to imitate sleep, to ease into oblivion as we continue, as the horse stumbles and flounders and toils up the sodden, rocky path.

That doughty soldier, Díaz, had warned me: ". . . We completed our ascent of the mountains," he said, "and entered uninhabited country where it was very cold, and where it rained and . . . a wind blew off the snowy heights on one side of us and made us shiver with cold. . . ."

Now I have a fearful notion. Honorio and Martín have been

conspiring. They will not wait much longer. I am completely helpless. That machete will do the deed swiftly. They will distribute my clothing between them, quarrel over my camera. Whatever pesos I carry are more than they have ever seen on one person in these gloomy hills. The solitude is complete. It has happened before. *Bandidos*—the breed was spawned in these sierras —*bandidos* will get me anyway. Why should these two not take me first?

The rain was cascading off the brim of my sombrero into my lap, into the knapsack that hung from the stock, soaking into my clothing, making paste of my notebooks. Now a fresh agony: the Muggy-Wuggies, those damned shoes, the ultimate evidence of my ineptitude! What foul part of the beast gives the leather from which they are made? The rain and the unscheduled dash across the river have soaked them and swollen them so that only the very tip-ends of my toes will go into the stirrups, and every muscle is tormented by new cramps as I try, by dull instinct, to hold some of my weight off the saddle. But it hardly matters. Perhaps this added strain will bring oblivion sooner. Before the machete falls . . .

What of those soldiers of Cortés who came this way so long ago? How they must have wondered what plots their Indian allies were hatching. How they must have feared the other side of each summit. What medicine did they take for *their* fever? Their spectral shadows were riding with me, huddled in the eerie mist, shivering as I did, frightened as I was to be thus, on the Pilgrim's Mountain of Doubt, or one very much like it—in the charge of that foul giant, Despair.

The first clue that we were about to top the sierra at last came with the perceptible thinning out of the woods. The trail then broke into an open, level plain and, for the first time in some four horrendous hours of winding and climbing and slipping and stumbling, the view ahead was not blocked by the dripping foliage through which so much of our path had tunneled.

We saw the first signs of human habitation, a few Indian huts standing bleakly on the bald pate of the mountain. Visible dimly in the distance through the gloomy mist and drizzle, the hovels had a ghostly look. No life stirred about them, and the only sound to be heard was my horse's dull, clopping hoof beats.

Wretchedly I hunched over on the saddle, trembling uncontrollably, praying that nightfall might hold off a little while longer so the darkness would not add still more oppressive weight to my burden of misery. Martín checked the saddle's cinch once or twice, but it was clear it was not the saddle but I who leaned so precariously on the steaming animal's back.

The plain was bleak and barren here, where the *norte* swept and raked it. It did not remain level for long; it began to slope, but gently, downward—an easy decline now. Had the setting sun succeeded in vanquishing the thick weather, the view must have been a splendid panorama of rolling hills, of *milpas* green and gold, of meadows flecked with mountain blooms; for we had at last completed our assault on the steep cliffs and bottomless ravines that form the monster bastions of Mexico's central plateau. Steadily I had been scaling this palisade since leaving Zempoala shimmering in the tropic sun. Each village since had been a rung on a gigantic ladder, until we topped the sierra two miles above the level of the sea.

If it were conceivable to describe as "blessed" the brutal weather of the past few hours, the opaque mist may have been a blessing in its fashion, for I had, unseeing, skirted many an awesome precipice. Prescott describes the route that the Spaniards (and I) had followed, winding along the shoulders of Nauhcampatepetl: ". . . Working their toilsome way across this scene of desolation, the path often led them along the borders of precipices, down whose sheer depths of two or three thousand feet the shrinking eye might behold another climate, and see all the glowing vegetation of the tropics choking up the bottom of the ravines. . . ."

I had passed this way blindfolded by Nanahuatzin—Old Thunder, the god who brings the *chipi-chipi!*

Nor would Nanahuatzin yet relent and let me see the great tableland or enjoy its temperate breezes. *Nunca en tu vida—*

never on your life! The icy drizzle continued as my troops and I moved down the long slope toward where Martín said we would find Los Altos. Would I find a hospitable village, as every village had been to me so far? If I must still perish, why, let me sit for a final time in some *campesino's* warm kitchen while the womenfolk bustle about me; while the tortillas toast on the *comal.* Let the *chiles* be afire when they are set before me. I'll not cry for water.

But I am not certain of lasting until we reach the pretty village. My teeth chatter. My foot throbs, my nose will not stop bleeding, and my very soul is ice.

The shadows of men move in the yellow light of a hovel among the other hovels. A *pulqueria!* Honorio and Martín help me off the horse for the last time. We are near Los Altos and the road is downhill now. If I can pour some *aguardiente* down my throat in this place that passes for a public house, I will walk —or crawl—down to the village. I cannot mount the horse again.

17

If the *pulquería* at Ixhuacán had been something less than prepossessing, the place we now approached was a setting for one
of the Grand Guignol's more frightening productions.

Two figures in dirty serapes leaned against the door frame
like pillars supporting the *pulquería's* entrance. I was struck by
their great size—or had my misery so shrunken me? Gog and
Magog, they surveyed me wordlessly as I sidled between them
with a stammered *con permiso* and entered the place while
Honorio and Martín tied up the horse.

Inside, the décor was classic for this order of entertainment;
it was a most dismal lair. The swollen pigskin, truly a funereal
appurtenance, hung on the wall, plumper now by far than when
the pig had been in it. The crude wood counter was damp and
malodorous with the spillage of the pulque. There were no
chairs or tables. The patrons, rough-looking men in gray serapes
every one, lined the walls of the place, standing in shadows
beyond the dim lamp's reach. There was no hint of joy as they
stood there, silently drinking from a miscellany of *jarritos*, eying
me dully as I entered. Unwillingly, it seemed to me, responding
mechanically to my nervous greeting, they murmured, " *'Diós.*"
There was none of the spontaneous grace that had characterized
those Indian greetings on the mountain trail. I sensed no welcome
here. It was not a place of fellowship or laughter. It was a den
for silent brooding by ill-used men.

I would understand the place and its mood shortly, when I
learned that Los Altos was not to be the "pretty village" of my

recent near-delirium. These robotlike men were the laborers, the *trabajadores,* who load the trucks with corn and the other staples of this high sierra region for delivery to distant Mexico. The gray of their serapes was the dust of the maize. Gray, indeed, was the color of Los Altos, a bleak staging area for the truckers.

How fitting it was that the purveyor of refreshment in this memorable establishment should turn out to be a witch! I exert every effort to be kind but cannot otherwise describe her. Her few teeth were coal black, and these were broken close to the gums. A stout old biddy, I have little doubt that the victory of those patrons who had broken her fangs had been a Pyrrhic one.

I was having difficulty convincing her that pulque was not the remedy for the ague besetting me when Honorio and Martín came to the rescue and persuaded her to produce some more authoritative liqueur. This was kept in one of those omnipresent demijohns, and was a clear liquid until milady agitated it by pouring some into the smaller bottle I contracted to purchase. This caused a great number of embalmed creatures to rise from what had been until now their final resting place at the bottom of the jug. As the liquid glooped from the larger vessel into the smaller, the action fragmented the corpses, so that my mates and I were able to share a fairly homogeneous product, no one getting all the meat while the others were left with the wing.

It was powerful stuff—*aguardiente,* a distillation of the sugar cane. Swallowing the "ardent water" seemed to have the sought-for effect and my shaking subsided at least for a little while. I did not insist on drinking the stuff down to the dregs, since the dregs were composed of a rather more concentrated collection of insect remains than I could properly swallow without damage to my reputation as a person of moderate appetite.

"*Bueno, señor,*" growled the lady, "*le gustó?*—was it to your taste?"

"I believe I have enjoyed better," said I, too sick to consider the possible consequences of a confrontation with her in her own arena.

"*Pues,* I told you to take the pulque," said she rightly.

Paying off this Hecuba, we departed the unholy place and proceeded on foot down the muddy hill toward an area where I could discern through the mist and the dusk of nightfall the blurred lights and the sounds of automotive traffic—I still thinking we had come upon a village that would offer at least the basic amenities required by a dying man. I was dismayed to find, instead, a collection of shabby warehouses, barnlike structures facing upon a few rough streets from which a succession of heavy trucks departed at uncertain intervals with their cargoes. The connection for Perote I was to make here would be some truck that might by chance be going that way and whose driver would be willing to take me.

My efforts to find one were less than encouraging. In the first place, we could find no truck whose cab was not already occupied by the driver's helper and one or two friends, leaving no room for a sick, unshaven vagabond of most unsavory aspect *plus* a hard-looking mountain Indian.

In the second place, none of these trucks was going by way of Perote, but were headed *exprés* for Mexico. Here was the cruelest of temptations. With pesos, I might persuade a driver to allow us to crawl under the tarpaulin among the sacks of corn and thus, in one night's ride, complete my pilgrimage. Vera Cruz to Mexico City! Done! Is there any question but that Bernal Díaz would have climbed aboard if there had been *camiones* then? Would not Cortés himself have expedited his mission to Moctezuma's citadel, sparing himself and his men the uncertainties, the bloody trials of Tlaxcala and Cholula? Who would condemn *me,* then? Justifications? For starters: a coronary history; a ruptured disk; imminent—if not actual—pneumonia; a torn and throbbing foot. More? I had done the difficult part, step by step, over the mountains. I had even sought out Xico Viejo when Xico *"nuevo"* alone should have qualified me for membership in the Explorers' Club. I had been in *terra incognita* on trails untrod *since*—or even *by*—Cortés. I could almost swear to that. Who could prove me false?

What does Honorio say about all this? He has done the worst portion of this *via crucis* on foot while I rode. And he has no esoteric point to prove such as has placed me in these unsalubrious circumstances.

"*Qué dices,* Honorio—what do you say? A truck ride straight through to Mexico. . . . We can be there in the morning to dine on beefsteak and good chocolate."

"*Como desea el señor*—whatever you say, boss," says he. We have not discussed the matter—not a word—but the compact whereby he was to accompany me only to Perote is forgotten. Having come so far—and having seen me suffer so much—he will be my *tamane* to my journey's bitter end.

But to arrive in such shabby fashion in Tenochtitlán? And what of Xocotlán, where the Spaniards saw the hundred thousand skulls? Not tread after all the hill where Xicotenga made his camp when he showed the foreign devils of what stuff the Tlaxcalans were made?

"No, Honorio," say I, for a venture such as this brings out the best—or maddest—in us, "*No, tenemos que seguir via Perote*—Perote or bust!"

"*De acuerdo*—right-o," says he (but I do believe that for one brief instant he hates me!).

We went from driver to driver seated high above us at their wheels like proud captains on their bridges—supplicating, begging to know if they would pass Perote, and if they would take us there. All the while Martín stood by patiently, his hand on the horse's bridle, waiting until he knew we had found our way. A sense of duty such as this can be found only in the old lays of chivalry. His assignment had been to accompany me to Los Altos and then return the horse to Ayahualulco. The ghastly journey we had made together he must now turn around and do again, alone and in the shadow of black night. True, he will ride—and sit more easily on the horse than I had done. Nevertheless, his is a heroic odyssey.

The situation was grave. No trucks were going to Perote and it was beyond any doubt I could not survive a cold mountain night on some warehouse floor. The delirium of that last hour on horseback would be as nothing compared to the night in the company of rats and scorpions that now seemed in prospect.

Then a driver, regretting he could not help me, mentioned that possibly the electrician's *camioneta* had not yet departed—and he was certain the electrician went to Perote. *"Ah, allí está* —there he goes! That *camioneta* just pulling out onto the street!" Honorio raced down the street and stopped the small, quarter-ton delivery van while I limped after him.

The electrician had *his* assistant with him. Drivers do not make their night runs alone in these desolate places. Yes, he was going to Perote, but first he must stop at Sierra de Agua with instructions for the electrician there. He regretted that this would be for me too great an inconvenience.

"No, no! It is exactly what I wish!"

"Bueno, señor. Accommodate yourselves." He tossed his thumb in the direction of the covered van behind. Honorio raised the back flap and climbed in over the tailgate, while I sought hurriedly to wish Martín God's company on his way back to Ayahualulco and pressed some pesos upon him.

"Adiós, Martín. It is incredible, what you have the fortitude to do! *Adiós."*

"But *no-o-o, señor,"* he laughed. *"Nada.* Nothing. Nothing at all."

Honorio pulled me up over the tailgate and we settled ourselves in the utter blackness of the van's interior among cables, tools, and some sacks of potatoes.

The mortification of my flesh was not yet done. Every wounded part of me was now subjected to fresh assault. The worst flagellations of the saddle were duplicated by the assorted hardware on which I bounced. It was not possible to tell how fast we went, but the corrugations of the road were transmitted to my spine with remarkably short intervals of relief, until we reached a highway about an hour later. Shortly thereafter I could feel the truck turning off the pavement and we stopped before a place whose bright illumination I was able to glimpse from under the tarpaulin's flap. Loud music, wild laughter, female shrieks—the sounds of the truckman's night—told me we had returned to civilization.

We stopped there for a half hour, so I suppose the electrician conveyed his message and had his supper. I had not the strength to crawl out from under the tarpaulin and felt incompetent at the moment to involve myself in a scene of wild Mexican rioting. A renewal of my shivering had been set off by the vibrations of this truck ride, and so I lay shaking and quaking, wondering what I would find in Perote, and when. Honorio, however, climbed out, and when he returned ten minutes or so later, I detected that he had taken a drop to drink. His day had not been easy either.

The electrician came out at last. He looked in on me to say we were now bound for Perote and, if I wished, he would drop us off at a hotel that had been opened recently on the road entering the town. If I wished? I wished!

Another half hour, this time on the paved highway, and we pulled up before a place of tile and glass, a sleek and glossy inn of the modern sort, product of Mexico's Olympic year and more suitable for a tourist than for a pair of unkempt mountain men.

A *caballero*—a gentleman in the honest sense—wields his pliers, snipping and crimping the cables that bring modern electrical power to the primitive reaches of the high sierras. He cannot know that, far away, in another world, I toast him. He cannot know that, when he delivered the raggedy mountain men to the inn that awful night, he saved a gringo's life.

The innkeeper was a great mustachioed fellow who recognized misery when he saw it—the talent is not universal. Perhaps as a reaction to my last-ditch rescue, the trembling took such hold of me that he rushed me up to a twin-bedded room, turned a shower on in the bathroom so the water would run hot while I shed my sopping clothes, left the room *con permiso,* and quickly returned with a bottle of what he called the *brandi del país*—Mexican "brandy." It was mezcal of a finer sort in a sealed bottle instead of the bug-congested demijohn of my last haven. I tried, but was unable to hold the glass steady as he poured, for the shaking was completely out of control. The good chap took the glass from my hand and filled it for me, checked the shower water, then went down to his desk to register me, leaving me to maneuver the liquid to my lips in my own time.

Perhaps the water *was* hot; I was that far gone, it felt cold to me. While I showered, Honorio emptied out the contents of the knapsack and found no clothing that the *chipi-chipi* had not reached. He took it down to be dried in the kitchen, at the suggestion of the compassionate innkeeper, while I added my sleeping capsules to the mezcal I had finally managed to swallow and sank still shivering, onto my bed.

The next morning the trembling had calmed. Honorio slept soundly in the other bed, his machete dangling at its foot. A rare picture of a couple of pitiful desperadoes, which my imagination could never have invented during the winter past when I had sat reading *The Conquest of Mexico* and formed my first notions of following in the footsteps of Cortés.

Sleeping pills and mezcal—*there* is a combination to indicate the extent of my exhaustion and the small compass of my judgment—and my roommate a primitive demonstrating a partiality for liquor. But, to be just, he had not done me in during our passage through the *mal país,* as he should have done had he had half the spirit of a *conquistador!*

When we arose the next morning and had dressed, Honorio's first concern was the Naturalist's Guide, which appeared to have been soaked beyond salvage. I explained to him how, when the book dried, the illustrated pages would adhere irrevocably. For the next two days he dedicated himself to keeping each damp leaf apart. Not that this newborn literary interest interfered in any way with his more basic appetite.

Never was a man more patient when he was beyond the reach

of food. Stolidly he strode or rode beside me, hour after hour, without complaint when towns and sources of refreshment were few and far between. But when we sat at table—well, let our first meal in Perote serve as a sample of his style.

It was breakfast. We entered the hotel's dining room and found it to be, if not elegant, at least dignified—white table-cloths, stainless-steel cutlery, a hostess—the manager's wife—of the *criollo* class, who was more accustomed to seeing Indians nibbling their tacos while squatting on the curb outside than at her proper tables. The waitress was a pretty girl in crisp apron who could hold her own in badinage with any passing salesman —which is what she was doing when we entered—but who it is doubtful had ever waited on an *indio* of the sierras.

I removed my sombrero as Señora led us to a table and placed it on an unoccupied chair. Honorio kept his headgear where he thought it belonged by its very nature—on his head—and there it stayed throughout breakfast. Señora handed me the menu and withdrew to allow me time to make my selection. I passed it to Honorio and told him to choose what he liked. He pondered it with knitted brow, a Euclid formulating some theorem. He then put it aside, looked over his shoulder, and produced an extraordinary sound. *Pssh!* What was extraordinary about it was that, while not loud, it reached across the room and through the kitchen door like one of those whistles audible only to dogs. This *Pssh* brought Señora back into the dining room and to our table, where Honorio enumerated the items he desired, *biftec* and bottled beer among them. I asked for *huevos y chorizo*— eggs scrambled with ground-up sausage—and chocolate. Señora, smouldering at the indignity of being summoned with a hiss by an *indio,* showed her mood by excessive politeness to *me* and gave the order to the waitress, who brought us the beverages while cook prepared the entree in the kitchen.

Honorio wiped off the rim of the bottle with the scrap of label, ignored the tumbler, and tasted the beer. He turned his head toward the kitchen door.

"Pssh!"

The waitress came to the table. *"Mande—*you wish . . ."* Her eyes were cold. Honorio muttered something to her I could not quite hear, and the girl left, returning immediately with another bottle of beer, upon which he performed the same ritual. Thus he had two bottles of beer on the table when the waitress brought him his *biftec,* with beans and rice on the side; and I, my eggs. She returned to her salesman friend on the other side of the room in rather less gay spirits than she had been in before our arrival. Honorio attacked his steak, at the same time eying my eggs.

"Pssh!"

The waitress came across the room and stood before him, her lips tight-pressed. *"Mande . . ."*

He pointed his forefinger at my eggs and his thumb at himself. No other command was needed so he spoke none, and the *muchacha* gave another order for *huevos y chorizo* into the kitchen. He had finished his *biftec* when this additional course was served him, and, putting aside his knife and fork, he used the tortillas that were being kept warm under a napkin to do away with the eggs. While so applying himself, he disposed of the second bottle of beer, leaving the first bottle untouched. I asked him if he desired anything more.

"Tsk." It was an economical way of saying, *"No, señor."*

I could not contain my curiosity. "Why," I asked, "did you order two bottles of beer, but drank only the second bottle?"

"Demasiado frio," he said. The first bottle had been too cold!

18

It was an amateur's inspiration that had led me to select Perote
as a target when I plotted my course through the *mal país*.
Perote does not figure by name in the history of the Conquest
—but it was approximately here the *conquistadores* arrived when
they had completed their passage over that trackless sierra. More
precisely, they emerged from the "badlands" at Punta de la Lena,
according to the Captain-General's report in one of his *cartas*.
Punta de la Lena is now known as Sierra de Agua, the place
where I had feverishly glimpsed, from beneath the electrician's
tarpaulin, at least one of its raucous roadhouses upon my own
emergence from the mountains.

So we were unquestionably on the trail. One needed only to
gaze at the panorama spread before us as we stood outside the
door of the hotel and compare it with the description of the
view Cortés saw as it was recounted by Prescott, that most
indefatigable researcher. The Captain-General had looked out
upon ". . . [a] great sheet of tableland [spreading] out for
hundreds of miles along the crests of the *Cordilleras*. The country
showed signs of careful cultivation but the products were, for
the most part, not familiar to the eyes of the Spaniards. Fields
and hedges of the various tribes of the cactus, the towering
organum, and plantations of aloes with rich yellow clusters of
flowers on their tall stems, affording drink and clothing to the
Aztec, were everywhere seen. . . ."

The highway, with its traffic of growling, fuming trucks, has
been added to the scene on which the weary adventurers had

looked, but little else would have been different to the *con-quistadores.*

And Cortés, per Prescott, shared with me—or I with him—the recollection of the country we had left behind when we started our ascent. ". . . The glossy and dark-leaved banana . . . had long since faded from the landscape. The hardy maize, however, still shone with its golden harvests in all the pride of cultivation, the great staple of the higher equally with the lower traces of the plateau. . . ."

This cool region had another moment in history, meaningful to *norteamericanos* though forgotten by them. It was here at Perote that a strong-willed retired general and statesman paused on his way to take control of a Mexico that had seen eight revolutions since the *"Grito de Dolores"* in 1810 first signaled to Spain that she had had her day in the New World. Now, in 1840, the statesman came out of retirement (Madame Calderón, his contemporary who had personally met him, compared him to Cincinnatus—he really was a prestigious personality then) to set things in order once and for all, to bring stability to the young and restless nation, and guide her to greatness. He said so in his speeches. There were many in the capital who, when they knew that General Antonio Lopez de Santa Anna was in Perote and would soon arrive in Mexico City, cheered and were comforted in the knowledge that their country would now move forward to her great destiny. What they did not know was that another young nation to the north was flexing *her* muscles, and had been making speeches about how manifest *her* great destiny was. . . .

It is highly unlikely that the tourists know, as they speed past Perote—it takes only a twinkle to streak past it in the air-conditioned tour buses, and they never stop—that "Santy Anny" slept here. Few natives know it either. Well, "Santy Anny" has gone out of fashion in the American demonology this long century past, though he had his day. There are only little echoes of that day now—but they are not entirely pleasant. As General Winfield Scott marched upon Mexico his soldiers sang "Green

Grow the Rushes, Oh!" and so we are still known as "Green Grows," sometimes good-humoredly, sometimes not. From time to time unhappy murmurings are heard from the Chicanos in the *barrios* of California, Texas, Arizona, and New Mexico, for whom the Guadalupe-Hidalgo Treaty has not proven a one-hundred per cent boon. Souvenirs of long ago . . .

Perote today is a typical high sierra town of ten thousand population, a good portion of which seems to be engaged in selling tacos at the bus station. The air is crisp all year round, for the town looks down on rolling country from an elevation of some eight thousand feet; and I found that, while the sun beamed warmly on my shoulders as I strolled down the road in search of a money changer, my chill of yesterday returned whenever I stepped into a shadow.

Yes, at the rate at which Honorio consumed food, I thought I had better find a bank and purchase some more pesos, for we still had a long road ahead of us. I needed very little money, really, as long as I was in rural Mexico, so I carried few pesos, for I had been warned it would be unwise to have any excessive sum of cash on me in the kind of ambient toward which I was apt to gravitate. For that reason I had exchanged traveler's checks for only a minimum amount of the local currency when I received that hard-won license to do so in Jalapa. I now thought it best to replenish my stock, in anticipation of my present hotel bill and the indeterminable expenses of the journey's next leg.

We found a bank—a store-front affair—and entered. Honorio waited by the door, for his intercourse with establishments of this kind has been largely vicarious and he sees the bank as a mysterious, unhallowed place, possibly Protestant, whose indecorous activities had best be viewed from a distance.

The total effect of our entrance tended to be provocative, for Italian and French films depicting clever bank robberies have had as wide a distribution in Mexico as elsewhere, and small-town bankers are nervous when dark strangers enter their premises by twos. By now Honorio and I shared a sinister appearance. Indeed, I had observed to my *compañero* that I had become *más indio* than he. His response, with his usual economy of expression, had been, *"Tsk"*—which I took to mean that I had a long way to go before I deserved the honor. Nevertheless, my untrimmed beard of dirty white, together with a burned, angry-red complexion, endowed me with the suspect look of someone who may not be what he seems to be.

The *empleado* of the bank looked at me uneasily as I approached his counter, then from me to Honorio, who remained near the door. While Perote is not the City of Light that Paris is said to be, neither is it a town whose banks are commonly entered by *indios* armed with machetes and obviously freshly arrived from the sierra.

I presented my book of traveler's checks and asked to purchase pesos. The checks were prima-facie evidence that I was a *norte-americano,* which at least partially dispelled the clerk's fear of an Indian raid. But I was not home free yet. Another ghost rose to haunt me.

"Su pasaporte, señor."

Good Quetzalcoatl! Here we go again, thought I. *"He perdido mis papeles . . ."* I started.

This earned for me the inevitable look that says, "What, lost your papers? That cannot be. Only a *ladrón* loses his papers. Surely not an honest man."

"However . . ." I continued, reaching deep, deep, deeper into the pocket where I kept the immortal "Acts" of Zempoala and of Jalapa. I suffered a moment of panic when I did not immediately feel them there. Finally I found them. They had been soaked, steamed, kneaded, then dried to the dimensions and consistency of a stale tortilla. I might have been tendering a cowrie shell in barter. ". . . However, these documents,"—I held out the tortilla—"have been prepared for me by the *presidente* in Zempoala and by the *Procuraduria General de Justicia* in Jalapa and . . ." Wearily, I told the old tale.

The *empleado* took the certified tortilla to another official, one who had the rank that goes with a corner desk. The two conferred at great length while I looked lamely toward Honorio and shrugged. The functionaries succeeded in picking apart enough of the tortilla to determine that possibly I was capable of the truth. Then, with such bravado as I could muster, I signed my name on the back of one of my business cards and offered it to them as irrefutable testimony that I could sign the same name on the back that was printed on the front. This precocious accomplishment swung the balance in my favor, and they sold me my pesos.

Honorio had been observing this transaction and must have begun to wonder if, in meeting me, he had not fallen in with bad company. But I was simply not in the mood to repeat the saga of the missing documents to him. I muttered, "*Maldito chipi-chipi*—that damned rain . . ." and we took our leave.

The fact that my shivering tended to recur whenever I stepped out of the direct rays of the sun made it advisable that we linger at Perote for a day before proceeding on in pursuit of *conquistador* ghosts. The hotel room's warm shower was a comfort and, as I had taken no bath since Jalapa, it seemed wise to stock up on this luxury while the opportunity was at hand.

The facilities were not perfect, in spite of the newness of the hotel and for all that it was the stately pleasure dome of Xanadu compared with the places we had been. While the bathroom was large, it was distinguished by a most curious feature: there was no tub or shower stall. Instead, the shower poured down upon one end of the tiled bathroom floor, in a corner of which was a drain. This arrangement is common enough and I have seen it in modern and even luxurious Mexican apartments. However, in *this* case the floor sloped *away* from the drain and toward the opposite end of the room where the sink and toilet were situated. Therefore, when the shower was used, the sink and toilet fixture were in several inches of water.

It is well known that parts of Mexico City rest on the unstable bed of a lake long since gone, so that some of its most historic edifices are sinking out of plumb. One of the most heartbreaking

Terrain of the Conquistador Trail

Above: Old Conquistador Chapel, Vera Cruz Antigua

Below: Where Cortés toppled the gods of Compoala

Above: Institution of learning on trail to Xico Viejo

Below: Ixhuacán de Los Reyes

Above: Market in Altotonga.

Below: Popo and Ixtaccihuatl, seen from Xicotencatl's "Tomb"

Above: What Cortés saw from the Great Pyramid at Cholula.

Below: Thriving market in lump sugar—Altotonga

Above: Cargador, on trail to Ayahualulco

Below: A short cut through Altotonga, but nearly vertical!

Above: Tlaxcala. Temple said to be "Tomb" of Xicotencatl

Below: Where Moctezuma reigned. Today, the Zócalo in Mexico City, on the "Day of the Revolution"

sights is that of the Shrine of Guadalupe, crumbling as, with the passing years, it lowers into the ground.

But we are now some 160 miles from the old lake beds of Xalcotan and Texcoco, where Tenochtitlán had sat glittering like a barbarous Venice when Cortés first saw it. Perote sits instead eight thousand feet high on the volcanic rock and has no possibility of settling at its foundations. The sloping floor of the hotel bathroom, then, is an unaccountable feature of its design, intended, we may cynically conjecture, to discourage repeated or prolonged use of the shower. Or do we have here a relic of some ancient and unpublished practice of the Aztec who, perhaps, brushed his teeth and bathed his feet simultaneously? Yes, the Aztecs brushed their teeth. Sahagun, a historian of New Spain, writing as a contemporary observer of Aztec customs, has recorded the admonition of an Indian parent to his son that, among other things, he pick up articles dropped on the floor, wash his hands before dinner—partcularly, we may suppose, if it was an important ceremonial affair and fat roast boy was on the menu—and, *"después de comer*—after dinner—clean his teeth. . . ." These disciplines are not peculiar to Scarsdale and our own enlightened age.

Our good boniface sent a *muchacho* up early in the morning to bail out the bathroom. But the problem remained that a late-evening shower left the toilet facilities submerged like the Temple of Philae all through the night, which was inconvenient for those of us who make nocturnal pilgrimages to the temple.

But one does not follow the trail of the *conquistadores* in order to discover perfect plumbing!

Dinner in the dining room was as much a trial for the help as breakfast had been. They could not very well throw Honorio out without losing my patronage—but he *would* keep his hat on at table, even during the quasiformality of evening dinner. I was naturally not immune to the strain of the situation and looked at my *compañero,* who sat imperturbably opposite me, the sombrero squarely on his head. Surely I had an obligation to lecture him, to improve him, to somehow direct his attention to my own properly bared head and awaken in him some awareness of the accepted etiquette. But his attention was single-mindedly on the food, which he ordered in his peremptory fashion. I thought hard on the matter, trying to persuade myself that I would be doing the *chamaco* a good turn by telling him to follow my example when we were in civilized places.

The more I thought about it, the more I convinced myself that it was the worst presumption to suppose I could tell a man how he should act in his own country. In the end, I reached for my sombrero, clapped it on my head, and thereafter hissed when I wanted the waitress.

19

Cortés wrote to his king that he next proceeded to Ceyconacán and thence to Caltanmi, but no such towns could I find on my maps, and I encountered no citizen of Perote who had ever heard of them. This does not mean Cortés invented the places. Were Don Hernán to turn about and try to follow my trail through Westchester County, he, too, would get blank stares if he inquired of my fellow townspeople for the whereabouts of the town of Kensico, which was razed not much more than a half century ago to make way for the city reservoir. Who knows what happened to Ceyconacán and Caltanmi after four and a half centuries?

I spent my last evening in the hotel room in Perote with Prescott in one hand, Díaz in the other, and a glass of mezcal in the third, analyzing, deducing, and weighing alternatives in preparation for the resumption of our journey the next morning. Prescott, who has wrung out every source and pored over countless documents and who is the master historian of the Conquest in spite of the fact that all his labor was performed in his Boston study, has the Spaniards proceed from Puerto de la Lena —our Sierra de Agua of the female's abandoned laughter— and coming ". . . suddenly to what seemed the environs of a populous city, which, as they entered it, appeared to surpass even that of Cempoala in the size and solidity of its structures. . . ." This, he says, is the town that today bears the delightful name of Tlatlauquitepec. It is understandably abbreviated to Tlatlauqui by its inhabitants.

On the other hand, Díaz, who marched faithfully behind his Captain-General, mentions a station in between, unnoticed by his leader in the latter's communiques to King Charles. I quote Díaz: ". . . We crossed a pass over some high mountains [high, indeed! They nearly killed me] and came to another town called Texutla, which we found well disposed to us also. . . ." In other words, the General saw fit to mention a "major" city (today's Tlatlauqui) in his official report. The lesser officer, if the doughty Díaz could ever be described as a lesser *anything,* remembered the then smaller town where he and his mates no doubt heard those blessed words that officers on horseback seem loath to speak to marching troops: "Fall out! Take a break! Smoke if you got 'em."

So, thought I, as I sipped the *brandi del país,* we now have two towns either named or described by eyewitnesses: Texutla— which has to be the Texiutlan on my map; and Tlatlauquitepec, which is also on the map. This provided me with a clear enough direction for the morrow.

I have seen this segment of the route worked out in a publication of Mexico's famed Anthropological Museum, but with an interesting difference. The author reasoned that through orthographic corruption (there certainly has been enough of that!) the name Texutla evolved from *Teixuacan* or *Teuhixuacan,* and is therefore none other than our old Ixhuacán! However, I myself climbed the mountain *after* passing through Ixhuacán, and it is after this ascent that Díaz speaks of Texutla.

Bueno. The route is the same in any case.

But we are not done with puzzles yet. Díaz says that from Texutla they next came to Xocotlán, and describes *that* town in terms that could fit the missing Ceyconacán. One name could be a variant of the other. Is this all terribly preposterous? Not when one considers the trouble soldiers always have with foreign names. After all, the best Díaz was ever able to do with Huitzilopotchli, perhaps the most important of all the Aztec gods, was "Huichilobos."

There are scholars who hold that Xocotlán is today's Zautla.

It is possible. But Prescott said "Tlatlauquitepec," and since it was his great history that set me off on this quest in the first place, it was Tlatlauqui for me. They are all in the same tight region anyway—all within walking distance of each other—as Aztecs walk!

How different was the mezcal I sipped as I puzzled out this confusion from that vile *aguardiente* we drank in the witch's *pulquería!* And how clear the route of the *conquistadores* became as I studied and sipped. There was Tlatlauquitepec, and here was Teziutlan. And since they both follow the old Indian trails, it was evidence enough for me that a road that went through the two of them had to be the right one.

The next morning, then, in considerably better condition than I had been in on the night of our arrival, we bade *adiós* to a relieved staff at breakfast and marched a mile down the road to Perote's bus station, where I had been advised to look for a *camión* for Altotonga, en route to Teziutlan and the very heart of *conquistador* country. The sun was bright and the air fine as we walked, and the temptation was strong to spurn the bus; but that would have meant a hike of some fifteen or twenty miles along a paved and much traveled motor highway, and there seemed little sense to deliberately exacerbate the aching tendon.

I anticipate an impatient question and answer it with another. What good would it have done to seek out a doctor to treat my foot? He would advise me not to walk on it! Imagine how a *conquistador* would have responded to such advice. "All of us were wounded," says Díaz after a skirmish, "but we pressed on." But would not a *médico* have bound up my foot, at least? Probably so, but I possess, among my other qualifications for the rugged, physical life, an extraordinary allergy to doctors' tape. The adhesive in a soothing plaster causes my skin to blossom out in great, angry rashes and loathsome pustules. In hospitals, of which I am a fairly regular client, nurses are obliged to pin little notes on me warning surgeons not to use surgical tapes when applying their dressings while I am under anaesthesia.

So my rationale in avoiding medical care was not all bravery nor all bravado. As for pain, I had become an habitué of the local *boticas,* which saw to it that my supply of pain pills never ran short. No, I do not know what the pills were composed of but, taken with a nip of mezcal or washed down with a swallow of beer, I was able, for the most part, to tolerate the pain. *Claro,* I do not give this account of a ramble through the hills of rural Mexico to provide guidelines for sensible self-medication. Good sense would have kept me at home in the first place. Nor is good sense the ultimate guide for an endeavor.

Not for an instant, as we walked along the highway, did Honorio stop riffling the still damp pages of the Naturalist's Guide, airing and sunning them with such patience and dedication that, finally, I told him the book was his. His pleasure was so great that he uttered an almost audible *"Gracias"* under his breath—a truly remarkable outburst of emotion.

20

The little bus we boarded for Altotonga was invaded by the motley vendors of comfits and comestibles minutes after we were seated. It would be as long as a quarter-hour before the *camión* made its next stop and, as has been already noted, an Aztec will not lightly chance so long a journey without assuring himself something on which to nibble. He had his usual wide choice. *"Chiles rellenos!"* the hawkers cried. *"Enchiladas de pollo! Empanadas! Dulces y refrescos!"* The style of the vendors was more musical in Perote than it had been in the more somnolent, tropical towns of the *tierra caliente.* Here they chanted their offerings with lively, almost oriental suasion difficult to resist and sparking a brisk trade. The pace of commerce reached a crescendo when the driver climbed aboard and the Indian women made their quick, flitting signs of the cross against the perils of the journey—for the passengers must buy their snacks now or never. *"Tortas distintas!"* was an especially alluring cry, tempting me to try a "distinctive" turnover just to learn in what way it distinguished itself, but I had already enjoyed a good breakfast of chilled papaya, eggs—always eggs—and that truly great Aztec gift to the world, the delicious spiced chocolate that Moctezuma was wont to sip in aristocratic ennui all the day long.

In keeping with my purpose that this account of a bumbler's pursuit of history be a source of enduring truths, I must observe that we all speak more Aztec than we realize, as when we ask for chocolate; it was *chocolatl* in meso-America long before the white man came. And who gave tomatoes and another word to the world but the Mexicans of old who named this exotic fruit *tomatl.* Our Aztec vocabulary is surprisingly large. We speak a bit of the Nahuatl tongue when we call a *coyotl* a coyote (the great Nezahualcoyotl was "Hungry Coyote," following the old fashion of naming Indian boys after animals of extraordinary talent). We have our ocelot from Aztec's *ocelotl.* For our Chiclets, we must thank the Mexican discoverers of *chicl* (what tourist in Mexico City has not been besieged by old Indian women crying, *"Chicles! Chicles!"*). And if Texans think *they* invented chilli, it was *chilli* to Moctezuma himself—or *quauchilli,* to be exact. Mesquite, that standard cowboy's shrub, was the Nahuatl *mizquitl.* We have already been introduced to the slippery *ahuacotl,* which anyone can plainly see is the avocado, the name less changed than the spelling would suggest.

I was not proof against all blandishments. A gaunt vendor boarded the bus at the very last minute, bearing a tray on which was arrayed a quantity of cheeses of a milky whiteness so manifestly proof of their goodness that I bought us a couple. They were *quesillos oaxaqueños,* and made, their purveyor said, after an old family recipe. I cannot claim to know what that particular family's tradition was, but it is well known that in the villages, señora will keep a dusty piece of cow's cud, usually hanging from a roof beam, which she adds to the milk in order to induce the curdling process in cheese-making. The cud does not look pleasant, but it possesses the precise kind of enzyme owned only by a cow's regurgitated juices that someone long ago determined was essential to good homemade cheese. The originators of the process could not have been the Aztecs— they had no cows, in spite of what Cortés said when he wrote King Charles that he had seen lush pastureland at Vera Cruz for ". . . all kinds of herds . . . grazing, and for use as beasts of burden. . . ." There were no such beasts in Mexico until the Spaniards themselves introduced them. Cortés was jumping to conclusions, and was turning in a report he thought would please the boss. The ploy is in the best business tradition.

I pinched off a bit of my *quesillo oaxaqueño* to taste as the *camión* started to roll, and we were not five minutes on the road before I had consumed the whole of it. What do I know, or care, about the origin of the *quesillo's* enzymes! Never again in my rambles did I find, and never have I since, a cheese its equal.

We were on the plateau, the tableland, and did not expect the bus would still be grinding out more altitude, but the visitor knows that, except for Mexico's flat desert regions, it is a land with mountains upon its mountains. We threaded through hills, around curves that bent the roads back upon themselves, alternately climbing and dipping and climbing again and dipping once more, gears grinding now to hold us back, to the end that we should reach Altotonga, which sat in a great dimple in the plateau two thousand feet *below* the level of Perote. It is a wondrous terrain.

To the *conquistadores,* this region was poignantly reminiscent of home. Cortés and Díaz both commented upon this similarity of topography. One of the soldiers, a Portuguese, recalled his native Castel Branco when they came to Xocotlán-Tlatlauqui-Zautla, whichever it was, and they so named the heathen city. They did this frequently, as homesick soldiers do. G.I.'s of World War II will remember their time spent in "Leghorn," possibly quite forgetting the Italian city was named Livorno. British soldiers knew Castellamare di Stabia as "Axminster"! Cempoala itself was baptized "Sevilla" by Cortés and, though a man educated in law and letters, it was the Captain-General who transformed Quauhnahuac—the forest land—into Cuernavaca—the "Cow's Horn."

This topographical resemblance of the territory near Teziutlán to that of Spain and Portugal came to my own mind while I was being gently rocked by the constant turns and stops and starts and heard a stout lady say, *"Qué vaivén!"* (It sounded like "by-ben".) I had heard the same expression once before in Andalucía, on the edge of Extremadura, the very province from which Cortés had come—make what you will of that—while dining with a young couple on a train from Madrid to Granada. On that occasion young señora excused herself suddenly and retired from the *coche comedor*—the dining car—while her husband explained to me that his wife was always affected by the *vaivén*. The word means, literally, "go-and-come." I was almost the complete *conquistador* now, sharing the same memory of the same distant homeland, though my nostalgia was prompted mainly by a pretty word.

I nodded dreamily as the *camión* proceeded northward (going eastward, westward, and southward to do so), watching the spiny rows of maguey go by and thinking, as always, of my predecessor *conquistadores*. I do not believe it impossible that we had bridged the centuries, they and I, and had become comrades.

And what, as we marched upon him, were the thoughts of the great Moctezuma? Consider the state of the omnipotent emperor's mind as the Spaniards, inching across these hills, neared Tenochtitlán.

Omnipotent? Even the king, born and reared to believe himself a person apart, something more than mortal, must privately feel pinpricks of mortality.

It must have appeared to Moctezuma that Quetzalcoatl had come at last to reclaim his own. To be sure, it was not the first time the god had come. Some twenty-seven years before, when Moctezuma was a boy, rumors had spread that white, bearded beings, fitting the traditional description of Quetzalcoatl, had been seen on the islands. (How could the awed natives who started the rumors have known they had seen Columbus and his crew?)

But Quetzalcoatl did not stay, and a quarter-century passed—time enough for the new emperor, the great Moctezuma, to fall into the complacent ways of earthly lords, believing quite sincerely in his gods and doing them proper homage but not seriously expecting a physical encounter with them. That was the kind of thing that would happen in someone else's—some kingling's—tenure. . . .

He grew to be a potent prince, and a pious one, too, for he fed Quetzalcoatl and Huitzilopotchli and Tezcatlepoca and the rest of the hungry gods generously with living, human hearts, seeing to it the cages were plentifully stocked with sacrificial victims so it could never be said that he and his priests were ever remiss in their pious duties. A good man from the very outset of his reign, at his coronation he sacrificed a whole host of men and women in order that the gods would smile upon his empire. The procession of the victims climbing up the sides of the great pyramid, at the top of which awaited the *papas* with their obsidian knives, was a sight to inspire in the citizens of Colhua thoughts both pious and patriotic.

Was it because Moctezuma had been so good a prince that Quetzalcoatl was repeating the visitation? (In 1517, Hernández de Córdoba, a hidalgo from Cuba seeking Indian slaves among the Bahamas, was blown by severe gales to the unknown coast of Yucatán but established no foothold. In 1518, Juan de Grijalva was seen at *Akimpech*—Campeche. Grijalva scouted the coast as far as Panuco, but circumstances forced him, too, to return to Cuba.)

Another visitation now, a year later—but this time Quetzalcoatl seemed to have come to stay. But was it truly Quetzalcoatl? He and his band were acting strangely. They had all the attributes of the expected god: they carried thunder and lightning in their hands; some of them pranced on four legs; they were white and bearded, as tradition required them to be, and they came from the sunrise. But all was not fully understandable to the sleepless Moctezuma. Why did these strange visitors go about toppling their own idols?

How restless were the nights for the great Moctezuma! He bade his priests tear the living hearts out of the choicest victims, captured at great cost from the neighboring nation of the recalcitrant Tlaxcalans—but found no satisfying answers. The strange visitors continued to move inland from the sea, toward Tenochtitlán, his beautiful city.

He should receive them, of course. One does not close the gate to god. Some of his priests and princes so counseled him. Others, less sentimental and boasting more political sense, said no, he should stop the strangers while they were yet beyond the gate, while it was still possible. If they turned out to be the gods —apologize! Plead ignorance!

What sleepless nights he spent! A great Moctezuma, who has quite his own way in all things, does not want even god to come along uninvited. It is a comfort to believe in the deity, to share problems with him; but a deity must not be . . . insistent. It had been a relief when god had gone away after his earlier visits and the Aztecs had gone about their business as usual, telling proper, inspirational stories to the children about supernatural beings who would someday come out of the sunrise. It was good in the talking about it, and in the praying and the preaching and the sacrificing.

Now god was nearing Tenochtitlán. What sleepless nights Moctezuma spent, and all the other princes who had things their own way. Gloomy, fruitless consultations with the priests, and Moctezuma decided—without decisiveness—to let god approach nearer and nearer. Perhaps before he arrived he would go away again. He had done so before. . . .

How does one manage god? The problem has presented itself before in the history of men, and will again. For all the reverence and awe men feel for their deity, they do not find it an easy matter to bid him welcome—nor ever will. Because of all the things that God is to men, God is most of all man's competitor.

21

It was almost as if there were a Moctezuma watching my progress, commanding vassals to greet me and bid me welcome as I moved from town to town, just as that doubt-wracked, nervous potentate had done for the advancing Spaniards.

Once again I reached a remote town, this time Altotonga, with not the slightest notion of what acceptance I would have as I invaded its privacy; of what facilities I might find for refreshment or repose. When the *camión* deposited me on the narrow cobbled street that entered the town, I was overcome by the same sense of loneliness I had experienced when I was left standing that first time in the plaza at Zempoala. Wise though I was by this time to the ways of villages and their people, *expertise* was now beginning to give way to fatigue.

Of course I had Honorio upon whom I was able to bounce off a rhetorical, *"Bueno.* What now?"

He shrugged his agreement that the question was a valid one, and we proceeded down the street knowing that almost any street in a small Mexican town is likely to lead to its *zócalo* or plaza—its heart. If we had stayed aboard the bus a few minutes longer we would have ridden comfortably to the plaza, but the stout lady who had been bothered by the *vaivén,* anxious to share a native's wisdom with a stranger, had excitedly told me we were in Altotonga the very instant we reached the town's outer boundary, so we hurried off, fearful that if we did not react immediately to the information it would cease to be a fact.

It was not a long walk and we were soon at the square, where we found Moctezuma's legate awaiting us!

It was incredible how I, deteriorating with each passing hour both internally and outwardly, always found someone waiting to be kind to me. I seemed to have, in all of these unheralded entrances into the by-villages of Mexico, an extraordinary propensity for human contact—not one of my more notable personal characteristics in my own world.

My own world . . . maybe this was it in fact—where I could saunter, in the sense of Thoreau's *sainte-terrer*—holylander —as I pleased, bearded and unbathed, where there was none to make demands upon me or to hold me in any way accountable; a wanderer from whom nothing was expected except that he wander.

Expensive guided tours, whose sleek brochures guarantee that expert, conscientious cicerones will be in the hotel lobby at the specified hour, do sometimes disappoint the tourist. But my record, for which I had no choice but to thank the old gods—I surely could not give the credit to my own astute planning—my record was truly remarkable. From the very beginning, in Zempoala, there had been Agustín, the town elders, the family Marqués— all appointed to my service. In Jalapa, José Antonio had been assigned to steer me through that proud city's bureaucratic toils; and the barber at the table had been there felicitously to guide my attack upon a *caldo Xalapeño*. In Xico, the judge and the *ex-presidente,* as well as all the cronies, had been waiting for my arrival as surely as there is a Huitzilopotchli. The *pochteca* appeared out of the pine-green mountains to lead me from Ixhuacán to Ayahualulco, where the family Cortés-Fuente—yes, Cornelia Otis Skinner, too, *bendita sea*—had been stationed to welcome and to succor me!

Who would dare to say that in my misery, in Los Altos where the world ends, the electrician happened only by chance to be departing at that grim moment for Perote?

Now, here in Altotonga, which has never seen a tourist— search the Baedekers or their Latin equivalents; no word about

Altotonga will be found—I walked down a forlorn street to find Don Platón Alvarez taking a half-hour's sun.

"Dispénse, Usted," I said, "but can you direct me to the *Palacio* of the government?"

"Su servidor—your servant," the old gentleman said. "I will be happy to accompany you there."

We strolled for only a moment or two before he had drawn from me, nor was I loath to be drawn, the fact that I was following in the footsteps of Hernando Cortés—Honorio nodding vigorously to Don Platón that it was true, true, incredibly true, the señor was indeed pursuing that forgotten trail. Honorio considered me his own by now, and felt he must champion my causes.

Platón Alvarez, it developed, was the one person in Altotonga who had a scholar's interest in the history of this region. He would show me things, he told me, that he was certain I would be the happier, and a more fulfilled man for seeing.

Walk! I will not soon forget Don Platón or Altotonga, and my exploration and circumnavigation of the place. It had not been my intention to do so thorough an investigation of the town, for after all, it is nowhere mentioned in the chronicles of the Conquest. But Don Platón, a *criollo* who was most proud of his Spanish forebears and their accomplishments in New Spain, was determined to prove that Cortés had come this way beyond all doubt. This he did by showing me the vestiges of ancient cultures on the site of Altotonga, arguing justly that the Spaniards could not possibly have avoided this area, which stood in the undisputed path of Tlatlauqui *or* Zautla. Whether the one or the other had been the Ceycconacán of Cortés (yes, that is how he spelled it), the Spaniards had needed to pass through what is now Altotonga to get there. Cortés was not the one to bypass this place knowing that here were the indigenous and unholy temples he was sworn to replace with the temples of the true faith. There never was so impatient a missionary, and more than once his zeal had needed to be curbed by Fray Olmedo himself, his ever-present chaplain, who counseled him that it would be more effective—certainly more discreet—to pacify the natives first and *then* convert them.

Don Platón took me to the high school—it was not far, he said, lying in his teeth. There the principal permitted me to inspect an enormous fragment of stone, a scaled, winged serpent that once had embellished some great edifice. It now lay beneath a window in the corridor outside the principal's office—a thing for school children to sit on while waiting to be summoned to the august presence. I ran a finger along its carved, worn surface, as I am always drawn to do with the artifacts of other ages, while bright teen-agers walked by, debating vital questions of the day. What were the vital questions when the sculptor was engaged in bringing this cold stone to life? Well, if vital organs have not changed, we can be confident that vital questions were about the same then as now!

The greater mystery is how the sculptor was able to carve the stone. Metal for tools was not known in Mexico before A.D. 950 or so, and the ornate pyramids as well as the other great structures of Monte Alban, Teotihuacán, Tajin, and Palenque were all built well before this time. Some speak of a now forgotten root juice of some sort that was able to eat into the stone. Others say there is no science known today not known in another time and we are advised to be modest about our accomplishments, for they, too, will in their turn be forgotten. No philosopher who deserves the title will assert that the wheel will *never* have to be invented all over again, or iron rediscovered!

Then my new friend insisted I should see the spot where the stone serpent had been unearthed. No, not at all far, he said, so we walked across the entire breadth of the city, until we were in the countryside. Then we walked over the rolling hills of the countryside until we reached a meadow. The meadow was pretty enough to have a picnic in, but really had no other single outstanding feature.

"Here," declared the old man, ". . . here is where the stone was found!"

I tried to show appropriate reverence toward the empty field, a difficult thing to do at the moment in spite of the awe in which I habitually hold meadows. Nevertheless, it was significant that such a relic of a vanished edifice should have been found there. The fragment was much too large to have been carried from some other site and left, discarded, in this place. The empty meadow, then, had been the ceremonial center for some ancient civilization.

I begged my friend to lunch with me, thinking by this stratagem to trick him into sitting down—but since we were near it now, he said, he would like me to see the airport. We tramped along a highway skirting the town for a league or two and reached another meadow nestling among the hills.

"*El aeropuerto!*" Don Platón announced proudly.

There were no airplanes and, indeed, it appeared to me that no wheels of any kind had intruded upon the virgin field within the memory of anyone but a booster like Platón. The point he wished to impress upon me, a visitor who might carry the word to the outside world, was that if someday an aeronaut should wish to fly to Altotonga, Altotonga would be ready for him.

My fatigue became at last apparent to my host, and he promised me a short cut back into the city. This meant that, instead of following the level highway by which we had reached the two astonishing meadows, we would follow a straight course, the shortest line between us and the city's center—climbing and descending a dozen hills to do so. It was, of course, the shortest way—and the most vertical!

Back in town, we sat at last to lunch in a tiny place of his acquaintance, occupying the only table. But it was impossible to keep the old fellow down. While waiting for the chicken to boil, Señor Alvarez asked that we excuse him for a moment or two. We were dipping our tortillas into the broth when he returned, staggering under the weight of a large, crescent-shaped stone. It, too, was a fragment of ancient sculpture that he himself had unearthed many years before and that now decorated his parlor. I caressed the piece, of course, and expressed my admiration of it, before Don Platón fetched it home again.

He was back shortly and I asked that he at least take a *refresco* with us, for it did not seem likely he could sit still long enough to take solid food. He accepted, and chatted pleasantly while we ate. It was inevitable, naturally, that I should remark upon the fiery character of the cuisine, for my tears were flowing as I swallowed the boiled *pollo.*

"Señor Alvarez," I squeaked to him, "I love the food of your country *con todo mi corazón*—with all my heart—but I do believe that even your ice cream will bring tears to my eyes!"

Up he jumped and, with a *con permiso,* disappeared again, to return minutes later with a bowl of ice cream, for he could not bear to think I should be under such a misconception. My explanation that I had spoken in jest accepted, I tried the ice cream and found it to be a pleasant concoction of milk into which the vanilla bean had been ground, then the milk frozen to a crystalline texture.

Luncheon over, Don Platón was ready to take us on a walking tour of Altotonga.

22

Altotonga was clearly not the drowsy, haunted kind of town through which I had become accustomed to wander in the wilder reaches of the sierras: the high school was evidence of that. The students could not have been distinguished from those breezy young scholars of any school district back home, being not at all the timid, curious little mountain creatures for whom my visit had been an event. The school's principal even had that harassed air our own school administrators have when they promulgate rules on the length of co-ed skirts and then receive anonymous letters in girlish scrawl warning that the institution will shortly be burned to the ground. A quick handshake, and he had turned immediately to his business of principaling, having little time to spend with an uncouth wanderer. We were nearing civilization!

But Don Platón more than made up for the pedagogue's neglect and saw to it that my canvass of his fair *población* was thorough.

Altotonga is a Spanish town, built after the Conquest upon the buried bones of older cultures. But, while its buildings and its homes are in the style of the typical Spanish community of colonial days, its heart—literally the inner core of the city—is as *indio* as those sierra villages; and its *tianguis*—the outdoor market—was precisely the colorful babble of commerce that had so impressed the *conquistadores*. The plaza assigned for this function was not large enough to contain it, the market spilling out into surrounding streets and alleys where only dainty-stepping burros could make their way among the wares on display, though an occasional battered automobile tried.

Such a profusion of goods for sale! A reincarnated Aztec or Totonac would find few unfamiliar articles of merchandise in this bustling outdoor emporium. He would have little trouble locating his favorite nostrum among the sacks and bundles and bunches of medicinal herbs displayed in the herbalist's stall. What need for him—or you—to suffer any ills of flesh or spirit? Here one can purchase an herb tea for an instant cure. There is *Té Cerebrina* for nervousness, insomnia, dizzy spells; *Té Azteca* for biliousness and colic; *Té Azaaro* for hemorrhoids. *Turnera Difusa* herb is effective against impotence; *Té Uva Ursi* cures "secret infirmities" (venereal disease). A "radical" cure for diabetes is promised by taking *Té Ytamar*. Perspiration odors and offensive feet are eliminated by taking *Yerba del Cura*. Rheumatism or aching bones? *Yodolfina* tea will quickly restore you. Falling hair or dandruff? *Té Verrome* will eliminate them. *Té Claudorita* expels kidney stones; *Té Guayaca* dissolves cataracts. Golden Rain Tea clears the urine and relieves flatulence. *Té Limpia Plata* is effective against excessive acidity and is unequaled for polishing silver, at least according to the meaning of the name. There was the *buro,* a pleasant-smelling herb crushed into rough powder, the ingredient with which my friends in Zempoala had concocted that pleasant nepenthe for me. The lady vendor, with a graciousness I had come to expect from these earliest of Americans, offered me a pinch of the powder to sniff which I did with the air of a searcher after truth. At a nearby stand was the other ingredient, *caña,* as well as that form of sugar offered in every village market I had ever visited in Mexico, *panoja,* dark brown, unrefined, and molded into hard, conical cakes. The old woman who ran this establishment pinched off a crumb for me to sample, and a more delicious confection I never tasted. No affected social proprieties here. As for sanitation, we are obsessed with it and are forever catching cold. Our good ladies back home are obliged to serve us our sugar with sterile tongs, as has been decreed by the sellers of tongs, most likely. Let my Ottelia serve me with her fingers, whereby I will know she truly loves me!

Elsewhere in this marvelous *tianguis* were the fruit stalls, displaying multicolored heaps—*montones*—of fruits known and unknown to a gringo. Bananas and oranges; mangoes and mameys; yellow, black, and white zapotes; guavas and papayas; apples and cactus figs—the variety is extraordinary. And why not? For in the space of a day one may be in three climatic zones, and at the foot of the plateau where Altotonga sits are the tropics with their limitless exotic bounty—with caravans of trucks and burros and *cargadores* carrying sacks and baskets on their backs, making delivery fresh daily.

Metatls of black lava stone for grinding the corn are a common article of merchandise now—and were when the *conquistadores* came gawking through the *tianguis*. Here are the wooden swizzle sticks, ingeniously carved, for foaming up the chocolate; and basketry of rush, maguey, cane, bamboo, and willow, roughly crafted and decorated—products of cottage industry that one may purchase as articles for honest kitchen use for pennies—or for dollars in the souvenir shops of Mexico City and Acapulco.

There is earthenware of every size and shape, carelessly glazed but enchanting to see en masse—which is not to say there are not pieces to be found to delight the heart of the collector—vases and bowls formed with enough fault to prove they are the work of man's hand and not of his machine, and hence beautiful. And flowers, flowers, flowers—but no, there is a bower not of flowers, though at first glance it seems to be, but of *huaraches,* under which the wizened merchant sits like a very cacique of the sandals.

True, the foodstuffs one sees in the *tianguis* will not always be of a character to tempt the fastidious. On a long table lay strips of meat drying in the sun. An open-minded viewer could at least thrill at nature's wisdom for, in making the meat so attractive to the black cloud of flies that fed upon it, the number of flies was thereby lessened at the neighboring displays of fruits that were not destined for purification by fire. By exercising a moderate degree of sublimation, I found the *biftec* cut from this meat surprisingly tasty, done in the usual sauce of *chiles* and piquant herbs. If the germs withstood the coals of the brazier, they could not possibly survive the *chiles*! One must grit his teeth a bit if he is to be a *conquistador*. Did not Díaz record that he and his comrades ". . . supped very well on some small dogs . . ."?

Don Platón was kind enough, when I had seen Altotonga as much to his satisfaction as to my own, to take me to his home to rest and to sip a cool *horchada*. The house might have been transported stair and stone from Seville. Its two stories surrounded a patio bright with vines and blossoms and sunshine, and only the *pajaritos*—birds like animated jewels chirping and trilling from a dozen hanging cages—were evidence that we were in New, not Old, Spain. By their profusion, songbirds and flowers should decorate the standard of the Republic—but then, men do revere sharp-taloned eagles more as symbols of their pride and glory.

Don Platón had a lovely granddaughter whose eyes, with a hint of an epicanthic fold, bespoke those times when caciques bestowed their favorite maidens as gifts to their bearded visitors, thus bringing into being the distinctive race that is the modern Mexican. Once more I quote Díaz, my favorite guide and chronicler: ". . . to prove still more clearly how much we love you and wish to please you in all things, we want to give you our daughters for wives to bear you children. For you are so good and brave that we wish to be your brothers. I have one most beautiful daughter who is as yet unmarried, and I should like to give her to you. . . ." Thus the Tlaxcalan, Xicotencatl the Elder, to Cortés.

Having had great success thus far by using the old chronicles to guide me, and having joined the *conquistadores* in spirit through the jungles, over the mountains, and in the villages—having, in sum, done all the things the *conquistador* did short of supping on small dogs (and there is no guarantee that, unwittingly, I had not done that too) was it not natural I should expect a maiden as souvenir of my pilgrimage?

But none had so far been offered, so I decided to broach the subject as I sipped my drink and looked fondly upon the pretty granddaughter. There were a number of ways by which I might have my wish fulfilled according to the rules followed by my predecessors. One was to deliver a *requerimiento*. This was the device used by the Spaniards to legalize their conquests. In the presence of a notary, his own of course, Cortés would announce to the puzzled Indians, who could not understand a word being said, that they were hereafter vassals of the Spanish king, and if they acquiesced peaceably, no harm would come to them. Since on several occasions they did not acquiesce peaceably, the order was given to attack and seize. Such seizure was now "legal." Is there no new villainy under the sun?

But no, I would not deliver a *requerimiento* to Don Platón; it seemed a bit harsh. Instead, I would ask for the girl forthrightly. My host must recognize my right—my *derecho de señor*. This was a well-established technique of "liberation."

"*Qué linda es,*" I said, ". . . how pretty. Don Platón, I desire to take the beautiful Lucecita with me to my country."

As expected, Platón was properly charmed by the flattery implicit in my request, and even his daughter, the girl's mother, was pleased that I should think her offspring beautiful.

"*Sus deseos,*" said Don Platón, "*para mí son órdenes*—to hear is to obey. But, alas, to give you Lucecita would be to defoliate our orchard!"

Though a *conquistador,* I have a better nature. I understood the family's feelings and did not press the issue. After all, I still had some wandering to do along the Cortés trail, and Lucecita was only three years old.

23

We have already quoted Bernal Díaz who, in his customary taciturn fashion, has spoken of Texutla, where the Spaniards found the inhabitants "well-disposed" toward them. Naturally, he says not a word about the horrendous abyss that, like a great moat, defended the eastern approach to the city (and defends it still—against tourists, apparently, though none find reason to wander this far off the suntan lotion and nightclub route). Our rattling *camión* swept around the rim of this awesome hole as blithely as a boy balancing himself on a rail fence, while I drew back from the window, afraid that mine might be the weight that would send us all hurtling off the narrow road.

Teziutlán—one wonders why the Mexicans bothered to alter the orthography—seen from across the ravine, had a gloomy, forbidding look. It seemed to claw against the mountain's crags to keep from tumbling into the *barranca*. The fact is, however, that the town's main structures—the cathedral; the municipal and commercial buildings; the old colonial residences rather gone to seed but still erect with a vestige of Castilian arrogance —are all built of the mountain's own substance and stand sturdily enough, having become one with the mountain itself.

But scattered about the edge of this old city of stone was an utter confusion of crazy wooden houses that have become weary of standing at all. They appear drunk with the pulque and teeter on the chasm's brink, where they seem about to plunge and end it all, restrained only by the persistent cajoling of their tenants who, with such cast-off splinters of lumber as can be found to prop against the walls, thus stand off the houses' suicide. These are the ramshackle homes of the Indians.

It is hard to look upon these poor people and see the proud barbarians who "paid no tribute" to Moctezuma. The ancestors of these soft-spoken, sombreroed and rebozoed folk, often bare-footed, *always* hard-working, the old caricature notwithstanding, provided the *conquistadores* with food and drink, but only when they were satisfied that the bearded strangers were no accomplices of the pious tyrant of Culhua.

To this point in their passage, be it noted, the Spaniards had not conquered so much with the power of their arms as with the eloquence of Don Hernando Cortés, an advocate *par excellence,* whether he was swindling the natives or persuading his own soldiers to contribute their share of the loot to King Charles to prove their patriotism. The forked tongue had more than one accent in the white man's salad days, though in this case the conquerors were certainly speaking the truth when they claimed to be no friends of Moctezuma.

Though seemingly forbidding from the distance, the city, even more than Altotonga, now pulsated with a zesty, restless life. Its shops under the porticos did a bustling trade; even its taxicabs still clung to some of their chrome. Teziutlán is home to some nineteen thousand people, and its cathedral the seat of the bishopric of Papantla. A lively town like this was not at all what one expects to find around the bend of the road in the high sierras.

Meandering through the country in this fashion of mine, with one eye on history and the other on the contemporary scene, had my head in a constant whirl, the rate of revolution no doubt accelerated by the constant ingestion of pain-deadening pills and whatever antiseptic liquid was available with which to wash them down.

Why, for example, did Díaz mention Texutla but once, and only in passing? Why did Prescott not mention the city at all? Cortés himself, as we have seen, omitted all reference to the place in his *cartas-relaciones.*

Yet, oddly, all sources speak of the trying time the Spaniards had with the weather as they passed this way. It was immediately after departing from Texutla that they entered ". . . uninhabited country where it was very cold, and where it rained and hailed. . . ." Uncomfortable it must indeed have been for the rugged Díaz to deign to record it!

I say "oddly" because the name Texutla, or Teziutlán, in Nahuatl means "the place where it hails," and if everyone had been so impressed by the nastiness of the weather, why have not all the chroniclers made more of the town's apposite name?

In the event that the reader may wish to use another bit of Nahuatl in social chitchat, now that French appears to be going out of fashion, consider that the name Teziutlán is said to be an abbreviation of the original Teziuhyotepezintlán. The "Teziuhyo" part is derived from *teziutl,* meaning "hail." The "tepe" is recognizable by almost anyone as being a hill or mountain, as in Popoca*tépe*tl, or Nauhcampa*tépe*tl, both famous and familiar landmarks on the route of the Conquest. "Zin" is a diminutive, making tepe*zin* a *little* mountain. Finally, *place where* is denoted by "tlan," a combination of letters found in a thousand place names throughout Mexico (including Tenochtitlán, for which we are bound). Put together all these pieces and we have Teziuhyotepezintlán, or "little mountain where it hails"! Now, if only Teziutlán were indeed the Tejutla (or Texutla) of old!

And how it hailed! The Spaniards were drenched and chilled by the driving sleet and hail, and several of the poor Indians who accompanied them, being from the *tierra caliente* of Cempoala, or from Cuba (some of the officers had brought along their personal batmen from the island), unused to the cold and without the advantage of the *conquistadores'* quilted cotton "armor," perished on the road.

As for me, the sun shone pleasantly and the air, at 6,500 feet, was heady; and my own purgatory in the *chipi-chipi* was behind me, though not forgotten.

Once the *conquistadores* reached this plateau, they were never again out of sight of some splendid, cloud-capped volcanic peak

—posing another riddle. The highest peak in all Mexico is the Pico de Orizaba—Citlaltépetl, the mountain of the star. The peak rises 18,500 feet, a spectacular sight in its serape of eternal snow. This glorious mountain is in sight from almost any point along the Cortés trail, assuming one does not have his view blocked by a banana tree or is not clambering behind some other mountain. Citlaltépetl is often visible from the sea even before the mainland heaves into view. For all this, not once is the mountain mentioned either by Bernal Díaz, whose comments as a rule ranged so widely, or by Cortés himself.

They had other things on their minds, I suppose, for soldiers have their own special priorities. I knew a man during the war who was on duty with me at the Mena House, which stands opposite the pyramids at Gizeh. For one week we reported daily to the old Victorian hostel, and not once did he ever turn his head to look at those great, melancholy monuments. He maintained proudly, and perhaps he maintains it still if some distraught romantic has not shot him, that he *never* saw the Pyramid of Cheops.

24

We found a hotel of sorts—"Hotel" was painted, like a kind of time-eroded graffiti, on the arch of the *portale* facing the square—and caused Señora not a little consternation by asking for a room. Our grizzly look possibly had something to do with her reaction but, by the evidence, it had been months, if not years, since any transient had sought accommodations there, and the event was momentarily upsetting.

When one traipses about in this hobo fashion, the world becomes larger, as it had been before "group travel" reduced it all to a pallid uniformity; before the condescension of "Tourist Menus"; before the proliferation of sterile motels by the invention of which Pago Pago may do no more to satisfy one's wanderlust than does Yonkers.

I enjoyed this freedom to take my rest in a place of the kind normally viewed from the distance as the awful abode of untouchables. One soon discovers that there are few untouchables, and those few are likely to be found among the ranks of such gypsies as myself, who wander unbathed along the Cortés trail.

"Sí, señor, hay agua caliente!" declared Señora, as if to assure me I was among gentlefolk. It was good to learn there was hot water, for old Don Platón had done for me in his kindness, and my foot pained me unmercifully. A warm bath would create the pleasant illusion of relief.

*". . . A las siete de la mañana—*in the morning at seven."

It did not really surprise me. Indeed, it had surprised me to find hot water—well, warm water—at the hotel in Perote, but that had been an establishment on the main highway to Mexico and had been artificially spawned by the prospect of foreign visitors during the year of the Olympics.

But we had a good *biftec* in señora's dining room, and cold beer from the refrigerator that stood against the dining-room wall as proud evidence of the town's modernity.

In the evening the plaza showed in microcosm what Mexico is when one dares to challenge the travel agent's recommendations.

The plaza of Teziutlán is not a rural marketplace, but a rather formal park. Nevertheless, one sees here the Indian women selling fruits and vegetables; the *tortillera* baking the corn cakes; the *ranchero* come to town to buy new harness; the vendor of pulque, which he has himself drawn from the maguey; the seller of rebozos, piled high upon his shoulder—woven to keep señora warm or to sling little Juanito over her back. You may purchase one for its true worth here, where swollen tourists' purses are unknown.

A vendor weaves his way through the plaza's evening throng, a large box slung on his back as he dangles a small metal triangle by a string. Striking the triangle with an iron rod produces a thin, penetrating "ping" that announces without words that he has hot *empanadas* for sale. These are the little meat pies Cortés described to persuade the Rey Carlos that, if given his own way, the Captain-General would add a nation of gourmets to His Majesty's empire. The *empanadas* are quite good, but not for the hamburger crowd, or, I must add, as regular diet for colitis sufferers.

Another fellow adds a counterpoint as he strides through the plaza. He strikes a cowbell he has fastened to his box. The cowbell says—again no words are necessary—he is a purveyor of *helado*—ice cream. From time to time is heard a doleful whistle—"O-o-e-e!" This proclaims the presence of an itinerant vendor of *camotes*—steamed sweet potatoes. He probably hails from Puebla, where the confection of *camotes* has been raised to the level of a distinctive art. A hurdy-gurdy man contributes to the symphony, churning a charming cacaphony out of his battered box.

Observe the fine lady there, taking an evening stroll about the *zócalo,* her children in the charge of a servant. Let us assume the lady is the wife of the merchant, Guzmán, to whose shop the townsfolk come to purchase an occasional shirt or a dress to wear for the *fiesta.* The shop deals also in the cheap, durable clothing the Indians wear, the trousers with the tapering legs, the sturdy, square-toed shoes. Señor and señora Guzmán are considered prosperous, and they are relatively so indeed, since more and more rural Mexicans favor "store-bought" clothing these days. As *criollos,* the Guzmáns belong to that fifteen per cent of Mexico's population that is white.

Their *criada*—their domestic—is an Indian girl. There is perhaps no servant in Mexico who is not *indio.* But she is very much a member of the family and could grow old in the family's service, sharing the family's heartaches or happiness, sometimes quarreling with the señora so that, but for the braids, one would be hard put to tell who was mistress and who was servant.

The girl—call her Esperanza—is likely to marry a mestizo boy, since hers is a town girl's life and mestizos constitute seventy-six per cent—the bulk—of the Mexican population. She may marry one of those vendors of foodstuffs whom we see in the plaza, a chap who knows the girl will be tireless as his production department while he concentrates on Sales. It is impossible to say how much he owns of Zacapoaxtla blood and how much of it is Spanish. Both strains are there, and their children will add, of course, to the dominant mestizo coloration of the country; for a mestizo nation it is—a unique, New World breed existing nowhere else on earth, with its own life style like no other, its own distinctive temperament, its own special expression of art. Just listen to Mexican music, comparable to no other, and brood over the murals of Rivera, Orozco, and Siqueiros.

Does this mean the Indian is disappearing—melting into the mestizo pot? Esperanza's sister, who stayed at home in the hills near Hueyepan instead of chancing the sacrilegious temptations

158

of "big city" life in Teziutlán, will marry an Indian boy of the sierra, to bake him his tortillas while he labors in the *milpa*—and *their* children will continue to maintain the ethnic ratio of the country, perhaps even adding more weight to the Indian balance as the services of the *curandero* give way to modern prescriptions and the effects of Mexico's Social Security (conceived in 1917!) continue to be felt. No, no vanishing Americans they!

Why did we choose to suppose the Guzmáns shopkeepers instead of important political functionaries? Does not everyone know the white man must be the political arbiter wherever in the world he plants his boot?

Benito Juárez, for one, did not know this. Mexico's first citizen president and great patriot, whose solemn portrait, like Lincoln's and Washington's in our own country, is hung reverently in the schoolhouses throughout the land, was a Zapotec Indian from Oaxaca.

Porfirio Díaz, no hero now but nevertheless one of the most durable of leaders, who controlled Mexico for thirty-four years —from 1877 to 1911—showed that a "lowly" Mixteca Indian could be as prepotent and ruthless a dictator as any Latin or Teuton. The railroads of Mexico date to his time. The Palace of Fine Arts in the capital was a *porfirista* project, and it was through Porfirio's ambitious, if self-aggrandizing efforts that Mexico City became the "Paris of the Americas" (which it truly is). But, alas, it was also in his time that, of the ten million inhabitants of Mexico, 9,500,000 owned no land.

Emiliano Zapata, another great Indian in the history of this nation, morose and selfless, taught his peon followers, Indians and mestizos all, to remedy this imbalance by taking back the ancestral land and shooting anyone who tried to stop them. This direct course of action helped generate the necessary revolutionary spirit in other more politic—and cautious—personalities, to set in motion reforms that are being felt today.

The fact is that the Indian is still very much a force in the New World, though one must travel south of the border to

see it. And one can see as if on a stage the patterns of relation-
ship set up by the Conquest of four and a half centuries ago,
relationships interacting still in Teziutlán and the other out-of-
the-way towns of Mexico.

I slip into the Cathedral. Its vaulted interior is dark and
candles twinkle starlike in the cavernous gloom, a galaxy of
them burning before the *Asunción*—the Virgin who is Patroness
of Teziutlán. I should like to be here in August when, on her
day, a fair is held and the native *tocotines* are danced. The dances
were once performed to honor the old gods.

The old gods! Is it not Quetzalcoatl there, in that large glass
case, before which stands suppliant a tiny Indian girl, her baby
dozing in the rebozo on her back? The case bears a plaque
labeling the statue *San* somebody or other, but the girl is per-
forming a rite that has a distinctly indigenous turn. She holds a
few flowers by their long stems and brushes the blossoms against
the plaque. Then she sweeps them along the frame that holds
the glass. I cannot hear her murmured incantation or make out
whether it is in Spanish or the old tongue. She looks about her,
sensing she is not alone—and espies me lurking beside the
stone column. She hesitates, as if what she is doing should not
be seen by a gray-bearded *teule*—a foreign devil; but she cannot stop now, for her plea to the shadowy figure in the case is
urgent. Our glances cross, but she turns back to the encased
figure, continuing her ritual at a quickened tempo. She touches
the flowers to each corner of the glass and to her brow. Then she
draws an invisible cross on the face of the case and kisses the
flowers. Another furtive glance at me and there is no help for it
—she must reduce her ritual into one quick, concentrated pleading. She rubs the flowers all over the glass, across her heart,
then, reaching over her shoulder, dusts her baby with the blossoms. Done! She looks at me for a fleeting instant, but we are
both in the shadows, and her look is too evanescent to say
whether it be a smile or frown as she passes through the ancient
wooden doors of the Cathedral.

Have I been eavesdropping upon a devout Catholic—or are

the old pagan idols still here, their names changed and saint-hood granted them, to whom the country people continue, in one way or another, to offer up their hearts?

God! Quetzalcoatl! It is no easy thing to be a human being.

25

The *Departamento de Turismo* produces a wide range of tourist literature, including some attractive booklets describing for the prospective English-speaking motorist several recommended itineraries between Vera Cruz and Mexico. (By now it is understood that when a Mexican speaks of *Mexico* he means the capital.) These itineraries are known by enticing, well-deserved titles, among them *La Ruta de las Flores*—the Flower Route; and *La Ruta de la Vainilla*—the Vanilla Route.

While none of these exactly duplicates that followed by Cortés—no motor highway can ever mount the escarpment on which sits Xico Viejo, or climb that tortuous mountain trail I followed, bleeding, from Ayahualulco to Los Altos—nevertheless, segments of these scenic routes sometimes parallel the *conquistadores'* trail and occasionally touch a site through which the passage of Cortés has been documented. The Flower Route, for example, will take the motorist from Vera Cruz to Jalapa (it is *Xalapa* in the guide book, which should be no surprise), thence to Perote, and, after passing through numberless highway towns, some looking out upon the identical panorama the Spaniards saw, will take the motorist through Texcoco, a city that played a very important part in the Cortés epic. From Texcoco, the Flower Route proceeds to Mexico.

The Vanilla Route, once it has left the sea behind and has passed through the vanilla country northwest of Vera Cruz, likewise coincides with at least two cities of the Cortés passage—Teziutlán and Tlatlauquitepec.

The authorized tourist booklets instruct the motorist on much that he may see in each of these towns. But never once do they mention the name of Hernando Cortés, or the fact that his *conquistadores* passed through these places. The snub is deliberate. As far as official Mexico is concerned, history leaps from the martyrdom of Cuauhtémoc to Hidalgo's *Grito de Dolores*—the cry of independence from Spain—and remembers the intervening time of Cortés and the colonial period, if it must, with wincing reluctance.

The tourist will learn from the official guide books that Teziutlán has well-paved streets, and that an agricultural fair is held here annually—but he will not be told that here was the Texutla of the *conquistadores'* visit. He will read that Tlatlauquitepec has a magnificent vista and many fruit trees— but not a word of Cortés's meeting with Olintecl, the chief who warned the *conquistadores* that all the world was vassal to the great lord Moctezuma.

Texcoco is described by local writers as the ancient capital city of Nezahualcoyotl, the Haroun al Raschid of the Aztec world—but no mention do they make of Texcoco's role in the recapture of Tenochtitlán by the Spaniards after they had suffered the reversals of the *noche triste*—that sad night of their expulsion from the Aztec capital.

Many pages of the guide books are devoted to Jalapa, justly describing its beauties, its flowers, its street named "Come-to-Jesus," its university and parks, not omitting a puff for its distinguished sons. The brochures will point out for the visitor the house of the great Mexican poet Salvador Díaz Mirón, and will even admit that Santa Anna himself began his career in Jalapa —though the city does not feel the circumstance cause for celebration, considering that "Santy Anny" lost more than half the nation's territory to the gringos. But not a word to remind the visitor that Jalapa was the first New World city reached by the *conquistadores* when they struck out for the interior on their march to Moctezuma's golden city.

In all of Mexico there is not a single monument to Cortés, and

163

pictorial depictions of him reveal the nation's disenchantment as the centuries passed. The tall, Caesar-like figure in glistening mail, which sixteenth- and seventeenth-century artists thought they saw, has disintegrated like Dorian Gray's portrait into that most unsavory ruffian one now sees in Diego Rivera's mural. Orozco shows him completely unclothed, but not in the nakedness of an Apollo—more that of the jaybird of unpleasant favor. But with the passage of those same years, his Aztec adversaries have become stauncher, taller, nobler in the national memory.

The cycle of changing images has, with one major difference, a parallel in our own country, which, too, saw a period when the redskins were considered vermin, when settlers rationalized how God had meant the land for the white man's usufruct, and society could believe, with no great offense to its sensibilities, that the only good "injun" was a dead one. Today the popular media begin to hint that the *Nez Percés* were something more than coyotes—some quite handsome, in fact, played by popular film stars in tales telling of the Indian's true nobility. No halfway measures when the public conscience murmurs—though the motive is more embarrassment than remorse.

The difference between our Indian's condition and the Mexican's is that the Nez Percés, among others, are no more, whereas the Zapotecs and the Mixtecas have sufficient potency, four centuries after Cortés, to have produced patriots and presidents; the Yaquis still man the Republic's army, build her roads; and there remains enough of the collective blood of the Aztecs and the rest of the olden tribes—with just enough of the impatient European variety stirred into it—to render it judicious that the bones of the greatest *conquistador* of all be well hidden, and moved from time to time (seven times so far), lest the people whom he conquered burn down the building in which the bones are housed.

We walked along the road to Chignautla, my poor foot swollen within the pitiless Pupsy-Wupsy. Not being above an occasional evil thought, it occurred to me to bestow the shoes upon the first Indian I could find who proved rude to me. I would then buy myself a pair of lowly *huaraches*. But I could find no rudeness in these hills. Besides, one must be born to the local sandals, made for the broad feet of *tamanes,* the bearers of burdens.

I could say this much for the Pupsy-Wupsies: that, having been soaked and dried and soaked and dried again, they had now acquired something of the property of orthopedic casts. Like fatal women who destroy strong men to enslave them— as I have read—the shoes had destroyed my feet but I could not now do without their unyielding support. The *conquistadores* marched along this road (sans macadam, it is understood) wearing *alpargatas*—hempen sandals—but they had the advantage of me. They could soothe their hurts with the fat of a rendered Indian. True, I had Honorio at hand—but with the national temper requiring that the bones of Cortés himself be hidden from the natives, it seemed more likely that, in a confrontation, my fat and not Honorio's would be put to therapeutic use. I certainly had more of it.

So, deterred from any rash act by such an oleaginous eventuality and inspired, as always, by the example of the intrepid Spaniards who had preceded me, I pushed on, resolved that I would reach Tenochtitlán in my malignant shoes; and if ever I should see home again, I would have them stuffed for display on a trophy-room wall.

I could record here that I was afoot on the highway because of a Spartan attitude toward pain. I could likewise assert that I was bravely walking because the soldiers of Cortés had bravely walked. The simple truth, however, is that I slept badly and was out of my bed a good two hours before the bus driver was out of his. Naturally, I awakened Honorio so I might share the sunrise with him. I do not believe the slaughterers of pigs in rural Mexico are by habit early risers and while, as a rule, it was difficult to distinguish between pain and pleasure in my *com-*

pañero's facial expression, there was a hint of shocked disbelief in his eye each time I shook him up at five.

Bathless and breakfastless, therefore, since it would be a good while before either our hostel or the *lonchería* under the arcade across the square would be astir, we had struck out for the open road, estimating we could breakfast at Chignautla, some five miles to the west, by which time the *camión* for Tlatlauquitepec would have caught up with us.

On this twisting ribbon of a road we strolled through traditional Mexico—that is to say, the Mexico of Spanish days—where the twin towers of one colonial church never passed out of view behind us before another pair came into view before us. The old chroniclers have recorded that *teocallis*—temples and pyramids—dotted the landscape of this region in like fashion when the Europeans first came. The maguey was everywhere on the convoluted scene—then, as now, lining the highway and bordering the fields. Sweeter than bee honey was the juice of the aloe, wrote Don Hernán, putting his discoveries in their best light as always for the approval of His Majesty Carlos V. I doubt that he had written the *carta* immediately after his first sip. Pulque grows on you, as we have noted, but if it is sweeter than honey, then a goat is more fragrant than the bougainvillea.

Nor, by tempering the Captain-General's enthusiastic prose, do I intend to minimize the generous character of that most versatile of plants. If we have noticed the important role played by the maize in the evolution of a civilization, consider then the maguey. Its leaves provided the Aztecs with their writing paper and roof shingles. Its thorns were their needles and nails. I watched as a field laborer nicked such a thorn at its base, leaving it just attached to the leaf's fiber. Then, by grasping the thorn and stripping it quickly from the plant, he had a needle complete with three feet of thread. Observing my interest, he gave it to me, concluding by my appearance that I needed it more than he.

The juice of the plant, of course, became the national beverage, the national solace of which, said the prissy New England historian, "the natives are to this day excessively fond." The plant's fiber was woven into cloth, and its root was cooked and eaten like a turnip, well spiced with *chiles,* one may be sure.

A self-contained supermarket it was—and so valuable that a landlord would "let" a plant or two to a *trabajador* in lieu of wages. Quite likely this arrangement survives today, a supplement to the Social Security, for it seemed very improbable that the Indian who gave me the thorn—the needle—had actual title to the property.

The sun came up to warm the morning's intoxicating air, and I slung my jacket over my shoulder as we marched on, a habit to which, possibly, I owed the loss of my documents, for things had a way of fluttering out of my pockets from time to time. I had and would have cause enough to regret my careless ways.

We breakfasted before reaching Chignautla—on fresh *tunas.* An unlikely article to encounter on the slopes of the sierras so far from the sea? Not at all. These *tunas* are the pear-shaped nodules sprouting off the edges of the fleshy nopal "leaf"—that species of cactus so characteristic of the Mexican landscape. Back home, these green, purple, or red protuberances are known as "cactus apples." Europeans call them "Indian figs"—from the days when the early explorers brought home stories of the wild, exotic novelties they had seen in the New World—the "Indies." I have seen the fruit on the Libyan desert, choice tidbits for the camels. Beware! for they must be plucked with care. Invisible, hairlike spines cover the thick rind of the fruit, and it is said there is no way that a *pecador*—a sinner—can take one without suffering its sting. His penance will last until the tiny spines are assimilated by his flesh and disintegrate; and the duration of discomfort is determined by the degree of one's venality. I itched for several hours—somewhat longer than average.

Honorio, demonstrably free of worldly sin, cut through the rind with his machete. When peeled away, a cool, moist, most delicious pulp was revealed. One would be wise to keep himself pure of heart in order that he will be qualified to enjoy a *tuna*— and he should learn from this to grant at all times the probable internal virtue of his enemies who, too, have spiny rinds. A half dozen of the fruit did me nicely, and we left those lower down on the plant for several sheep that had joined us for breakfast.

I recorded this pleasant moment in my notebook and handed it to Honorio, custodian of the knapsack and its contents, observing that he examined with much puzzlement what I had written before he tucked the book back into the sack. There was little doubt he would have great tales to tell at the monthly meetings of Xico's Loyal Order of Totonaco Pig Assassins; for what in the name of Quetzalcoatl could it be that this gringo etched in cabalistic characters in his book upon eating so simple an article as a *tuna?*

It was under this very sky that Cortés had penned a message in Spanish and placed it in the hands of four messengers ". . . natives of Cempoal . . ." to deliver to the people of Tlaxcala in order that he might learn if they would be his allies against Moctezuma. The wily *conquistador* knew the Tlaxcalans would no more be able to read the message than Honorio was able to read my notes, but he reasoned that indecipherable writing has an occult force and lends its own persuasion. See how chairmen of the board, and would-be chairmen of the board, sign their letters.

We did not need to walk the rest of the way to Chignautla. Not five minutes after we had resumed our march, a gentleman came along, a Spaniard—or mostly a Spaniard—in an automobile of hoary age, who pulled up beside us and asked if we would ride or whether his offer would "molest" me. Was it my *teule's* beard that made rural Mexico treat me with such grace?

He heard the explanation of my journey's purpose in good humor, putting up his hands in mock dismay. "Señor," he said, "for my part I am not Cuauhtémoc, on my word of honor!"

"Nor am I Hernando Cortés," said I. "On the contrary, my own feet feel as if they have been put to the famous torture."

Honorio, with unexpected haste assured the gentleman I spoke the truth: I was not Cortés but merely an *Americano* possessed of odd whims and caprices.

I reassured my humorless *compañero*. *"Es un chiste, nada más* —we were only joking, my friend."

Honorio received the clarification reluctantly. *"Bueno,* if you say it is so. . . ."* Nevertheless, he persisted, in his sober fashion, in explaining to our new acquaintance how I had hurt my foot by neglecting to recognize the limitations of my venerable years, and that truly I was not Cortés—far from it. This defense of me he conducted in fewer words than has the recounting of it, but with assorted *humphs* and *tsks* and tosses of his head, and rolling of his eyes in my direction, as if he were revealing the truth to our friend in strictest confidence.

We turned off the highway after a short while and drove for a quarter-hour or so on a dirt road that passed among some cornfields, our driver assuring me this was a preferred route to Chignautla. He did not explain why the dusty road was preferable, but I, too, have done as he was doing to outmaneuver the toll-takers. We were soon back on the highway and reached our destination in short order, a Mexican highway town that would have held no surprises for Pancho Villa, were that lusty *bandido* to stop by today—and, for that matter, few surprises for the *pochtecas* of an even earlier epoch.

Neither Cortés nor Díaz mention Chignautla in their accounts of the march on Mexico. It may not have existed by that name in their time. Yet, during their passage through this region, people had been hereabouts, and a strong-willed people at that, for it has come down to us that their tribe resisted conversion well after the subjugation of Tenochtitlán. It was the familiar story of new settlers having a temporary problem with the Indians. If we say "injuns," the ring of the story will be more familiar. Once the Indians had submitted to being converted from their old heathenish ways and the promise of a proper Christian hereafter held out to them, it became easier to dispossess them of their more worldly assets. The old saying puts it well: First the white man had the Bible and the native had the land; then the native had the Bible and the white man had the land.

The *camión* for Tlatlauqui was not long in coming by, and

169

we climbed aboard. It was standing-room-only for a while, until the excess population was shaken off like fleas from a dog—my good friends in the mountains will forgive the choice of figure —at the various way stations, unmarked as such except for the roadside tramplings where the disembarking countryfolk were accustomed to disappear into the corn.

Cortés wrote that somewhere in this locality he saw ". . . a small tower almost like a roadside chapel, in which certain idols were kept and around which more than a thousand cartloads of logs neatly cut had been piled, for which reason [the Spaniards] called it the *Paso de la Madera*—the Pass of Wood. . . ."

I have quoted this observation, which is of little consequence, only because Bernal Díaz, writing as an old man fifty years after the Conquest, said ". . . we entered another pass, where we found some groups of houses and large *cues* with idols, and they had great piles of firewood for the service of these idols."

If they could agree on such a detail, why, then, did each call the town they now entered by a different name? Cortés called it "Caltanmi"; Díaz said it was "Xocotlán." Prescott, as we know, identified it as today's Tlatlauquitepec.

In any case, an impressive town it must have been, and the first place the Spaniards came to where they were told to their faces that any courtesies they might receive would be subject to the approval of Moctezuma. Food was grudgingly given, and not of the best, the chiefs making it clear that the emperor had his eye on all these goings-on and would be quite upset at any favors that might be given to the strangers without his prior clearance.

Like the three blind men who touched the elephant, each *conquistador* remembers best what impressed him most. The Captain-General recorded that he asked the cacique, Olintecl, for gold in the name of Carlos V, to be told quite bluntly he could have it, and anything else—if Moctezuma gave the word. "Why," asked Cortés, "do you set this condition? Are you a vassal of Moctezuma?"

"Who is not?" replied Olintecl.

What remained vivid in Díaz' memory—and it seems reason-
able enough—was that in the square where one of their temples
stood were many piles of human skulls, so neatly arranged that
the Spaniards were able to count more than a hundred thousand.
"I repeat," says Díaz, jealous of his reputation for veracity,
". . . I repeat that there were more than a hundred thousand."

And what do *I* remember of Tlatlauquitepec? A thing or
two. . . .

26

A hundred thousand human skulls, together with the related thighbones recalled with such emphasis by Bernal Díaz, would have fairly paved the length and breadth of Tlatlauqui's plaza, if this had been the site, and roofed its arcades as well. Say what one will about the Spaniards—and it is agreed that not everything that can be said will accrue to their glory—they had at least replaced this edifying spectacle with a bandstand for the entertainment of the citizenry.

We have had occasion frequently along the trail to observe how lavish Nature is with her paint pot—but could it be the lime of those human bones that made the flowers bloom so richly red in the park where I now stood? No wonder the Indian's solemnity persists even to this day, his blood remembering how dispensable a quantity it had been. No wonder Honorio's phlegmatic ways. No wonder the melancholy air about the raggedy women who squatted in the shade of the *portales,* passively awaiting purchasers of their assorted foodstuffs.

I succumbed to one of the least likely of these offerings, which was inevitable, I suppose, considering that I was bent on knowing all I could about Indians, including what went into one.

There were no restaurants we could see under Tlatlauqui's arcades, but there was an abundance of dilettante restaurateurs who had set up their kitchens *al fresco* on the sidewalks. One of these attracted my particular attention. It was a crate behind which an old woman sat tending a tin brazier over whose charcoal embers a dish of something indefinable was warming.

Beside her sat a child, a miniature of herself, black braids, red ribbons, and all; and both were dipping their tortillas into the dish.

Atop the crate was a row of pigs' feet, glowing with the pink and white of brand-new babies. I have always been partial to pickled things and have nibbled many a cold, jellied knuckle with my beer. Having for so long come close to being cremated by the cuisine of the villages, I felt a sudden craving for one of the innocent articles here on display. I indicated to Señora, therefore, that I would have one. She removed her fingers from the stew she was eating, wrapped a pig's foot in a tortilla that at the same time served her as a napkin, and handed me the ensemble.

Telling myself that the woman was, after all, someone's sainted mother and that there was implicit love in her greasy hands, I brought the trotter to my mouth, to discover a barnyard fragrance lingering on it still. It was not pickled after all, but boiled—though not enough to have killed it if it had not already been dead from recent amputation. The flesh did not fall from the bone as it does from the properly marinated variety; instead, it was resilient to my bite, as a live, if slumbering creature would be.

I gnawed at it as bravely as I could, for the eyes of the populace were on me and I did not wish to give offense to a race already too sorely tried! but I succeeded only in extracting some vile, raw porcine juices. With all good will I could not continue and looked to throw the thing somewhere, but this would be too cruel an affront to the chef. Lamely, then, I held it out to her so she might dispose of it with her own trash.

Good Honorio, as always ready to explain my oddities to his countrymen, told the woman I was suffering from a broken foot, which made mastication difficult for me. Loyal in turn to my defender, I asked for a boiled egg in order to support his story and demonstrate that I had no general prejudice against Tlatlauqui cookery. The patient woman, assuring me there was no harm done, crushed an egg onto a tortilla for me and put the pig's foot, which my gnawing had only slightly damaged, back among its fellows. It was good to know its career had not ended with me, and that it would go on to nourish someone with a keener appreciation.

Not even the *conquistadores* had tried to eat pigs' feet *à l'indienne,* fresh from the sty and underdone. (Pigs, like cattle and horses, were unknown to the indigenous Americans until the Spaniards themselves subsequently imported them.) Soon I felt disquieting symptoms in my bowels and could only hope it was Moctezuma's standard scourge to which I was at last succumbing, and not the trichinosis one invites by such unconscionable adventurism. There was nothing to do but wait and see; and meanwhile continue to test the antiseptic properties of *aguardiente.*

But there is no human experience that does not have its interest, and if I must be sick, I would rather it be among the Aztecs than, say, in Ashtabula, Ohio. I will go further and say I would rather be very sick in Mexico than slightly ill in Ashtabula. I could go even further and affirm that I would rather die in Mexico in pursuit of a ghost's footsteps than be alive and well in Ashtabula, though that might strain the credulity of those in Ashtabula who had been my friends until just recently.

To be sick in Mexico could have a special flavor. I had been terribly ill in Egypt many years before and recall the time with nostalgia, muezzins' calls to prayer surviving in my memory, a leitmotif to my fever. Interestingly, the malady I suffered at that time was close kin to that which, to the Mexican Tourist Office's despair, is popularly known as "Montezuma's Revenge" or "Tourist's Trot," among other affectionate titles. It was called "Gyppy Tummy" in Egypt—and I suppose still is, for that much cannot have changed along the unchanging Nile.

Hernando Cortés implied that one might fall ill in worse places than Mexico when he described, four and a half centuries ago, an Indian market's "pharmaceutical department." ". . . There is," he wrote, "a street of herb-sellers where there are all manner of roots and medicinal plants that are found in the land.

There are houses as it were of apothecaries where they sell medicines made from these herbs, both for drinking and for use as unguents and lotions. . . ."

With such facilities, all was not lost for me yet.

A word about disease among the Aztecs. Many of their maladies were common to both the New and Old Worlds. Perhaps the germs were dispersed in the boat in which Tezpi escaped the Great Flood, together with all manner of birds and beasts. (The tradition of the Ark in pre-Hispanic America!) At any rate, the Aztecs had their malaria, grippe, rheumatism, and the like, for which the *ticitl*—the doctor—might prescribe steam treatments wherein aromatic leaves and the pouring of water over hot rocks would have done what plugged-in vaporizers and Turkish baths do today. If drums and incantations were deemed necessary to the cure among the Indians, one also hears arguments for the therapy of our bedside radios. The Aztecs had their share of intestinal problems in their time, but so do I in mine. As for exotic diseases, it is said, though it is not firmly established, that syphilis was the red man's unique gift to the European. If so, the European decimated the Indian population with smallpox and measles, against which it had no immunity, thus more than balancing the ledger. Boils and warts and itches were common, judging by the categories of medicines sold. Equivalent salves have a large market in our own smart society today, perhaps with cosmetic value but with no more curative powers than had the magical herbs of the Aztecs.

We have eradicated some diseases with our science, and "miracle" drugs have put off our departure from the scene for a while longer, so I suppose it must be conceded that our situation is better than it had been for those less-improved peoples of long ago. But, just the same, our hospitals are unable to accommodate the sheer numbers of our sick, and in the end we who really do consider ourselves evolution's ultimate masterpiece are vanquished by our mortality no less conclusively than the Aztec was by his.

". . . Since good on earth is insecure,
And all things must a change endure
In dark futurity."

So spoke Nezahualcoyotl nearly a century before Columbus.

The rate at which my infirmities were multiplying rendered
it prudent that we accelerate our survey of Tlatlauquitepec and
push on without undue delay.

The physical aspects of the place the reader already knows,
for he has seen its cobbled streets in Xico; its plaza in Ixhuacán,
though better tended here and more brightly bespangled with
blossoms. He has already seen its arcades in nearly every town
we have passed through so far, from Vera Cruz to Teziutlán.

Tlatlauqui boasted a motion picture theater, the world's tiniest,
judging by the space its box office occupied beneath the portico,
where a poster announced a film for the coming Thursday. The
theater opens one day a week in the smaller towns—those that
have one—and the films shown are more often Mexican productions than imports. This would surprise the homesick American traveler of a generation ago who, at a time when there was
no tourism to speak of in Mexico, could always have his heart's
cockles warmed by the sight of a familiar American face on a
theater poster. Today, Mexico City has become the "Hollywood"
of the Spanish-speaking world and a prime source of taped or
filmed programing for Latin television. Mexico exports her
telenovelas to wherever in the United States there are enough
Chicanos or Puerto Ricans to support a *bodega* that sells canned
mangoes and rice in ten-pound sacks. Fine, sensitive films they
often are, too. For one thing, they have a kind of built-in authenticity. No ersatz settings need be built for the production of their
Gothic tales of the colonial days (I have rarely seen a comedy
set in that era), or for their "Westerns," the latter filled more
with *ranchero* songs than gunshots. A drive just a few miles
outside the capital will show that Mexico is like one vast sound
stage, with properties ready-made for any setting and super-
numeraries ready-costumed for virtually any of her historical

epochs. And always, always, that fabled backdrop of slumbering volcanoes.

The history of the people, an unhappy one, is subtly reflected in the country's drama, even in her television "soap operas," which, I would add, are a cut or two above what we are accustomed to understand by that term. Rather, they are, in a legitimate literary sense, serial novels; thus the term *"telenovela."* These productions frequently have a twist most unexpected to the *norteamericano* viewer. The "good guy" can lose *everything* in the last reel, and not even die as a proper tragic hero should to bring his sorrows to an end. Thus the viewer may be left with the frustrating feeling that the "good guy's" bad luck must be going on and on after the show is over. This is apt to shock the American who has been taught the Horatio Alger morality that, at least on film, virtue must prevail. Our films, if not by law at least by accepted code, have always had Good ultimately triumph over Evil. The murderer must always be captured, his retribution shown or intimated. We have always had the comfort of knowing the heroine would be freed from the railroad track in time. To the degree that this pat morality is being upset today, to that degree one hears murmurs of discontent from our bourgeoisie with how badly art is faring. In a Mexican cliff-hanger, however, the hero arrives an instant too late, which is no surprise to the audience, though hope had been held out to the last that all would be saved—which is how life really is, sad to say, and not only in Mexico.

The presence of television in Tlatlauquitepec was announced for me in touching fashion when I saw a small *cargador*—a boy who could not have been ten years old and who could not have weighed as much as the cargo he bore on his back. The customary tump line across his forehead helped him sustain the burden while he stood, leaning forward as the bearers—the *tamanes*—do, transfixed before the door of a shop. He was watching a television screen on which *vaqueros* on horseback were thundering through the *paso*. The boy was, to the life, one of the laborers of Moctezuma come face to face with the electronic present. His silent fascination had a hint of the wonder his ancestors had felt when they first saw the *conquistadores* curvetting their horses on the beach at Vera Cruz.

So far I have mentioned only a few of the gods who controlled the lives and destiny of the pre-Hispanic Indians. They are, in fact, a numerous pantheon and in my own way I tried to give offense to none of them. Until now, all had responded with apparent solicitude for my well-being. But there was one, a lady, whose jealous pride I had neglected to take into account. She was the goddess Teteoinon, Mother of the Gods, who was also worshiped under the names of Ixcuina—Four Faces; Toci—Our Grandmother; and, most important to me because in this personification she made me feel her wrath, Tlazolteotl—Eater of Filth. It was the extraordinary function of Tlazolteotl to eat refuse, whereby she consumed the sins of mankind, thus cleansing the men and women who paid the obeisance that was her due.

In her view, my dietary indiscretion was an unholy usurpation of her prerogatives, and any court of law, upon applying its nose to the pig's foot, would have upheld her sternest judgment. My punishment came swiftly.

I had left Honorio munching a taco while I explored the sundry *bodegas* in the shadows of the porticos. Coming out, then, into the bright sunlight, I was momentarily blinded and mistook a high wall for a step. In full view of some hundreds of Indians who had not had the pleasure of seeing a white intruder bite the dust in a precious long time, I went hurtling down to the cobbled pavement four feet below, taking the greater force of the fall on my left knee.

No grown man has ever tumbled publicly off a four-foot wall and succeeded in letting it appear a normal course of conduct; yet, if he is not completely stunned, he will invariably say to whoever chances to witness the catastrophe, "It is nothing— nothing at all!" as if this will preserve his *amour-propre*. This I said, of course, to Honorio, who came at a hurried pace across the square, though not running, for that would look as if he thought something unusual had happened.

"*No es nada—nada!*" I said as he looked down at me, recognizing my wounded pride and allowing me time to rise by my own efforts if I was able. This I managed to do, but barely, for the fall had been hard enough so that the cobblestones had torn through my trouser leg and I could feel a sickening moistness on my knee.

Fortunately—or unfortunately—a *farmacia* was not far. It was on a corner of the plaza and looked out on it—or the plaza looked in on the *farmacia,* which had an open front. My *compañero* helped me hobble toward it and there, as if on a stage, the plaza a well-attended pit and the arcades crowded loges, the pharmacist sat me down, unstuck the trouser leg from the wound, and bared my leg. He determined quickly that it was a job for his *muchacha,* whose longer fingernails were more suitable as pincers to free the deep abrasion of grit.

This she did, kneeling on the floor and looking up at me with pretty malice from time to time so she might gauge the depth of her probing by the reaction on my face. When I cried, "*Cuidado, por amor de Dios!*—careful!" it encouraged her to pick a little deeper. Her *patrón* took a vial from his shelves and gave it to her with appropriate instructions; then he averted his eyes, for he had a delicate stomach. She touched a drop of its contents to the wound, and I delighted the gallery by nearly dying.

"*Qué dolor*—what pain!" I gasped, suppressing a scream with difficulty.

This was apparently the desired reaction, for she now covered the entire bleeding area—the whole of my knee—with the frightful stuff. It was a clear liquid and only the fact that the bottle had been sealed and labeled persuaded me it was not some unrefined *aguardiente.*

The *muchacha* seemed for a moment to lose the audience when I did not fall at least into a dead faint—but interest in the drama quickly revived as the pharmacist handed her a box containing a yellow powder. The gallery could sense, with me, impending crisis. She dusted the wound with the powder, but too generously, causing much of it to spill to the floor.

"*Por Dios! Espera!*—Stop!" I spoke too late. She had gathered the spillage from the pavement and dusted that onto the hurt too.

My foreboding of the girl's next maneuver changed to relief when she now proceeded to wrap the knee with fresh gauze, but too late I realized she was anchoring it to my skin with adhesive tape—to which, as I have said, I have a severe allergy. There was a good possibility that the plaza would become the scene of a glorious *fiesta* were the girl now to pull the tape from my leg, considering the hair she would take with it. The association such an operation might have for an audience of Indians is obvious. I therefore chose the evil that was already accomplished, and let her leave the bandages on.

The pharmacist took only a peso or so for an operation in which materials and the rarest talent were lavishly used, and the *muchacha* smiled sweetly when I thanked her. She had done her work on the gringo well. She had pleased Xiuhtecuhtli, the Fire God, when she dabbed me with the burning liquid. Ixtlilton, God of Health and Cures from Ill, had been well served by her cool competence. Favorite handmaiden of Patecatl, God of Medicine, was she, for her faithful observance of his decrees. A moment of pleasant anticipation she had surely given to Mictlantecuhtli, Lord of the Region of Death. And happiest of all was Tlazolteotl, Eater of Filth, who was now avenged.

27

If I had taken that tumble at home, hurrying, let us suppose, in dreary pursuit of a commuter's train, it would have meant a week or more of immobile convalescence with light broth for supper and the clucking ritual wishes of visitors for my improbable recovery. Instead, I stood on the edge of the square in remote Tlatlauquitepec, a sorry-looking *conquistador*—but a *conquistador* all the same (that was the important thing!)—plotting my next move to attain the Tenochtitlán of Moctezuma. To be for a little while a *conquistador*—what better motive for abandoning one's accustomed road, one's day-to-day ways, and strike out for some romantic and improbable trail? For all the throbbing in my foot, the battered knee, the suspicious churning in my stomach, I felt strangely happy. My footprints were on the floor of some wooded chasm. Someone in a distant and obscure village perhaps remembered my brief visit; remembered laughing with me.

In a man's lifetime he must climb a mountain. This I had done. I was happy—and could hereafter scorn those who had not.

My next objective had been determined for me long ago— Tlaxcala. This was the "independent territory" to which Cortés had sent his emissaries—*Cempoalan* emissaries, because it was his Cempoalan guides who had advised him that in Tlaxcala the Spaniards would find allies. Therefore, to test the accuracy of his guides' estimate, Cortés sent *them* ahead.

While awaiting their return, the Spaniards rested—a relative term, for during that week or so they explored the neighboring communities, probing, proselytizing. The Captain-General visited around with the caciques of the nearby towns, who spoke to him in awesome tones about the might of Moctezuma. They told him of the wonders of Tenochtitlán; of its houses built upon the waters of the broad lake; of the veritable fortress the great city was, proof against all enemies.

If Olintecl was not overly friendly, his awe and pride of Moctezuma made him overly talkative. He was egged on, to be sure, by Don Hernán's own grand claims. The Emperor Carlos had the whole world as his vassal, Cortés told the Indian chief. But what red-blooded chauvinist of any epoch will listen to such boasting without setting the boaster straight? It was *his* master who was the world's most puissant lord, asserted Olintecl. Moctezuma had warriors beyond counting, he said—and he went on to tell the attentive *Conquistador* how they were deployed; the various and wondrous ways by which Tenochtitlán was defended; where the causeways were situated—three causeways situated oh so cleverly here and there, with removable bridges placed thus and so, so that one might enter the city only by will of Moctezuma. Imagine the wily Cortés and his lieutenants nodding their admiration—and making mental notes.

To prove further that Moctezuma was the mightiest of princes, Olintecl described the gold and silver plate, the precious stones and other wealth his master had at his command. All this he told proudly, with little notion he was thus helping to seal the fate of Mexico.

Cortés was not easily overawed. He replied, as the chronicler recalls, ". . . I would have you know that we have come from distant lands at the bidding of our Emperor who has sent us to command your great prince Moctezuma to give up sacrifices and kill no more Indians, and not rob his vassals, or seize any more lands. . . ." Cortés knew well the technique of planting the seeds of disaffection. ". . . And now I say this to you also, Olintecl, and to all the caciques who are with you, that you must give up your sacrifices and cease to eat your neighbors and cease to practice sodomy!" Díaz has made note more than once of this particular predilection, and we must wonder whether the vice was as common as he makes it out to be or if he exaggerates its prevalence as propagandists are wont to do. No less an authority on pre-Hispanic American history than Vaillant has stated that sodomy was not only quite illegal, but was dealt with in an especially "revolting" fashion by the dispensers of Aztec justice.

". . . Then," continues the chronicler, "Cortés said to us soldiers who were standing by: 'Now, I think there is nothing else we can do except put up a cross.' "

We can hear Fray Bartolomé de Olmedo gasp upon hearing this, and, saying the Castilian equivalent of "Omigod! Not now!" he persuaded his zealous commander that, since they would soon be moving on, the cross was likely to be defiled by the unsympathetic, unregenerate pagans the instant they were out of sight. This argument swayed Cortés more than did the fact that the Spaniards were outnumbered by a thousand to one; that a garrison of Aztec warriors was stationed in Olintecl's province; and that, on top of all this, with colossal nerve unmatched in history, Don Hernán had ordered most of his ships sunk at Vera Cruz just in case the men got any ideas about returning home before the mission was done. Not even the sea now offered escape in the event of a miscalculation on the part of the strong-willed *Conquistador*.

With no news yet of the messengers, then, Cortés decided to proceed to Mexico without delay. (The caciques should *never* have boasted of Moctezuma's treasury!) He asked which was the easiest, speediest route, and Olintecl recommended they go via Cholula. The Cempoalans again warned Cortés not to do so, as the Cholulans were particularly cozy with Moctezuma. "They are very treacherous," they said, "and Moctezuma keeps a large garrison in the town." On the other hand, the Tlaxcalans had a long history of hostility toward Moctezuma, so the small body of Spaniards would be better advised to travel among Moctezuma's enemies than among his friends.

And so it was that Cortés and I directed our next steps toward

Tlaxcala. The Spaniards proceeded two leagues along the valley southward to what Díaz called Xalacingo, but that Cortés referred to as Ixtacamaxtitlan (I beg to be excused from trying to explain this!). It is Ixtacamaxtitlan to this day, though the present village is not on the original site. The *camión* rolls past it faster than one can say its name, which is enough time to contemplate the mood of those young Spaniards as they moved on, knowing they were surrounded at all times by the architects of that display of the hundred thousand skulls!

As for myself, I dragged my lacerated leg into the *camión,* headed likewise due south, so that I might look out, on my right, upon the country through which the *conquistadores* had marched, their "musketeers and crossbowmen in regular order," cautious, alert every moment of the day and night. We were knocking on the very gates of Colhua-Mexíca—the domain of the dread Moctezuma.

It was "not far," Olintecl had said, and though I had been misled so often by those soothing words, I, too, with those adventurers of long ago, began to feel the proximity of Tenochtitlán. The towns succeeded one another with increasing frequency along the road—with fewer of those long, unpeopled stretches along which we had ambled between the isolated *pueblos* of the sierras. Tenextatiloyan, Ocotepec, Libres, and a dozen places in between that no maps name, known only to those who dismounted the *camión* as we passed along the avenues of maguey and cactus— the little women making their quick signs of the cross when we halted too close to some weatherworn wayside crucifix.

The rattling bus would go on to Puebla, where I too must go, but later; for in order to adhere to the Cortés trail I must frequently forego the luxury of direct bus routes and wearily descend at some crossroads to seek another rural bus, if there was one, that would take me along a rutted spur along which the *conquistadores* had gone. This I did at Oriental and headed westward now, leaving behind me noble Orizaba, the star-mountain, suspended pink in the evening sky.

We passed through Huamantla, I dozing feverishly, my fitful

dream peopled with the ululating warriors who, believing the Spaniards were allies of the cursed Moctezuma, fought them gallantly among the knolls outside my window. At Apizaco the *camión* paused long enough for the usual incursion of vendors, and I responded almost mechanically to the hawker of *papitas* —certainly not because I hungered after the potato chips offered in a cone of newsprint, but because the vendor squeezed a half *limón* over them as he handed them to each purchaser. I had to sample *that*. It is clear enough by now that I must share in native pleasures under the same kind of compulsion that had moved Byron to swim the Hellespont. I found the *papitas* quite improved by the juice of the *limón*—as everything is. Just a taste sufficed, and at least I broke bread, so to say, with the actual, existing descendants of the only tribe that stood up to Moctezuma (and to the Spaniards as well). The remainder I passed on to Honorio, who was, of course, immune to the plague boiling inside me.

Then, turning southward, we proceeded on for another half-peso's worth, collected en route, and reached Tlaxcala in the gathering twilight.

I was quite ill now from any one, or more, of the wide choice of afflictions at my disposal. With a hot fever mounting, I sought out a hotel without delay so I might lie down and attempt to generate the perspiration necessary to bring relief in situations of this sort, according to both Aztec and Madison Avenue medicine men.

To a vagabond by now used to the most modest of quarters, the hotel to which a passer-by directed us was an imposing place —a sprawling structure with terraced gardens stepped against the hillside. A balcony ran along the building's length, giving access to a row of some half-dozen rooms. Around the entire premises ran a high iron fence, separating the establishment from a rather disreputable street. A block away, out of sight but not out of hearing, was the plaza.

Impressive as was the exterior of the hotel, its clientele, until we entered, consisted exclusively of ghosts from some epoch long past. The great iron gate groaned when we pushed it open to enter the grounds, and we walked up a path that led to a porch well hidden by untended vegetation. I propose no personal identification with the fairy-tale prince—but if a princess lived there, she had slumbered for a long time before my visit.

The lobby within was unlighted, gloomy, to all appearances abandoned. When this place was new, in *porfirista* days perhaps, elegant ladies and *caballeros* drew up in carriages and lolled in this entry hall, then aglow in gaslight, while their Indian *mozos* carried trunks and portmanteaus up the long stairway to the *habitaciones* on the floor above.

Why a hotel in a city so close to the nation's capital should have this haunted air about it can be explained by the demographer. In Mexico, as in our own country and elsewhere, there has been a steady migration of people into the metropolitan centers (Cortés was not the last to seek gold in Tenochtitlán) and, as a consequence, much of the energy has been drawn out of the previously self-sufficient cities of the provinces. Where once these were focal points for provincial activity, more and more this activity is channeled directly into the metropolis. The snarling trucks at Los Altos, it will be recalled, were headed *exprés* for Mexico City rather than for Perote.

Since these once grand little subsidiary cities are largely bypassed by commerce now, their dust tends to rest undisturbed, unless they are susceptible of being tidied up for tourists.

But what is there for the resort-minded tourist in Tlaxcala unless, eccentric soul, he thrills to breathe the air the *conquistadores* breathed? He will hardly know that here was the stage where one of the great dramas of the Conquest was played unless he reads Prescott or Díaz, both absent from the best-seller list lo, these many years. The travel agencies do not tell him. As we have noticed, references to the events surrounding the Conquest are only grudgingly made by the Government's official bureaus, which see a better possibility of retrieving the Aztec's stolen treasure by enlarging the resort facilities in the likes of Acapulco.

186

In doing so, they gauge the tourist's preferences accurately, so who can blame them?

There was no one at the reception desk, and if anything was in the pigeonholes on the wall behind it, it was nothing so inanimate as a key or a piece of forwarded mail. I shrank a little from striking the desk bell and so harshly shatter the dark silence, but did. Presently a door opened off one side of the room, spilling a shaft of light from the custodian-family's quarters, and a young señora came out to click on the ceiling fixture and question me. She was unsure of me, naturally, but pleasant. Doubtless she had come to think that no one—least of all an *extranjero*—would ever push his way through the garden's brambles to her door. Other voices could be heard in the family's room. "*Quién es? Pasa algo?*—Who is it? Has something happened?"

Señora summoned Esperanza, who came out wiping her hands on her apron, and despatched her to prepare Number 6. Away went Esperanza, her glossy braids flying, to find a key that would open Number 6, while I settled with Señora in advance (it was my custom to do so since, insomniac, I usually made my departure before the management wakened).

"*Sí señor, hay agua caliente . . .*" I am informed as I tender payment.

"*Yo lo sé*—I know—after seven!" I anticipate her instructions regarding the hot water, which it is unlikely I shall use anyway. I have come to view my dirtiness with the same appreciation and reverence in which the holy men of old held theirs. Dirt has a far more hallowed tradition than is normally attributed to it. Few hermits who had any principles at all would allow water to touch them. The basic rationale was, I believe, the mortification of the flesh—and none could be much more mortified than mine. But yes, there have been more splendid examples. There was St. Simeon Stylites, who spent thirty years squatting atop a Greek pedestal in prayer and meditation. Even I shudder to think of his condition at the end of the first week—speaking only from the sanitary view, of course—let alone thirty years! But it does give a contemplative man a goal to strive for.

Our room had the musty smell of Tut-Ankh-Amen's newly opened tomb. It was furnished with a small wardrobe that was not deep enough to allow its door to be closed if a suit were hung in it—but I had no suit and so there was no problem. A chest of drawers with loose, white ceramic pulls, and a home-made table between two beds completed the furnishings.

Honorio said he would visit the plaza and return shortly. It was unnecessary for him to say he needed a snack and a drop of something. *"Bueno,"* said I, and threw myself upon the mildewed bedding to seek relief from the headache my fever had added to the inventory.

It was impossible for me to sleep, and so of course I slept. It was that feverish sleep in which one hears the buzz of insect wings as flights of dragons; in which one's awareness is borne by a gossamer filament, making and breaking contact, alternately igniting and extinguishing consciousness. The contact at last burns short and there is blessed, timeless oblivion. . . .

28

A stirring in the room awakened me and I was in a strange, dark world. How long I had slept it was impossible to tell. My first thought was that the combination of fever and exhaustion, not to mention the accumulative effect of sleeping capsules and pain killers, had kept me blissfully unconscious all the night, through the next day, and now it was night again. Did I hear a rat? I had seen none in all the rustic places I had passed through, but my good fortune must have its limits. Was it the fabled *eslaboncillo* I heard scuttering along the floor beside me? This was the species of lizard of which Madame Calderón had spoken, which throws itself upon its victim and, if it is prevented from biting, dies of spite! I drew up my feet at the thought—cracking the clot on my hurt knee.

The noise seemed to come from something—or someone— making guarded movements. Honorio, of course! But why did my *compañero* move with such stealth? I held my breath and searched the dark. At last he had come to the decision to rob me before we reached the end of our journey! Only I in all Tlaxcala could identify him, and therefore he would need to seal my lips. How better could he do this than by opening my skull with the machete! How skillfully he had peeled that orange with it, so long ago. I crossed my forearms defensively over my forehead to ward off the impending blow and called with a subdued voice, "Honorio?"

"*Señor . . . Ha descansado?*—Have you rested?"

He turned on the light and stood at the foot of the bed, a

cool bottle of *cidral*—an apple-flavored *refresco*—in his hand. He had brought it up for me, knowing that, in my feverish state, it would please me.

"*Qué hora es*—What is the time?" I asked, squinting at my watch. It took a while before I knew that not twenty minutes had passed since I had dropped to the bed! Honorio was only now returning from his visit to the plaza.

Unaccountably revived by the brief nap—and relieved that Honorio still had not undergone the atavistic reversion that seemed to threaten each time I had a spot of fever—I returned with him to the plaza where I weighed the pros and cons of dinner before retiring for the night. I elected to feed the devil some of his own fire—a homeopathic style of treatment that has many champions among those who have survived it.

We found a little restaurant among the shops along one side of the square. At one of its three or four tables were two young women whose relative chic was another reminder that we were fairly within the capital's orbit. Hereafter, if we were to take our refreshment in earth-floored kitchens, it would be by choice and not necessity. (The choice was always there. No matter how close to Mexico City one may find himself, he can always find people living in the most squalid circumstances. Incredible slums exist no farther than an arrow's flight—to use a *conquistador's* phrase—from some of the world's most elegant hotels. In this, Mexico City is not greatly different from New York, London, Rome, Paris, Cairo, Madrid—it is quite unnecessary to name the other thousand. *En todas partes se cuecen habas*—in the most affluent societies, some must content themselves with beans.)

The *muchacha* took our order, unperturbed by Honorio's sibilated command for a preprandial beverage, possibly being herself of a family that communicated by hisses; and when dinner came, the *patrón* of the place—the proprietor—came with it. No doubt the girl had reported the arrival of a couple of *tipos raros,* a pair of customers that must be seen to be believed. He was a hearty fellow who accepted my invitation to sit down at table with us and was much interested in the *extranjero* who had selected his small establishment in which to dine. The story of my pursuit of the *conquistadores* delighted him and he expressed the opinion that if more foreigners—he did not have in mind foreigners as ragged and penurious as I—could be induced to follow, it might be good for business in Tlaxcala.

We have already observed that Tlaxcala's role in the Conquest is distinctive. The distinction lasted throughout the three hundred years of the colonial period. The Spaniards never forgot Tlaxcala had helped them win New Spain; nor did the Tlaxcalans themselves ever completely lose their sense of identification with the victors. The province—now a State—was granted a coat-of-arms by Spain, and after the Conquest there was considerable intermarriage between the two victorious allies, Spanish officers finding convenience and often even prestige in marital alliances with the landed Tlaxcalteca aristocracy. This minimized the fragmentation and dissolution of Indian properties that occurred everywhere else in Mexico. As a result, the Indian bloodline survived in somewhat greater dignity here than elsewhere in the empire, and a multisyllabic name or two, complete with "X's" and "Tl's" may still be found. The little city of Tlaxcala—it is *Tlascala* in the old Spanish writings, as you would expect—is the State capital. One can tell this by the presence of the military guard at the portal of the *Palacio de Gobierno.*

Tlaxcalans tend even to this day to speak with pride of their role in the Conquest, for they were, after all, enemies of the Aztec lords of Mexico long before the Spaniards came.

"Por supuesto—certainly the Spaniards came this way," my host said enthusiastically. *"Mire*—see, there across the plaza, through those *perus*—those trees with the red blossoms, just to the side of the bandstand—there is the first church in all Mexico, built by the personal direction of Hernando Cortés."

I could see a church, its stones bleached by the weather of centuries. The lights illuminating the plaza were reflected by the white façade, lending it the spectral air the night enhances in ancient places. We have not lost the habit of thinking of our hemisphere as "new," as if the New World has all its life still before it and that we must cross the ocean to brood upon true antiquity. Yet when this obscure church was built, Elizabeth I was queen of England, Ivan the Terrible ruled Russia. The Taj Mahal did not yet exist, nor St. Paul's Cathedral, nor the Palace of Versailles. The New World became very old as I peered through the plaza's foliage at Tlaxcala's parish church.

We did a turn around the square after dinner, but I was still too ill to enter into the Friday-night spirit beginning to brew. A bonfire had been started in the middle of the dark street on which our hotel was situated, and ragamuffins in makeshift costumes representing nothing that I could associate with events of Mexican history—though such association was surely there— howled around the blaze and prowled up and down the street carrying torches lighted from it. A few *cohetes*—firecrackers— were exploded under discarded tins in order to wrest the maximum decibel level from a minimum of ammunition.

Perhaps the most terror-inspiring noises came from a corner *cantina,* where such howling could be heard as to freeze one's blood, particularly the blood of a sick, exhausted traveler upon whose system the recent homeopathic experiment was beginning to have an adverse effect. Blood would be shed in the *cantina* before the night was done, I had no doubt; nor would everyone necessarily be secure outside the *cantina* either, for, from time to time, through its doors would fly a celebrant whose behavior, it seemed, was too antisocial even for the roisterers within.

As we made our way to the hotel gate, one of these outcasts —not an example of the world's most notably prepossessing creatures—staggered toward us on a tacking course. His eye was upon me, and I felt a great pessimism over the outcome of this meeting.

"*Amigo!*" he shouted, and enfolded me in an unfragrant embrace. I did not understand at first what he saw in me. Honorio tried to insinuate himself between us.

"*Amigo,*" I returned weakly.

He reached out toward my face and I dodged his hand. Honorio was now locked between us, so that the fellow had one arm around the two of us while he kept reaching for my face with the other. We danced around a bit, an awkward tango, until he succeeded in penetrating our defenses and managed to stroke my beard. He rubbed his own hairless cheek with an idiotic grin, reached again, and gave my whiskers another caress.

He wanted nothing more. He tipped his sombrero at me with a drunken flourish and wove his way back to the *cantina,* where there was the distinct possibility that he would hurl into the faces of his fellow celebrants the challenge to stroke, if *they* dared, the beard of Quetzalcoatl as *he* had done! Honorio and I, reaching our hotel, clanged shut the gate behind us and retreated gratefully to our room.

Abed, I stared at the ceiling waiting for sleep and marveled at the situation to which I had been brought by the fireside reading of a nearly forgotten book. It was sobering to consider how the wildest improbability could become fact. What sayer of sooth could have forecast my present curious circumstances?

Honorio, as far as I could tell, allowed no such ponderings to defer his slumber, and he lay there, in the deep sleep that comes only to those who enjoy a total innocence.

The night air was cool, for on reaching Tlaxcala we had entered the Valley of Mexico and were at an elevation of 7,400 feet. But the air in the room was oppressive. As I focused my attention on it, it became unbearable. Presently I thought I had discovered the cause. My *compañero* had been steadfastly by my side these many miles, but, more than that, he had marched patiently behind me during my unforgettable hours on horseback. Moreover, his boots had done yeoman duty carrying him forward without reck where the mules and burros of the *arrieros* had left their trail. The sturdy footwear, having earned their rest, were taking it where their owner had dropped them, on the floor beneath my nose. Quietly I moved the boots down toward the foot of the bed and resumed my quest for sleep. But the air continued oppressive, and I sighed and turned my back to what I thought had been the source. Now the odor was so vile, I knew that the rotting remains of some dead thing must be on the other side of the bed. I was essentially right: my own shoes lay fermenting there. Removing them as far as the limits of the small room permitted offered some relief, though not as much, to be sure, as if I had pitched them out the window.

It remains, now, to relieve the reader's curiosity on another intimate matter, which relief he is not likely to get elsewhere.

An Indian of the Sierra Madre Oriental wears a two-piece suit of underwear consisting of a "tee" shirt that can be buttoned at the throat in inclement weather, and close-fitting shorts that reach the knee. The stuff is a very hard cotton of extraordinary durability, as long as it is not washed too often. If a machete stroke does not damage it prematurely, therefore, it may well survive the wearer and do subsequent service keeping tortillas warm in the manner of a tea cozy. I offer no other justification for imparting this esoteric information, since any knowledge is its own reason for being, except to point out that one does not travel hard miles with an Indian as I had done without learning *something*.

My own practice on this expedition was to wash nothing, and to throw away my linen when it got patently offensive. Honorio, however, scavenged every scrap I discarded, and so my thoughts return from time to time to that assortment of socks and underwear, and how it may now be faring in those distant hills.

29

The *patrón* of the little restaurant greeted me with the affable *"Qué tal?"* of an old friend when we stopped in for breakfast early next morning—for Honorio's breakfast, that is. I limited my refreshment to a cup of chocolate, and even that lay uneasily on the stomach.

"Estoy enfermo," I said to my host sadly—"I am not well."

He was politely sympathetic as I ran down the list of ailments until the litany reached the intestinal problem and I expressed the opinion that a pig's foot had not sat well with me. He winced as if with pain. Disgust was there too.

"Hombré! Es una cosa muy india," he said, shaking his head. The translation, taking into account the look on his face, was that it had been a damned stupid *Indian* thing to do!

Honorio, who invariably lost his habitual taciturnity whenever he had the opportunity to explain me to his countrymen, contributed the information that the señor was beyond redemption, for he *must* try everything and then write it all down!

"But," announced the *patrón* after lecturing me gently on the advisability of leaving Indian things to the Indians, *"no se preocupe*—do not concern yourself. It is something we can cure."

This was good to hear, since paragoric was doing nothing for me. My friend recommended that I stroll over to the *Palacio de Gobierno,* where I would find in the inner courtyard a collection of murals by a certain Xochitiotzin, a contemporary artist, the pride of all Tlaxcalans. The murals would interest me greatly for, said he, Xochitiotzin had dipped the brush in his own blood to create them. When I returned, his señora would have prepared for me an *atole de avena.*

"*Qué es eso*—what is that?" I asked.

"A gruel of hot milk and new wheat—an ancient recipe."

"But hot milk has the contrary effect," I protested, "and the roughage of the grain will also aggravate my condition."

"*Tiene razón*—you are right," he said. "Separately you must by all means avoid them in your present state; but taken together they will cure you."

Since I could not conceivably get any sicker, I agreed to try the *atole* and, while his lady prepared the concoction, I wandered across a corner of the plaza to the Government Palace, into which the guard passed me with a languid salute.

The murals that covered the courtyard walls were truly formidable, and it would take a more pedantic scholar than I to notice if any detail of the Tlaxcalteca role in the Conquest, or any of its *dramatis personae,* had been omitted. It is a vivid tableau in which the epic contest lives as if, truly, the blood of the artist pulses through every scene.

If anything can be considered the "native," characteristic art form of modern Mexico, it is the mural. Her great muralists are well known—for their smoldering revolutionary spirit no less than for their art. Rare is the new building whose walls do not speak to the people of Mexico's history, of her pre-Hispanic dignity, her more recent revolutions, her aspirations—and even the illiterates find the stories eloquently told and the lessons clearly stated. The nature of the medium itself, the sheer size of these paintings, tell the people that the work was done for them, for their inspiration and enjoyment; they have no need to pad about quietly in subdued, expensive galleries to squint at miniatures.

The *atole* was waiting for me upon my return to the café and was served me in a large bowl. Not only was it delicious, but its warm smoothness was soothing—an experience I had not known the Mexican kitchen to be capable of producing. It was effective,

196

too. If Moctezuma had handed down his curse, his *ticitls* at least were considerate enough to hand down a remedy. The *atole* was *atolli* to the Aztecs who, since milk and wheat were unknown to them, prepared the gruel with water and corn to produce the identical effect. (Interestingly, the Somalis have traditionally used rice and sour milk to cure dysentery.)

My benefactor would take no payment.

"*Mira, señor*," he said, running his finger down the menu, "it is not listed."

The story is told that Samuel Johnson and Oliver Goldsmith were seated in one of their favorite taverns when a stranger entered.

"I hate that man!" said Johnson.

Goldsmith, startled, asked the good Doctor how he knew the fellow.

"I don't know him at all," Johnson replied. "If I knew him, I would love him!"

Xenophobes, heed the words of the irascible Doctor Johnson.

Tizatlán is a slumbering, pastoral village. "Village" is perhaps not the precise designation, for there is no concentration of shops or dwellings and, incredibly, no plaza. There are only a country *bodega* or two and a few scattered houses and barns strung along a dirt road leading out of Tlaxcala.

It was in Tizatlán that Cortés, his forces temporarily expelled from Tenochtitlán, caused to be built thirteen brigantines that were then carried, in pieces, eighteen leagues overland to Texcoco. There, reassembled, they were instrumental in recapturing the Aztec capital in—who would believe it on seeing, today, the aridity of Mexico City's environs?—a naval operation!

Tizatlán was "not far," the *patrón* had told me, and to my astonishment it was as he had said, in all a pleasant walk of but two or three kilometers. On the way, we crossed over a fresh-looking stream by means of a narrow suspension bridge that swayed just enough to induce an irresponsible *aventurero* to pause for a moment at its middle and say happily, "*Vaya* —look here now. It sways!" There are people who would complain to the town's aldermen and demand that such a bridge be reinforced—and we know what kind of grumpy spoilsports *they* are.

A few yards downstream, some chattering Indian women were scrubbing laundry on the glistening rocks. No wonder Honorio's underwear must be of sturdy stuff, for they pounded the wash with a will on the abrasive surfaces, laughing, dear aboriginal souls, as if life held no greater pleasure. They paused momentarily to return my "*'Diós*," then resumed their labor, giggling more merrily than ever for having been waved at by a foreign monster. I must remember, thought I, to offer a comment on the subject of attitude toward chores to our ladies in the electronic kitchens when they are peevish on laundry day. That should assure me a benediction or two to help see me to . . . to heaven.

We plucked a few *tunas* by the roadside, I, intoxicated by my victory, at least for the time being, over the intestinal difficulty; and we were at our destination as the sun sprang clear of the mountains on the eastern horizon. I sobered quickly upon learning we must now climb a hill—a small one, but any departure of the terrain from absolute level was now a severe trial to me. The encrustation on my knee that cracked and oozed. . . . But, as old Bernal Díaz himself has said, "Why should I repeat the old story?"

Atop Tizatlán's hill, my *patrón* had said, I would find the tomb of no less a personage than Xicotencatl (Xicotenga, to Díaz; and to Cortés, Sicutengal), discovered when a peon far gone in pulque—a *borracho*—boasted in Tlaxcala of a gold coin of curious mintage he had uncovered while scratching at the soil with his *coa*. The area where he found the coin was subsequently excavated, bringing the tomb to light. The story is commonplace enough so far—but wait! So noxious were the gases generated by the corpses of Xicotencatl's slain warriors buried there with him that to this day no way has been found to reach the remaining treasure deep in the subterranean warrens.

My friend's story is far better than the true one, so why believe the inferior article? If we were to worry the tale with facts, we would be obliged to consider that in pre-Hispanic times gold was not made into coins but into pretty ornaments and utensils for the nobility. The Indians did not use the metal as a medium of exchange in minted form. Instead, they kept it as dust, stored in turkey quills for convenience, and on occasion might barter it by the quill-full. As for the "tomb" itself, the ruins are those of a temple—a *teocalli*.

Nevertheless, they were of Xicotencatl's time—earlier, probably—for most of the monuments the visitor sees as "Aztec" date from a thousand years before the Aztec era. But Xicotencatl and his fellow "senators" had certainly trod the stones of this temple, and so must I.

The crumbling chapel has altars showing the god Tezcatlipoca in fresco whose colors survive still. I did not see the painted surfaces—they are below, in a kind of cellar, and my entry was barred by a large, tin, padlocked door—but I do not dispute the fact, for when it comes to paints there never was an ancient culture worth its salt that did not beat us hands down when it came to putting out a superior product. *Everybody* seems to have made paint better than we do—from the Egyptians to the Pompeians—and including, no doubt, the ancient Chinese. Makes one wonder about our vaunted modern technology each time we pay the housepainter.

The custodian of the place lived in an adobe house that by neglect had come to look very much a part of the ruins themselves, and yet was quite pretty, as vine-enlivened ruins have a way of being. Some turkeys—*guajalotls*—and pigs gave me noisy leave to knock upon his door, for I had a yearning to sniff Xicotencatl's gases for myself, but the custodian was not at home and his black-braided señora did not have the key to the padlocked tin door. The lady was quite calm about the existence beneath her feet of reeking specters, for she was hanging out the family wash over their heads!

A few paces away from the ruins, and sharing the hilltop

with them, stands the Church of San Estéban, built—parts of it, at least—in the sixteenth century by Indian hands under the direction of those padres who followed Cortés, to supplant the heathen temple. The church is a gaunt skeleton, its stones bare of plaster, its lofty arches vaulting over emptiness. Our footsteps echoed as we searched the cavernous interior, but we found none of the ornamentation of the kind such as usually typifies the baroque churches built by the Spaniards in the colonies. There were signs that services are presently held in a cranny of the place, as if in a great, cold cave rather than in a church. I am unable to say if San Estéban's should be classified a ruin from Conquest times or simply a very old and rundown church whose list of parishioners has dwindled. It could qualify as either. In the graveyard are some stones whose names time has erased, while others bear twentieth-century dates. That forgotten *hidalgo* upon whose stone I sat to scribble unforgettable thoughts in my notebook lest I forget them—does his spirit get on well, do you suppose, with the spirit of Xicotencatl? The two would have a deal to talk about if heaven is what it should be, where all misunderstandings are put aside and old foes—their phantoms, anyway—can reminisce together over the events of their brief, contentious sojourn on this planet.

A monumental misunderstanding it certainly had been that brought the Spaniards and the Tlaxcalans into collision here, in these same fields and on the very hills I scanned from amid the relics at Tizatlán—for if ever two factions needed each other as friends and allies, it was these two against Moctezuma.

When Cortés and his men had proceeded some six kilometers from Ixtacamaxtitlan (the reader will recall that I hurried on ahead by *camión*), they encountered two of their Cempoalan emissaries who had a story to tell that would have been disturbing to the ordinary run of men. The four messengers were seized and held captive by the Tlaxcalans, who had not been impressed by the fine Castilian letter Cortés had written, or even by his gifts (including a tall felt hat in fashion at the time—at least in the Old Country). On the contrary, the chiefs of Tlaxcala accused the Spaniards of being allies of "that traitor Moctezuma," and if they should be caught within this territory, the Tlaxcalans intended to vary their diet with brisket of Spaniard!

These two of the four emissaries had managed to escape, to warn the approaching Spaniards of the culinary preparations underway. We are not surprised at the reaction on the part of the audacious *conquistadores.*

"If it's like that," said they, "then, Santiago and at them, for God is on our side!"

How did it come about that the Tlaxcalans, traditional enemies of Moctezuma, had made the fateful decision to resist the Spanish advance—particularly since, to this point, nothing had happened to prove these bearded strangers were not gods? Well, for one thing, in dealing with men, to be a god is just not enough. Even a divinity had better show that his partisanship is slanted in the right direction. The Senate, so called, of Tlaxcala was well aware of the fact that these strangers had once or twice received favors from Moctezuma. They could not have advanced so far into the interior if this had not been the case. What the Tlaxcalans did not know, of course, was that the vacillating emperor ordered these favors—at Cempoala and elsewhere en route—in a torment of indecision, hoping vainly that the "gods" would leave him alone. Nor could the Tlaxcalans know that the Spaniards' acceptance of these courtesies only meant that, with their appetites so whetted, they had no intention of stopping until they had seized all of Moctezuma's Colhua-Mexíca. As far as the caciques of Tlaxcala were concerned, then, whether these were gods or men, they were new allies of their old foes.

30

The territory of Tlaxcala, though completely surrounded by Moctezuma's empire, had vigorously and successfully resisted domination by the Aztecs for generations; and the hatred that existed between them was all the more bitter because the Tlaxcalans and the Aztecs were of the same stock, spoke the same Nahuatl tongue, and followed the same religion and customs.

Cortés reported Tlaxcala's government as resembling "very much the republics of Venice, Genoa and Pisa"—high praise, to say the least, for the redskins encountered by the first Europeans in the New World. They had a Senate, composed of the caciques of four provinces: Topeticpac; Ocotelolco; Quiahuiztlan, and Tizatlán (in whose graveyard I now sat ruminating), and it was before this body that the poor emissaries of Cortés presented themselves—or, more likely, were dragged the minute they were caught—to announce the Spaniards' intention of entering their territory.

Something like the following deliberations now followed, which we know not only because some of the Senate minutes have been handed down to us, but because down through history statecraft has not varied so much that we cannot make our own deductions.

The opinion of Maxizcatin, the cacique of Ocotelolco, was that the Spaniards should be received courteously, particularly since, if they truly were the gods whom tradition said would one day arrive with Quetzalcoatl, they could not be stopped anyway.

Xicotencatl, the chief of Tizatlán, agreed it would be indeed a pious act to be hospitable to strangers, but not when they brought trouble. Besides, who could be sure these were truly gods? Better to stop them. Gods or men, consider what the effect of their presence, in alliance with Moctezuma, would be on the national security—and the corn market. Predictably, Xicotencatl's argument prevailed and the Tlaxcalans prepared for war.

Warned, then, by the emissaries that a less than cordial welcome awaited them in Tlaxcala, the Spaniards now advanced cautiously, with mounted scouts in the van. They had not gone far when the scouts reported a small party of Indians on the lookout, in plumed headdress, bearing fearsome clubs and lances tipped with wicked, flesh-tearing obsidian. Cortés ordered an attack in order to take one alive for interrogation, but the Indians resisted fiercely and five died. This skirmish was only a prelude, for now a host of Tlaxcalans, about four thousand who had been lying in ambush, leaped forward, showering the Spaniards with lances and fire-hardened arrows. Up came the main body of Spaniards with artillery, muskets and crossbows, and the battle raged until some fifty or sixty Indians had fallen. The Spaniards, too, felt their first sting: four wounded, one to die a few days later. Poor Pedro de Morón, forgotten soldier of long ago. . . .

At dusk the sides retired, and the Spaniards rested that night near a stream where they dressed their wounds with a dead Indian's fat and supped on passable dog. Guards were posted and sentinels both on foot and horse patroled the camp throughout the night.

The next day Cortés ordered a resumption of the march to Tlaxcala, ranks in good order and cavalry well rehearsed in the use of their lances. It was not long before two armies of Indian warriors in even stronger numbers came up to meet them with fierce shrieks and flying arrows. The extraordinary Don Hernán writes: ". . . I began to deliver my *requerimiento* in due form by means of the interpreters with me and in the presence of a notary. But the more I endeavored to admonish them and treat them with peaceable words, the more fiercely they attacked us.

203

Seeing, then, that demands and protestations were alike useless, we began to defend ourselves as best we could, and thus they continued attacking us until we were surrounded on all sides by more than a hundred thousand men, with whom we contended throughout the day until an hour before sunset when they retired. . . ."

Was it as self-defensive as all that, and the Captain-General so forbearing? It is interesting to search for nuances in the version of the same incident as his observant soldier, Díaz, tells it: ". . . He [Cortés] told one of our soldiers, Diego de Godoy, the royal notary, to watch what happened so that he could bear witness if it should be necessary, in order that we should not be made responsible at some future time for the deaths and destruction that might occur, for we had begged them to keep the peace . . . [but] the Indians became much more savage and attacked us so violently that we could not bear it. Cortés shouted: 'Saint Jago and at them!' and we rushed at them with such impetuosity that we killed and wounded many, including three captains. They then began to retire toward some woods where more than forty thousand warriors under the supreme commander, Xicotenga, were lying in ambush. . . ." A hundred thousand? Forty thousand? Well, there is no question that the fierce warriors of Tlaxcala were in such numbers that they covered the rolling fields, so serenely bucolic now as I looked out on them from the hilltop graveyard at Tizatlán.

A significant consequence of this battle was that the Tlaxcalans managed to kill a horse, pieces of which they took pains to distribute throughout all the province to show that the beast which had helped give the Spaniards their supernatural repute was but flesh and blood after all. To their own temple idols, the Indians offered the horse's shoes, the gift felt hat, and the letter Cortés had sent them! One may imagine that they handled these articles, the horseshoes particularly, with the same breathless, gingerly awe with which we handled the first rocks brought back from the moon.

That night the Spaniards made themselves secure in and

about one of the hilltop temples, and before sunrise next morning Cortés, taking with him his horsemen and a hundred Spaniards on foot, together with four hundred Cempoalans and three hundred friendly Indians whom he had persuaded to join him in Ixtacamaxtitlan, proceeded to burn down some five or six villages, each of about a hundred inhabitants, taking the latter prisoners. The taking of prisoners was the *Conquistador's* regular practice, since they were useful for carrying messages to the enemy, an assignment for which there were few volunteers. Woe to the messenger if the message displeased the recipient!

The Tlaxcalans responded to the burning of their villages by marching an army of more than 139,000 warriors against the Spaniards, ". . . so many," quoth Cortés, who made this interesting numerical estimate, "that they seemed to cover the whole plain." The battle raged anew and the next morning Cortés again took his horsemen, a hundred foot, and his Indian followers to burn down ten more towns, some of them consisting of more than three thousand houses. After all, he had conscientiously delivered that *requerimiento* in the presence of a notary!

It must be said for Don Hernán that he was no G.H.Q. hero. Believing it was God's work being done, he was in the thick of each battle, wielding sword and lance with the best—and the least—of his soldiers. And he takes full responsibility, in writing, for the destruction he wreaked—though Díaz, who wrote fifty years later and felt obliged to alter history a little (in the national interest, as it is said) blamed the Indian followers for running amok and burning down the towns.

And so the war went on, gathering momentum week after week, the Tlaxcalans so numerous, so reckless, so brave, too, that the Spanish crossbows, muskets, and cannon trained on the teeming fields and hillsides easily found a mark. Cortés could say early in the campaign, ". . . as we bore the banner of the cross and were fighting for our faith and King, God gave us such victory . . . that we killed many Indians without ourselves receiving any hurt." (He appears to have forgotten the soldier who had died after that first skirmish.)

But, as the days went on and the battles waxed, God, who is not all that partisan, allowed Spaniards to fall too; and the *conquistadores* buried more than one of their own comrades deep in an Indian's underground storehouse, so that the enemy should not smell the corpses and know that white men were common flesh.

Numbers are impossible to compute accurately, battlefield "bodycounts" being more for political effect than for the public's information, as any leader knows who courts the approval of the electorate; but long before Xicotencatl's initiative showed any sign of abating, Díaz records ". . . [The Spaniards] had lost forty-five men in all, in battle or from disease and chills, while another dozen were sick from fever, among them Cortés and the Mercedarian friar [the chaplain, Olmedo]. What with our labors and the weight of our arms we carried on our backs, and our sufferings . . . it is not surprising that we wondered how these battles would end, and what we should do and where we should go when they were done . . . and what would happen to us when we had to fight Moctezuma if we were reduced to such straits by the Tlascalans who had been described as a peaceful people. . . ."

With the satisfaction that comes from personal participation, I, too, record that the ailment afflicting these worthies was the identical one that had afflicted me. Let no one expect that I, who shared so much with Cortés, including the same disease and in the same territory, should be the one to deny the plausibility of metempsychosis. (I wish I could add that he had been cured with an *atole,* but we have the report of his chronicler that ". . . he purged himself with camomile"!)

If forty-five casualties seem few, we must consider there were four hundred *conquistadores* against the numberless warriors of proud and independent Tlaxcala. As for the seven hundred "friendly" Indians who helped to even the odds, Cortés must have had his uneasy moments over the steadfastness of that alliance.

Messengers—poor wretches—went back and forth. Cortés

communicated to Xicotencatl at Tzompantzinco—how still the hill is now!—that the Spaniards desired only friendship and peace. Xicotencatl replied with ten thousand warriors whose fire-hardened arrows fell "like corn on the threshing floor" and the promise that they would make peace with the foreigners by eating their flesh with *chiles* and honoring Huitzilopotchli with Spanish hearts and blood! Artillery, musketeers, and crossbowmen riposted, and so it went, day after day.

Then the Spaniards received word that Cichimecatecle was refusing to send further aid and manpower to Xicotencatl, the first clear indication that Tlaxcala's solidarity was crumbling. This welcome news was given support when fifty Tlaxcalans asked leave to come over for conference. Cortés received the delegation. But they were discovered by their actions to be spies, so Don Hernán ordered their hands cut off and sent them back to Xicotencatl. Men were almost as savage in the sixteenth century as they are in the twentieth!

The Tlaxcalans were now advised by their priests, who had analyzed the situation by studying the entrails of a sacrificial victim, that *teules* are vulnerable to night attack. But the *conquistadores* slept in their armor, their weapons at hand and their horses saddled; so the Indians met fresh disaster. In their turn, the priests were sacrificed for giving bad advice, a procedure not without its merit and highly recommended for moderating the zeal of those who pursue their brave deliberations while safely out of the line of fire.

The *conquistadores* had not expected so intransigent an adversary. The countryside continued to echo the war cries of Indians; the curses and prayers of the Spaniards; the crash of smoking ordnance; the groans of the wounded of both sides.

Then another hint of the struggle's finale, when some of the other caciques persuaded Xicotencatl to make a propitiating gesture. That stubborn chieftain agreed to send forty men ". . . with supplies of fowls, maize cakes and fruit, four miserable-looking old women . . . and incense." The women were for the Spaniards to sacrifice and eat! (The unkind description of them was a soldier's.)

But Cortés discovered that these bearers of gifts were also spies, so he picked seventeen of them, cut off the hands of some, the thumbs of others, and sent them back with the final ultimatum that the Tlaxcalans accept his proffered friendship or see the whole province become a handless society and worse.

This and the loss of his fellow caciques' support convinced Xicotencatl at last, and he capitulated after three weeks of the bloodiest, bravest resistance yet offered to prepotent European in the twenty-seven years of his presence in the New World. Cortés wisely—even affably—accepted Xicotencatl's explanation that it had all been a misunderstanding; that he had thought the foreigners to be friends of the cursed Moctezuma; and that it had been those low-life Otomies, a nearby tribe, who had killed the horse. From here on to Mexico, the Tlaxcalans would be the staunchest of allies to Cortés. Without them there could have been no Conquest.

31

We drifted back to today's Tlaxcala along the lane that led to the little suspension bridge. The highway to Puebla, thence to Mexico City, ran roughly parallel, but it was hidden by the hills and we could not see it or hear its occasional traffic as we walked; and I was able to enjoy without distraction that aspect of the country that is so much as it must have been in the days of Xicotencatl.

There had been more people around here then—Cortés estimated thirty thousand trading in the marketplace on a single day. Bigger than Granada, he said Tlaxcala was, and we will allow him his hyperbole, remembering that the *conquistadores* were coming upon real cities in a world they were the first to unveil.

The population has had ups and downs in the intervening years. By the early nineteenth century, Humboldt, the indefatigable measurer of everything his eye ever fell upon, was estimating that Tlaxcala had 3,400 inhabitants. Today there are some 7,500. There are probably not as many towns throughout the State as there had been when the Spaniards came—not with Cortés's penchant for putting them to the torch.

But the countryside still rolls gently, with here and there a hill into which an old hacienda is notched. There always was a good deal of corn grown in this region—*tlaxcali* means "corn house" in the first place—and the "Land of the Tortillas" continues still to be a pleasant patchwork of golden and green cornfields, punctuated, of course, with the spiky maguey. How beautiful and tranquil it is. Is there not virtue in repose?

"*Amigo,*" the *patrón* greeted me. "You have visited with our spirits, then?"

"I was much affected," I said. "It is with regret that I must now move on and follow the *conquistadores* to Cholula."

"*Adónde vamos con tanta prisa?*" he asked. The translated words, "Where are we rushing to," do not seem to convey his whole meaning. The *patrón* was expressing a general skepticism regarding life's currents. "You will, of course, not go without first a visit to the Convento de San Francisco?" He was not inquiring; he was delivering himself of an imperative. To say I conducted my expedition without a guide would be less than accurate. The *patrón* was only the most recent of a long series of "friendly natives" who had put me in the way of seeing the true essence of their country.

My first question was, of course, "*Está lejos*—is it far?"

"No, not far." The question really had been superfluous.

"And what is it about the Convent of San Francisco I must see?"

"*Hombre!*"

You have never known a Mexican's hearty friendship until he addresses you in this fashion.

"*Hombre!* It is the first church to be built in America."

"But that church across the *zócalo*—did I not understand you to say *it* was the first?"

"*Claro,* it is so."

"*Entonces*—well, then?

"The Convento de San Francisco was built even before."

"It was built *when?*" I asked.

"As to that, I cannot say. But Hernando Cortés himself baptized the *Senadores* there."

Of course! The fantasies that had beguiled me on those winter evenings, reading and dreaming of the Conquest of Mexico! Prescott had told how Xicotencatl and the other senators, to seal the bonds of friendship with their erstwhile foes, offered them the royal daughters—which tasty gift the single-minded Cortés declined in behalf of the company unless and until the Tlaxcalans gave up their false religion. He must have had charisma by the barrelful to hold the affection of his men!

Let us view the scene through a soldier's eye: ". . . The caciques [brought] five beautiful Indian maidens, all virgins. They were handsome for Indian women, and very richly adorned and each one being the daughter of a cacique, brought a maid to serve her. 'This is my daughter,' said Xicotenga to Cortés. 'She is a virgin. Take her for yourself'—he put the girl's hand in his —'and give the others to your captains.' "

Cortés expressed his thanks but asked that delivery of the merchandise be deferred until Tlaxcala gave up its idols.

"Don't ask us to do that," Xicotencatl said, his manner hardening.

Replied Cortés, "Our God and our King have sent us here to make you give up your idols, and cease to sacrifice human beings, and cease the other abominations you practice."

Xicotencatl looked somber. "Can you ask us to give up the gods whom our ancestors have worshiped? If we omit to make sacrifices to them, the whole province will rise up against us!"

Father Olmedo sensed trouble. "Don't press them, señor," he warned.

The other officers agreed with the chaplain—not a common event—and offered what they thought would be the best way out of the impasse. Just baptize the girls!

Father Olmedo, described by Díaz as an intelligent man as well as a theologian (the irony was unconscious—at least I think it was) considered the proposal a good one, discreet, and, in the long run, a more effective insinuation of the true faith into the volatile community. So it was done. The caciques agreed to allow a temple to be whitewashed and converted to Christian use, Mass was said, and the maidens were baptized. Their fathers and friends found the rites quite inspiring and not altogether incompatible with their own. Xicotencatl's daughter became Doña Luisa (but Cortés arranged to have her given to Pedro de Alvarado, for the Captain-General had another attachment of which we shall have more to say later). Gonzalo de Sandoval, Cristóbal de Olid, and Alonso de Avila, all gallant captains and favorites of Cortés, received one apiece, and it was not long before these gentlemen were witnessing the baptism of their fathers-in-law. The general populace followed suit, and Christianity came to Tlaxcala without the toppling of the idols *a la* Cempoala.

It is not recorded if a similar distribution of brides, baptized or no, was made to the enlisted men on this occasion. They foraged for themselves, no doubt, as they always did. But it must be said that their Captain kept them under firm discipline, and the respect and admiration the Tlaxcalans developed for the Spaniards within the three short weeks after the *conquistadores* stopped slaughtering them was truly extraordinary. This may be deduced from a statement by the historian Camargo that Prescott gives as a footnote, since it was significant enough to record, though too naughty for the Victorian to translate. I bravely translate: "[The Indians surrendered their daughters willingly, even enthusiastically] . . . in the hope that they would become pregnant and thus leave in Tlaxcala the seed of such brave and valiant men." (Camargo was himself an Indian, writing shortly after the events of the Conquest, so we may take this as a more objective view of his countrymen's position on these delicate relationships than if a Spaniard had stated it.)

Fifty years later, Bernal Díaz remembered it all as a beautiful affair. He kept in touch, too, and was able to hand down to us the following pleasant gossip: ". . . Pedro de Alvarado, who was then a bachelor, had a son by her [Xicotencatl's daughter, Doña Luisa] named Don Pedro, and a daughter, Doña Leonor, who is now the wife of Francisco de la Cueva, a nobleman and the cousin of the Duke of Albuquerque, who has had four or five sons by her, all splendid gentlemen. I should like to add that Doña Leonor is in every way worthy of her excellent father."

Here I must adjoin my own footnote. Pedro de Alvarado subsequently went on to become, in his own right, the Conqueror of Guatemala. When he died in 1541, it was Doña Beatriz, his *Spanish* wife, who succeeded him as governor—the only woman ever to head an American colony.

And while we are in this gossiping mood, let us say a word about the later career of another of the favored bridegrooms, gallant Cristóbal de Olid. About five years after the Conquest, while Don Hernán was busy consolidating Spain's territorial gains, he sent Olid down to Honduras to supervise matters for him there. Olid took a leaf from his chief's book and decided to set up his own little empire. But Cortés was no Velasquez. He sent an expedition down after his renegade captain, caught him, and had gallant Cristóbal de Olid decapitated. *Sic transit* . . .

32

Not all my infirmities could keep me from visiting the scene of these baptisms and weddings, where coy, timorous Indian maidens were handed over to the bearded, thunder-bearing demigods—and Christianity.

We had to climb another hill, of course. Temples were almost always on hills, and if suitably lofty locations were not available, the pre-Hispanic Americans built them—thus, the pyramids. We have already seen that the Spaniards routinely replaced each heathen temple with a church, and so it was that the Convento de San Francisco was situated atop a prominence overlooking the town.

The drive that rose steeply to the hilltop started from a point not far from the *cantina* where the pulque awakens memories of the old religion—on Friday nights. The *cantina* seemed subdued enough by day; it is by moonlight that tippling Tlaxcalans are moved to stroke Quetzalcoatl's beard. Now, as I explored a street or two in order to discover the drive leading up to the church, there were only sedate citizens abroad who responded to my *"Buenos días"* with a courteous tip of their sombreros.

The drive had been paved with cobblestones, in the pretty Spanish style we have seen so often, for the carriages that once delivered haughty *gachupinos* to services in colonial times; and we mounted easily to the tall iron gate of the cloisterlike courtyard. Crossing this patio, we then passed through the ancient wooden door of the church.

Entering here, one steps into the oldest operating edifice in all America—North or South. Consider that in 1521, when the Convento de San Francisco was built, Christopher Columbus himself had been dead but fifteen years. It would be twenty-two years until Copernicus published the outlandish theory that the earth went around the sun.

Who could enter this place and remain unmoved? For all its years, it is not a crumbling vestige of antiquity, but a living place. Whisper to the walls—they return no hollow echo. They have heard the voices of Cortés, Alvarado, Sandoval; of Xicotencatl, his princes and princesses. Their voices and the voices of all their successors through time whisper back at you their welcome into their company. One may read books, know history—yet remain a stranger to an epoch until he treads in this fashion the very stage of its events.

I moved down the nave of the unlighted church with only Honorio's silent company, but there was no sense of loneliness here; none of the feeling I had felt so often elsewhere, that I was in a haunted place. There is a continuity here, as if the votive candles flickering at the altars have been lighted by those wondrous characters whose footsteps I had followed and I may light my own flame from theirs.

The cedar ceiling overhead has looked down upon four and a half centuries of christenings, weddings, funerals—during which time the whole world of the West—our world—came into being, grew great and mighty, and became old and tired, too. The pulpit was the first to be erected in the Western Hemisphere. We wonder if Hernando Cortés, Marquis of the Valley now, ever fidgeted at the length of the sermons delivered there—but no, there could not have been a more devout parishioner than Don Hernán, who never set torch to a village in his life unless he first heard Mass.

But my brooding introspection was nothing until I went into a gloomy chapel in the right transept. There, in the shadows—one could easily pass it by—was the stone font at which, according to tradition and the marble plaque set in the wall, the chiefs of Tlaxcala were baptized. It is the first, the only place along the route I have followed where I have seen engraved the name of Cortés. The plaque reads like a routine announcement in a home-town newspaper:

". . . In the presence of *El Capitán* Don Hernando Cortés and his distinguished officers, Don Pedro de Alvarado, etc., etc., were baptized the Senators of Tlaxcala into the Catholic faith. Maxixcatzin became thereafter Lorenzo; Xicotencatl became Vincente; etc., etc., in the year 1520. . . ."

How hard to think of those fierce Indian chieftains as Lawrence and Vincent! Once the heads of state had accepted Christianity, the rest of the population came over wholesale, so that, for convenience all around, all the men baptized on St. John's Day became Juan, and on St. Peter's, Pedro, and so on, which explains why Mexican Indians all seem to be named Juan or Pedro.

The *conquistadores* spent about twenty days in Tlaxcala after Xicotencatl had capitulated—busy days cementing relations with their new allies. Great fellows, the Indians appear to have been. Prescott certainly thought so, though in describing their character the historian seems to be saying more about the New Englander of the early nineteenth century, as he saw him, than the Tlaxcalan of the sixteenth. He contrasted the geography of Tlaxcala with that of tropical Cempoala, coming to the predictable conclusion: ". . . although the bleak winds of the sierra gave an austerity to the climate, unlike the sunny skies and genial temperature of the lower regions, it was far more favourable to the development of both the physical and moral energies. . . ." (How did the Egyptians do so well in their "genial" African clime while Prescott's sturdy ancestors were huddled in their "austere" caves?) ". . . He led a life of temperance and toil . . . driven chiefly to agricultural labor, the occupation most propitious to purity of morals and sinewy strength of constitution. . . . Such was the race with whom Cortés was now associated. . . ."

I hope it was not such a life of temperance and toil that led to other habits which we, at least in our time, would describe in less glowing terms, for the Spaniards found wooden cages convenient to the temples in which men and women were held and fattened for sacrifice. While Cortés had agreed not to be too adamant, for the moment, about the removal of his hosts' idols, these cages he would not tolerate, and he released the poor wretches who thereafter kept as close as possible to their liberators for, while the caciques promised, after a proper scolding by Don Hernán, to discontinue this particular custom, they were likely, as honest Díaz observes, to resume the practice as soon as the Spaniards turned their heads.

I must have walked on the site of those grim cages during the days I spent in Tlaxcala, but there is no way now of knowing exactly where they had been located. For all anyone can tell, victims might have been fattened on the very spot where Señora prepared my soothing *atole*.

Cortés tied up the loose ends of his knowledge about the Aztecs during his stay here. The Tlaxcalans, old enemies of Mexico, could tell him much about the tactics, the weaponry, the fighting style he might expect. Cortés learned still more details about those drawbridges that controlled access to the golden city. He was briefed about the Aztecs' water supply ". . . a spring called Chapultepec, about a mile and a half from the city . . ." (today Chapultepec is one of the world's most delightful parks, at the head of the busy Paseo de la Reforma, a boulevard now—then one of those causeways connecting the island city to the mainland), and other information useful to prospective visitors, particularly visitors who recognized the possibility of a less than cordial welcome.

The chiefs tried every argument to dissuade the Spaniards from proceeding to Mexico, naturally concerned that a meeting between Cortés and Moctezuma might, in the end, prove disadvantageous to Tlaxcala. Their attempts to keep their new friends (and "in-laws") from marching on to Tenochtitlán were hardly less determined than those of Moctezuma himself.

Poor Moctezuma! He was falling to pieces completely, and the news that the foreign *teules* were now related by marriage to, of all people, his old enemies in Tlaxcala was the final cruelty.

The distraught emperor sent Cortés a message via six delegates and a cortege of some two hundred men, offering to pay him an annual tribute of gold, slaves, and goods—*anything,* on condition that the Spaniards not enter his territory because, he said, the land was sterile; there was a lack of food; and the Spaniards would be "inconvenienced." With these delegates Moctezuma sent Cortés a thousand pesos of gold and a thousand suits of clothes—of the latest Aztec style. Not only did the emperor underestimate Cortés; he was not, obviously, the greatest student of human nature. The Tlaxcalans, naturally, advised Cortés not to trust Moctezuma. The Captain-General scarcely needed the advice. In any case, if Moctezuma was offering to pay this price to influence him to stay away, Tenochtitlán was surely the place to go.

Back to Moctezuma sped the delegates with a kind and courteous message from the Spaniard. To have come so far and not salute in person the emperor, whom he truly loved? Cortés would not think of it! Let the emperor not concern himself with the scarcity of food; the Spaniards would take pot luck!

Back to Cortés came the harried delegates, with a cordial welcome, now, from Moctezuma, who could hardly count the hours until he (Moctezuma) embraced him (Cortés), for he (Moctezuma) had a matching love. He would arrange to have an escort meet the Spaniards at Cholula, so they might enter Tenochtitlán in the style suitable to their lofty station.

"Not in Cholula!" warned the chiefs of Tlaxcala. "Especially not in Cholula. The Cholulans are his henchmen, and the invitation is a trick."

"Don't worry," said Cortés, no doubt the most self-confident manipulator of men the world has ever seen.

How masterfully he played the dangerous, deadly game! The Tlaxcalans now insisted, if he must go, that they be allowed to lend their strength to his. Cortés, after making them understand he did not need them—the very quintessence of arrogance!—agreed to let a hundred thousand Tlaxcalan warriors accompany him (Díaz says ten thousand!), but only as far as Cholula, not more than five or six thousand to enter that city with him.

And so the little band of *conquistadores* set forth for Cholula, trailed by colorful legions of Indian warriors and *tamanes* (I thought I had been so clever in enlisting my single Honorio!), not one of whom had any love for Moctezuma—despite all the living hearts that sad potentate had conscientiously offered to the gods.

33

My *tamane* and I rose early, breakfasted with the *patrón*, bade
him farewell—another good friend who had given a heartbeat
to an ancient place—and were off ourselves for Cholula, as
anxious as Cortés to see that legendary city.

Cholula, in Aztec times, was one of the most important cities
in the empire, with about twenty thousand houses inside its
walls and as many in its suburbs; and four hundred temples, by
the Captain-General's own calculations. Appropriately, it was
considered the Holy City—the Rome of Anahuac—a great religious center even long before the Aztecs had risen to power.
In honor of Quetzalcoatl, who was supposed to have spent twenty
years here before disappearing into the East, the Toltecs erected
what is possibly the greatest pyramid ever built by man. It was
177 feet high, and its base 1,434 feet long—twice as long as
the Egyptian Pyramid of Cheops. This stupendous structure
covers forty-four acres. For these measurements we must thank
—but the reader has already guessed—Humboldt. It was a sight
that Cortés in his time, and I in mine, had to see.

But could it be expected that I, ever prone to collect wounds
and ailments, should have left that haunted hotel in Tlaxcala
without bearing with me some fresh and exotic stigmata to commemorate my stay?

I had not realized—such were the distractions of the injured
tendon; the scarred knee; the livid eruption of my skin caused
by the poisonous adhesive tape; the intestinal scourge; the fever
—I had not realized that the musty hotel bed had been a game

preserve. My legs and shoulders attested vividly to the appetite of its denizens. Well, I will wager that my predecessor *conquistadores* were bug-ridden too.

The day loomed hot and the temperature of the *camión* corresponded, so I scratched for the seventeen or so miles to Puebla —which is the way Cortés would surely have gone if there had been a Puebla in his day.

This city, now a great and bustling metropolis of some 300,-000 (its own boosters say a half million), was founded in the sixteenth century by the *padres* who arrived with the Spanish colonists after the Conquest. It is one of the few cities in Mexico that does not have pre-Hispanic foundations, having been built instead on the site of a few scattered Indian huts on the outskirts of Cholula. In the course of these few centuries, the upstart city has so far outstripped the old religious and commercial center Cholula had been that the latter is now the drowsy suburb.

Puebla's avenues are broad, its streets thronged with people, automobiles, trucks, and buses. Its seventeenth-century baroque cathedral is even larger than that of Mexico City. Puebla is an industrial center, too, with textile and earthenware factories and automobile assembly plants (Volkswagen)—but still has its *zócalo* surrounded by porticoes, lest anyone forget he is in Mexico. The city has its own proud history, independent of that associated with Cortés. Mexico remembers her share of figures in her past as villains, Cortés and General Winfield Scott ranking quite high among them, but Puebla's favorite miscreants are probably the French. The forts of Loreto and Guadalupe, scenes of the victory of a small Mexican army under General Zaragoza over the invading French on May 5, 1862, are maintained as museums commemorating that successful struggle of the Mexican people against foreign intervention. While the French returned with reinforcements the following year and took the city against gallant resistance, in the end they were expelled, poor Emperor Maximilian was executed, ambitious Empress Carlota went mad, and Mexico had a Lincoln of her own in Benito Juárez. *Cinco de*

Mayo—May 5—is now a street sign in virtually every town and city in the Republic.

My first impression of Puebla was a gloomy one. We left the *camión* at the terminal and set out on foot to find the smaller bus station, in another part of town, from which the local buses depart for Cholula. I cannot say how many miles we walked—a different kind of hike than I was used to—along a heavily trafficked street that had no end, tenanted almost exclusively by the makers and vendors of coffins. (I had checked in Coatepec, in a moment of depression, to learn that funerals for the lowly in Mexico start at about $32.00. This includes rest for the deceased in a proper plot for a stipulated number of years—seven, I think—and then into the common bone pit with him.)

We strode grimly on through rushing tides of *Poblanos* as if we were indeed bearing down on Moctezuma (else why the machete at Honorio's hip?), and, perspiring, gained the bus station. Presently we were speeding along a straight road, the driver sworn to knock down at least one pedestrian to maintain his daily quota, burros counting only half a point.

The road is flat on this way to Cholula. Looking back, one can still descry Orizaba, receding, while closer to us another mountain, Malinche, rises to keep us company nearly all the rest of the way to Tenochtitlán, as its namesake kept the Captain-General company.

It is appropriate at this point to speak of languages. *Claro*—clearly, that is to say—this odyssey of mine, on which I spent pennies instead of dollars; dined in country kitchens instead of sterile tourist traps; drank like the proverbial four hundred rabbits of Centzon Totochtin with great, amiable rascals instead of sipping effeminate concoctions at prices a tourist is expected to pay in some pitiful imitation of a *yanqui* cocktail bar; tramped dusty, happy miles through the unspoiled countryside, chatting pleasantly with good friends whose paths may never cross mine again, yet whose memory shall give me companionship forever—*claro*, all this would have been denied me if I had not possessed at least a little of the language. I possessed a good deal more, needless to say, after I had marched awhile, than when I started. In keeping with my habit of voicing only moderate opinions, I do hereby declare that anyone who has the time it takes to drink his two beers daily at the local pub and does not take half that time to learn a neighbor's language is a cretin for the delights from which his poor judgment excludes him. There! I almost broke a promise never to preach.

What of Cortés, then, in this strange world? How was he to deal with the *Xitl's* and *Xochtl's* of the place? How was he to ask the way to Teziuhyotepezintlán and Tlatlauquitepec and Ixtacamaxtitlán when his holy mission and his very life depended on his ability to do so? That itzcuintepotzotli he encountered in the woods might be edible—or it might be rabid. It was imperative that he have help with the language, Piltzintecuhtli only knows!

How fate delivered to the *conquistadores* an interpreter—an interpreter of *parts*—is a story too romantic and too implausible for fiction.

The earliest written reference to the existence of this remarkable person is found in the second letter written by Cortés to the king, in which he tells his version of what has come to be known as the Massacre at Cholula. He notes that the Cholulans are becoming quite cool toward the Spaniards, providing them with "indifferent" food; and the chiefs of the city are staying away from him. ". . . And being somewhat perplexed by this," he wrote, "I learnt through the agency of my interpreter, a native girl who came with me from Putunchan (a great river of which I informed Your Majesty in my first letter), that a girl of the city had told her that a large force of Muteczuma's men had assembled nearby, and that the Cholulans themselves, having removed their wives, children and clothes, intended to attack us suddenly and leave not one of us alive."

A native girl! Cortés makes only one more reference to her in all the voluminous five letters by which he reported the details incident to the acquisition of New Spain. This was five or six years later, when he was expanding the empire southward.

Writing in his fifth letter about some local chieftain who denied that any Spanish captain had delivered a *requerimiento,* and was therefore insisting on his own sovereignty, Cortés said, ". . . the captain [who delivered said *requerimiento*] was none other than myself, which he might verify by speaking with the interpreter, Marina, who has ever accompanied me, for it was in Tabasco that I had been given her, together with twenty other native women. . . ."

It is a sly bit of indirection Cortés tries in that first reference. "There was this girl . . . you know . . . from the river. I told you about her . . . well, I told you about the *river,* didn't I?"

But it was as he said. The girl was one of several given to the Spaniards on an earlier stop along the coast after coming down from Yucatán. There had been a battle near Tabasco, and the Spaniards had won. The girls were gifts to the victors from the defeated caciques.

On an even earlier stop, at Cozumel, Cortés had found two shipwrecked Spaniards who had somehow survived among the natives. These were Jeronimo de Aguilar, who had been a seminarian; and Gonzalo Guerrero, a sailor. Aguilar was overjoyed at being rescued, but not so Guerrero. "Fray Aguilar," he said to his fellow Crusoe, "I have my native wife and three children. I'm a big man here." Guerrero's face had been tattooed, his ears pierced for ornaments, and he found his jungle life congenial. He pointed to his children—this Adam of modern Mexico— and continued, "Look how handsome they are. Just leave me some of those beads for them. I will tell them my brothers from the Old Country sent them. You go back. I'm staying." So Aguilar joined Cortés as his interpreter, while Guerrero went back into the jungle to increase the mestizo population.

But the only Indian tongue Aguilar spoke was a Mayan dialect of Cozumel. As the Spaniards sailed down the coast, they moved into country that spoke another language, Nahuatl— the language of the Aztecs—and Aguilar's usefulness was considerably diminished. Then came the slave girl, Marina, who spoke both Nahuatl and Mayan. The chain of communication

224

was now complete—from Cortés to Aguilar to Marina. But it was not long before Marina spoke Spanish, and Aguilar passed out of history.

How did this bright Indian girl come to be a slave—a disposable commodity—in the first place?

She appears to have been of a well-to-do family residing in Painala, in the province of Coatzacoalcos. When her father died, her mother remarried and, in order to secure the family inheritance for her son by her second husband, she sold the girl to some itinerant merchants. By a convenient coincidence, the child of one of the family's slaves died just at this time, and Marina's mother was able to publicize the funeral as that of her own child.

The itinerant merchants—*pochtecas*—in turn sold Marina to the caciques of Tabasco who, as we have seen, gave her and twenty other girls to the Spaniards.

Marina—the Indians called her Malinche—was first given by Cortés to one of his captains, Puertocarrera—but she was too nobly endowed a young lady to remain long in any echelon less than top rank, and soon became not only the Captain-General's interpreter, but his confidante, advisor, and most effective advocate in his dealings with stern, sometimes dangerous native chieftains. It was through Doña Marina's mouth that Cortés spoke—even to Moctezuma. So closely did Malinche and Cortés come to be identified by the Indians that Cortés himself became known to them as Malinche.

Doña Marina is regarded differently by different people. Madame Calderón, who, for her Victorian time could have given our modern "liberated" ladies a lesson or two in spriteliness, speaks of her as ". . . Cortés' Indian Egeria, the first Christian woman of the Mexican empire." (I am inclined to believe she meant first in rank and quality, rather than merely first in time.)

Prescott was Calderón's contemporary, but was more the scholar than he was the man of the world. He admits Marina's qualities, her uncommon personal attractions (just hear him, "ahem"), her "generous temper." ". . . Her knowledge of the language and customs of the Mexicans, and often of their designs," he said, "enabled her to extricate the Spaniards more than once from . . . perilous situations." Regarding her accomplishments as linguist, he makes this delightful commentary, more original in his time than in ours: ". . . It was not very long . . . before Marina, who had a lively genius, made herself so far mistress of the Castilian as to supersede the necessity of any other linguist. She learned it the more readily, as it was to her the language of love."

Prescott was not the type to intend the word-play—but in fact Doña Marina did become mistress of the Capitán, as well as of his language, and had a son by him, Don Martín Cortés, who in later years was involved in one of the earliest shows of discontent on the part of the *criollos,* the Spaniards born in Mexico, toward the *gachupinos,* the prideful colonists born in Spain.

"She had her errors," says prissy Prescott, "but they should be rather charged to the defects of early education, and to the evil influence of him to whom in the darkness of her spirit she looked with simple confidence for the light to guide her. . . ." Echoes of an era when sin was sinful!

Díaz has nothing but good to say of Malinche—and we are grateful to him for a most melodramatic sequel to the story. Years later, when Doña Marina was established as an important and famous lady, she chanced to be in Coatzocoalcos with Cortés on a mission, and fate brought her mother and half-brother on their knees before her. Hear Díaz, who knew the family: ". . . When Doña Marina saw her mother and half-brother in tears, she comforted them. . . . She told her mother that when they handed her over to the merchants from Xicalango, they had not known what they were doing. She pardoned the old woman and gave them many golden jewels and some clothes. . . ." What a woman was Malinche!

Today, Malinche's name is a Mexican's term of contempt for those who have truck with foreigners at the expense of their own country, or who affect foreign ways.

Another necessary postscript: About a year after the fall

of Tenochtitlán, when things had settled down, who should arrive from Cuba but Doña Catalina, the wife of Cortés. She had been a merchant's daughter, he an army captain, and Doña Catalina's brothers had welcomed young Cortés into the family with shotguns (or whatever they used on reluctant grooms at the time). With Doña Catalina's unexpected appearance, Cortés gave Malinche to a gentleman named Juan Jaramillo, and the two were married at Orizaba. They appear to have lived happily ever after.

If Cortés, too, lived happily ever after, it was not with Doña Catalina. Within weeks of her arrival she died under conditions that gave rise to rumors that he had dispatched her in favor of a lady more suitable to his own newly acquired rank. More likely she died from the "vómito," as newcomers to Mexico frequently did in the old days. Nevertheless, one of the most popular subjects in the sensational periodicals, to this day, is the story— with "new and awful disclosures"—of how Cortés murdered his first wife. One may still see the house where he is said to have done the deed. It is now the police station in Coyoacán.

With Malinche's mountain outside our window, perhaps we have not wandered too far afield with this story of a girl who had a flair for languages.

34

It is said that the Spaniards built a church on the foundation of each and every temple in Cholula, and that three hundred and sixty-five churches now stand—one for each day of the year. I did not count them—though I have no doubt Humboldt did. A flat-faced individual who had sat near me in the *camión*— he had been noncommittal all his life but decided to make an exception in my case—said I could believe it if I wished, but as far as he knew, there were about forty. "More than enough," he said.

Soon I was climbing another mountain, muttering and moaning, my knee suppurating, my small resistance to pain entirely spent.

It is not at all true that persistent exercise hones the body and rejuvenates the limbs. Exercise piles ache upon ache. One becomes weaker, not stronger. Of life's delusions, one of the saddest is that a man can keep the suppleness of his youth by doing kneebends, breathing in deeply through the nose and exhaling through the mouth, and other such idiocies. I did these things scrupulously all my growing years and had a heart attack the earlier for my pains. The wiser man (I exclude myself from the category, having delayed my reflections on this subject until rather late in life) keeps his mortal frame in proper harmony with his years by reading good books that open up for him new worlds undreamed of; and maintaining a lively interest in the stars so he will know how contemptible are his worldly concerns. The odds are he will live no longer and no shorter a life than the chowderhead who does push-ups and takes cold showers when he needn't.

I *had* to climb this hill. A number of placards, starting at Cholula's plaza, indicated that by following them we would find the Great Pyramid. The signs continued to point the way through three or four nondescript streets until we were face to face with a wooded, hilly park, so there was nothing for it but to enter. It turned out to be a rugged climb, up a steep and twisting path overhung with the branches of trees and wild growths of shrubs and flowers. An enormous sheep blocked the path at one point. I had not realized how huge an animal a sheep can be. A little shepherdess would have been hard put to handle this one with her crook! The beast gave way stubbornly when I pushed its rump, and we continued up the hill.

I met a seedy, uniformed, civil-servant type who appeared to belong to the mountain.

"I am looking for the pyramid," I said. "The signs have guided me this way. . . ."

"It is so." He gestured toward the higher reaches of the hill.

We climbed on. It was like striving once again for the escarpment of Xico Viejo. I came upon a skull.

"What creature was this?" I asked Honorio, moving the thing with my toe.

"Caballo, puede ser," he said, shrugging. My God! Was I involving myself, in my condition, in an expedition where horses could expire and return to dust?

We reached the top of the hill at last. A substantial church stood there—La Virgen de los Remedios. It looked out upon Cholula, where the domes and campaniles of smaller churches were everywhere—and here and there a factory's chimney, too, to profane the storied holiness of "The Rome of Anahuac."

Behind the church of Los Remedios, I could see in the distant southeast shapely Malinche still with us in her dress of shimmering green. But to the west, seeming not so far away that it would not echo back a shout, was a breathtaking sight indeed. I was gazing upon what many consider to be the world's most beautiful view, almost as Cortés had seen it. ". . . Eight leagues from this city of Cholula," he said, "there are two marvelously high mountains whose summits still at the end of August are covered with snow so that nothing else can be seen of them. From the higher of the two both by day and night a great volume of smoke often comes forth and rises up into the clouds as straight as a staff. . . ."

Popocatépetl—the "smoking mountain." He is quiescent now, though he seethes within himself. A puff of cloud perched on his head like a sombrero worn at a debonair tilt. Beside him rested Ixtaccihuatl—the "white woman," whom the Indians hereabouts call, with equally descriptive legitimacy, *la mujer durmiente*— the sleeping woman. As the eye rests on her silhouette, one fancies he sees her bosom rise and fall. I know I did. The *campesinos* can tell much about the prospects for their crops from the varying length and décolleté of her snowy gown that, by its melting, influences the rush of water down the *barrancas*.

Tenochtitlán lay on the other side of "Popo" and his *mujer,* and it was over the saddle between these two sublime spouses that the *conquistadores* at last entered the Aztec capital. From this hill on which I stood I could see the route along which they had marched as on a great relief map. The countryside is green with dark pine forests that crowd the feet of the volcanoes, with here and there a lacuna of gold where the maize ripens. A few towns or villages dot the scene—Zacatepec; Huejotzingo (the Guajocingo whose men joined hypnotic Cortés as he proceeded toward his rendezvous with Moctezuma); Ixcalpan (today, Calpan). . . . With this panorama at my feet, I had followed (and survived!) the length of the Cortés trail.

But back to the search for the Great Pyramid of Cholula. We were on top of the hill and there was no place else to go. The only edifice here, imposing enough, to be sure, in its cypress park, but no colossal heathen monument, was the church of the Virgen de los Remedios. There was no other hill or building within this vista large enough to obscure from view a pyramid twice as large as Cheops. A mystery . . .

We started wearily to descend the mountain in order to make further inquiries. In a clearing just off the descending path a couple of Indian girls lolled prettily under a bowed and venerable oak.

"*Permiten sacar un foto, señoritas?*—may I take a picture?" I asked.

"*No, no,*" said they, and hid their faces.

"*Para una revista*—for a magazine," I fibbed.

"Then you most certainly may not," was the firm reply.

I continued down the path, a new regard grown in me for two Indian maids who scorned to be seduced by dubious offers of fame or fortune. Halfway down the hill we met a party climbing up, a guide from Mexico City with his two customers in tow—the first Yankees I had seen since departing from Vera Cruz a lifetime ago! There was no mistaking my compatriots.

"Americans!" I cried, quite excited, expecting them in turn to fall upon me with equal pleasure.

"Humph!" grunted my countryman. His face was red from his exertions and I allowed him a moment to get his breath.

"There's only a church on the top of this hill. No pyramids or ruins." I was anxious to share my veteran's wisdom. "But the view is fantastic. . . ."

"Stay close to the guide, Ruthie," he said, ignoring me. They edged past on the narrow path to continue their ascent. Possibly, when they had thought about the encounter awhile, one might say to the other: "Do you suppose the tramp was an American?" And the other might reply: "Don't you believe it. These people are sneaky." Their guide would agree, having almost certainly considered my few words gratuitous, and he would tell them: "Ah, señores, you are wise not to engage yourselves with these vagabonds. We have, I am afraid, a long history of banditry, and you do well always to make your arrangements with a travel service of repute. Tomorrow I shall take you to breakfast at Sanborn's, where you will have orange juice, waffles, and real American coffee, and then, as you have chosen Number Three, we go to the Floating Gardens of Xochimilco. This will give you plenty of free time for shopping in the afternoon. I have a friend who deals in . . ."

As for the long history of banditry—it is so. When the Mexicans succeeded at last in winning their freedom from Spanish colonial rule, thousands of heretofore downtrodden peons, having flexed their muscles, knew what to do when nothing better came along. They took to the road, superb horsemen now (how their ancestors had marveled at the four-legged Spaniards!), and the tradition of the *bandido* was born. By the mid-nineteenth century, the Puebla road had earned fame as the Robbers' Highway. To this day, Shrove Tuesday is celebrated in Huejotzingo as the anniversary of the capture of Agustín Lorenzo, the *bandido* who made his headquarters there and sallied forth, the scourge of the Mexico-Puebla diligence.

In more recent years, Porfirio Díaz controlled the *bandidos* by the then unique stratagem of swearing them in as police— the *rurales*—so that what they did they now did "legally" and in behalf of the Government.

I have already confessed my nervous expectation that some scoundrel with a sense of the romantic—and with a coincidental need for a peso that a gringo surely needed less than he—would waylay me in the sierra's solitude. Why not? It is done in our own cities every day even without the justification of swashbuckling tradition.

But, as we have seen, I ambled along, sanctified perhaps by my beard—or my smell—meeting only kindness.

We reached the bottom of the hill and began to circumnavigate it until we found another civil servant in threadbare uniform.

"We have seen nothing of the great pyramid on the hill," I complained.

"I will be your guide, señor," he said, "and you will see all."

I pleaded exhaustion and said I would look him up later, when I had rested.

"*Bueno,* you may find me just there, by the *entrada* of the tunnel into the pyramid," he said. "There the tour begins."

It dawned on me as it has dawned on the reader long since. I had already climbed the pyramid.

Excavations into the hill's interior show that this prodigious monument, so large that it was known as Tlachihualtepetl—the "man-made mountain"—is built up, layer upon layer, of bricks and plaster. Time and weather have eroded its surface (with help from generations that used it as a stone quarry), and the wind-blown dust of ages has settled upon the pile so that oaks and cypresses now grow out of it, and sheep graze on it, and Indian lasses picnic upon it. The church of Los Remedios, dedicated to the Virgin Cortés carried during the Conquest, the Patroness of the Spaniards in Mexico (as the Virgin of Guadalupe is the Patroness of the *Mexicans*), stands in the place of the Teocalli of Quetzalcoatl—which fact is almost as much an indication of the size of the pyramid as was the circumstance that I should have stood upon its peak, unaware the Great Pyramid was under my feet.

35

Puebla and Cholula are listed in the tour brochures as day trips out of the capital. Encountering the American couple, therefore, however minimal its satisfaction to the soul of a wanderer lately emerged from the lonely mountains, was evidence that my trek was approaching its end.

To some small degree I was able to share the anticipation of those *conquistadores* of old whom I now knew as men of flesh and blood, having swallowed dust with them on their own trail. While I had not felt the sting of heathen arrows nor, happily, attempted to give any hostile native a taste of my cold steel, I knew something, at any rate, of the Spaniards' earthier pains, their fatigue, their pleasure upon discovering unscheduled hospitality, their intercourse with assorted caciques.

That catalogue of ailments by which I have fulfilled an obligation to keep the reader current gave me added reason to celebrate my arrival before the volcanic sentinels of Moctezuma's city. I have reached strange cities before, but never with the sense of delight, expectation, and relief that the little agonies of this *wandervogel's* experience had earned me.

We walked back to the plaza, my mind as usual set to churning over past events. The place has a less frantic air about it now than on that early dawn in the autumn of 1519 when the pavement ran with blood and the air was rent with screams. Opinion has shifted somewhat, and "infamous" finds its way into the accounts of that day.

The facts seem clear. The *conquistadores* had been three days in Cholula, the first day or so receiving adequate if not outstanding hospitality from the inhabitants. We have already heard from Cortés himself how this hospitality was abruptly withdrawn, and how Marina, in a conversation with a lady in town, learned that a plot was afoot to surprise the Spaniards and destroy them. Gossip over the teacups (or cups of chocolate) never had more dire consequence.

When Cortés heard Marina's story, he quietly sent his Cempoalans to see what they might turn up. The scouts came back to him with disturbing news.

He now confronted the ambassadors of Moctezuma, who were in Cholula for the purpose of arranging his escort into Tenochtitlán. They declared the emperor innocent of any involvement in such a plot. Cortés knew better but, master of men and intrigue, he feigned acceptance of the ambassadors' protestations of innocence —with a view toward facilitating later dealings with Moctezuma.

Cortéz then interrogated the caciques of Cholula, who could not deny the evidence uncovered by the Cempoalan scouts: of camouflaged pits in which sharp stakes were set; of arms and stone missiles readied on the *azoteas*—the flat rooftops of the houses on the roads along which the Spaniards would pass; of the presence of twenty thousand Aztec warriors on the outskirts of the city, with whom the Cholulans had been detected in furtive communication. The caciques, astounded by the thoroughness with which the foreign *teules* knew everything, lost all presence of mind and could deny nothing. They placed the blame on Moctezuma who, they said, had commanded this desperate ploy.

Cortés listened and made his decision, which was to go far beyond merely countering the plot of the moment. It would impress upon Mexico for all time the Christian's determination and purpose.

Let the Cholulans provide him with a thousand *tamanes*, he told the caciques, and the Spaniards would depart next morning, for they would not stay where men were capable of such deceit.

Let the nobles and officers meet with him in the plaza to hear his farewell.

At dawn, after deploying men and cannon at all points of egress from the plaza, Cortés addressed the Cholulans:

He knew their every thought, he said. What had he done to them that they should behave with such treachery? At this very moment their kettles were ready—let them deny it—with salt and pepper and tomatoes to spice the cooked flesh of the Spaniards! Yet all he had asked of them was that they give up their false idols, their obscene habits, their sacrifices. He knew very well that just three nights ago they had sacrificed seven Indians—children—so that their false gods would assure the success of their treachery. He would now show whose god had the better credentials!

A musket shot was the prearranged signal, upon which ". . . we fell upon the Indians in such fashion that within two hours more than three thousand of them lay dead . . . in which task I was helped by some five thousand Tlascalan Indians and three hundred from Cempoal. . . ."

Thus, coolly, Cortés reported the affair to his king. Throughout the subsequent three hundred years of Mexico's colonial history, the emphasis was ever placed upon Cholulan "treachery." To this day, an echo lingers in the Mexican's own playful rhyme: *"Mono, loro o Poblano, no se tocan con la mano*—monkey, parrot or Pueblan, do not touch them with your hand!"

It is completely unfair, of course. One man's treachery is another man's strategy. Says Aeneas, "Courage or cunning—who cares which, when dealing with the foe?"

Here is how a local author states the case: ". . . In Cholula, out of fear to be attacked, the invaders made, by surprise, one of the most infamous and unhuman slaughters. The news of this monstrous butchery spread rapidly through the empire, contributing to make the march of the army, from there on, a military parade, since nobody dared to oppose their advance. . . ."

It was the fact. When news of the holocaust in Cholula reached Moctezuma, he resigned himself with sad finality to the termination of his reign over the lands of his forefathers and prepared to receive the *conquistadores*.

Indignant, we stare at the sober-faced people moving across the plaza, so bowed by history; and we meditate upon the horrors their race has borne. We are tempted to lay a heavy liability upon the heads of their conquerors—and the conquerors of any place or time who have ever moved into the land and way of life of other peoples.

But we must wonder whether the subjugation suffered by the Mexicans was not brought upon them by themselves—that is to say, by their own leaders. Without suggesting the least sympathy for the missionary spirit, that great presumption which has often motivated zealous men more to their own advantage than to that of their charges, we nevertheless cannot pass over the one great blot on the pre-Conquest Mexican's own escutcheon. In Cholula alone, on Quetzalcoatl's pyramid, as many as six thousand sacrificial victims were offered up annually. At the dedication in the capital of a temple to Huitzilopotchli in 1486, a procession of victims *two miles long* is said to have been led up to the sacrificial stone. All sources, whether Spanish or Indian, while not always agreeing on precise numbers, agree that many thousands of men, women, and children were sacrificed each year, and on particularly holy days might be lightly roasted *first,* before being killed! Motives can explain but not excuse these enormities. The Conquest was only the instrument; ancient Mexico fell by suicide. The sadness in the Indian face is due more to the low esteem in which his own leaders held him throughout his early history, than to anything the Spanish conqueror ever did.

There never was such a country as Mexico to set one brooding; and if the reader believes I am overly susceptible, let him take knapsack and pen on the trail of Cortés and test for himself his own discipline.

Fortunately, there was always one alternative we could depend upon to lead our thoughts into less melancholy channels— lunch. This one would be our last on the march, for if all went well we would be in Tenochtitlán by evening—but no eating place could we find around Cholula's historic plaza. I wondered where the guide would take the *Yanqui turistas.* Into Puebla, probably, where civilized ham and eggs and "safe" instant coffee were no doubt to be had. But Honorio had labored too hard toting my pack up the pyramid to be subjected to any unnecessary delay of lunch.

We searched in vain among the *bodegas* that ringed the plaza and extended the quest into one of Cholula's busy side streets where, impatiently, I looked in on a cobbler's shop for help. The *zapatero* stopped what he was doing (I almost said he lay down his last, the Virgen de Guadalupe forgive me!) and stepped out of his shop with me, making that odd (to us) "go-away" gesture that all the world except Americans employs to indicate "Come here" or "Come this way." He led us down a short alley behind the shop to a small, hidden patio, off which was a room furnished with a linoleum-covered table and some benches. A woman came out from some other sanctum—her kitchen, I suppose— and replied to our request for lunch by enumerating a number of dishes she was equipped to offer on this short notice.

They were all familiar enough to me by now, the *chiles rellenos* and tacos; *huevos ranchero; chorizos; biftec;* beans; and so on. Honorio acquiesced to every one of them. I asked if she could prepare an *atole de avena* for me, but she regretted that this would involve considerable time. I contented myself with chocolate. Even behind the shoemaker's shop the chocolate was a delight and, as I sipped, I watched the parade of homely Mexican dishes appear out of the kitchen and disappear into Honorio. There is an economic advantage in being ill, I thought, wondering what the half-dozen courses and accompanying beverages would cost me.

While Honorio was satisfying his every heart's desire, no doubt for the first time in his life on this grand a scale, a shoeshine boy entered and offered me his services in that mechanical way that foresees rejection. Reject I did, for my Huggly-Pugglies were of ersatz and untreatable "suede." He headed for the door with the air of Mexican resignation for which, depending on the historical preconceptions of which we have spoken, he may thank either Cortés or Moctezuma. I can recall the gypsies of Granada who are not so docile and will grip their victim's ankle to prevent his escape as they lecture him on the necessity of keeping shoes tidy.

The *muchacho* had reached the door.

"Pssh!" Honorio stopped him short, and with princely mien commanded the boy to do his boots. They were of the tall "western" style and bore the dust of many kilometers, not to say the traces of considerable zoography.

The boy looked them over with the view of offering an estimate of costs before committing himself contractually. Then he measured me with his sad eyes to assure himself the business risk had a banker's backing.

"Proceed," I ordered, fascinated by the cool manner of the monster I was creating out of the simple *chamaco* I had brought out of the sierra.

The job done, I grandly allowed the *muchacho* to keep the change from the peso I paid him—the equivalent of eight cents. I turned then to the more complex financing of the lunch. All of six pesos, it was! I gloated malevolently over a vision of those compatriots who had spurned me on the pyramid and who, I suspected, would be paying sixty pesos for their lunch—with none of the fun of embracing the very soul of Mexico.

36

Malinche, we know, was able to expand her Spanish vocabulary all the more rapidly because it was to her "the language of love." My own fluency, such as it was, evolved from a more heterogeneous collection of causes. As I carried no dictionary, I paid a price, usually in fatigue, to acquire each new word.

One comes to believe he knows a language passing well until he needs to purchase some such trifle as a paper clip ("el clippo" will not do!) and must resort to drawing sketches of the item. The product of this hasty art is more often than not a hieroglyph —not always decipherable. I have seen a salesgirl's eyes light with understanding—and construe my depiction of a rubber band as a tortilla. Then, by dint of increased linguistic effort—consisting mainly of raising my voice—she understands at last, and brings out a leather belt.

The word that cost me most dearly to learn was the Spanish for "safety pin." I had tried in several villages to purchase some, in order to prevent my wallet from falling out of an inside coat pocket when I slung the jacket over my shoulder—but without success, a failure I must partly ascribe to poor art work. My sketches of this domestic item suggested eternal Priapus. A young lady in a shop in Jalapa, where I made my earliest attempt at such a purchase, had been so scandalized (at least she had seemed so to me—*honi soit qui mal y pense*) that I, awkwardly stammering some exculpatory explanation, only ended in convincing her I was a ribald scoundrel.

When we reached Cholula, so many kilometers later, I still

had not managed to buy a safety pin. I thought of this as I threw the coat over my shoulder as usual, taking care to notice that the billfold was still in its place when we boarded the *camión* for the short ride back to Puebla. When the fare-taker came through, I peeled off the paper pesos and carefully replaced the wallet. The pocket gaping open, my thoughts reached back warmly to the countless mountaineers, *campesinos,* drunken Tlaxcalans, swarthy Zempoalans—all who had permitted me to pass through their hills and villages with wallet inviolate.

On the Puebla road my eye scarcely ever left that money. During those intervals when I shed the coat, I did not neglect to give my pocket the instinctive pat that told me the wallet was still there. In the *camión,* I folded the coat on my lap, and when we reached Puebla and dismounted, the feel of the little lump in the cloth still reassured me.

We began to walk along the street of funerals, but to gain the main bus terminal where the final leg for Mexico would begin required that we plow through throngs of Poblano citizenry as if through fallow soil.

I had reached the limit of my endurance. Here there were no grassy roadside meadows where I might recline to refresh limb and spirit. The jostling city masses—civilization—vanquished me and I capitulated. I managed to conjure a taxicab out of the mass of traffic, and we climbed aboard, even knowing that the terminal we sought must be just around one of these teeming street corners. It was.

"Gracias a Dios—Thank God!" I said, reaching into the coat pocket to pay the fare. The wallet had flown.

It had fallen to the floor of the cab, of course. No, it had not. It had slipped behind the seat cushion, then. No, *tampoco.* I had tried Providence beyond her patience.

Did ever a traveler into the past so literally ape its incidents? In Zempoala, the affair of the Fat Cacique; in Tlaxcala, the dysentery of Cortés himself; in Cholula-Puebla, treachery! ". . . *Mono, loro o Poblano.* . . ."

The driver was sympathetic. "You must not be upset, señor."

He was unable to keep a note of pride from creeping into his voice. "Our pickpockets are artists."

I showed him the gaping pocket. *"Mira!"* I cried. "It was here —here, only this moment past." He believed me, he said. "And now you must come into the station with me," I said, "for I must change a traveler's check to pay you."

The checks were in my trouser pocket—I clapped my hand to it and found them safely there.

"No vale la pena, señor," said the driver, with a shrug, "— it is not worth the trouble. But hereafter you must fasten your pocket—like this . . ." His fingers pantomimed what I had been unable to sketch. ". . . You see?—with a *seguro."*

Puebla's main bus terminal is a kind of Grand Central Station, where *camiones* arrive and depart each minute from and toward every compass point. Long queues of Mexicans—they are gloriously picturesque with no intention of being so—form at each departure gate, through which they are fed like raw materials to be emulsified and sprinkled all over the country. Mexico had no viable network of roads until fairly recently—well into the present century—to link her towns and provinces; and with their coming the population seems to move compulsively, on bus, on burro, or on foot. Move it must. Continuously the lines move out and the travelers swarm, chattering cheerfully, into the buses. Laconic by nature or habit, the roll of wheels, unknown to their ancestors, does wonders for their humor. One imagines that if the buses were suddenly to cease running, the gathering pressure of humanity would burst the terminal building in one ineffable explosion, filling the sky with baskets, sombreros, and golden infants.

A new horror was in store for me when I took my place on the queue before the ticket window. Each traveler before me engaged the ticket seller in complex debate, the transfer of funds being an action not lightly undertaken. But who am I to mock my fellow travelers? No debate was more prolonged or frustrating than my own when my turn came at last. The ticket seller would not accept my check. I must cash it at the bank, he told me. But it was Saturday afternoon and the banks had closed.

"And therefore they will be closed tomorrow, Sunday, as well!" I cried.

"*Lástima*—a pity," the agent said, but there was nothing he could do. It was the rule. The queue pressed impatiently behind me. I had no ready money and no will to pass the weekend in this restless city, with Tenochtitlán there, on the other side of Popocatépetl—my goal within tantalizing reach.

"I will go to the police," I said, when no other argument, no other pleading or cajolery would prevail. "I will tell them that the Mexico I love, and that I found to be so good and kind, is not Puebla, which robs an *extranjero* and then treats him so!"

"The police is having his *merienda*—his tea, in the *restorán* upstairs. Hurry, señor, and you may catch him." So much for the ticket agent's concern when I threatened to paint his city in its wicked colors.

I found the police officer seated at a luncheon counter, his considerable girth bristling with cartridges, his pistol ready for a fast draw on such as me. His brown face hovered low and intently over his soup, and his spoon moved in its short arc with a cadence my sad tale was impotent to stay.

I was not seeking recovery of the lost purse—my purpose was loftier than that. It was to persuade a minor bureaucrat to depart so short a way from the rules as to accept a perfectly valid check. The officer, perhaps moved at last by my strange accent, promised me the limits of his great influence, but first he must finish his meal. Honorio stood beside me, the knapsack at his feet, as I sat fretting at a vacant table. The policeman consumed his soup and then turned his attention to his beans and *chiles,* eating them ever so slowly so he would not lose a modicum of their savor—and maddening me in the meanwhile.

"See, then," I said to Honorio bitterly. "Now I cannot even buy a *refresco* to pass the time."

I regretted my words as soon as they were spoken. Now, for

certain, seeing he had nothing further to gain from me, he would abscond with my kit, clothes—my notes. . . .

Disappear he did, to return shortly with a *refresco* for me—*his* treat. My weariness had caused me once again to unjustly apply my white man's standards to an Indian.

The officer at last finished refreshing himself, hiked up the sagging weight of his armaments, and, sucking his teeth, returned with me in full constabulary majesty to the ticket office—where the bureaucrat gave him even shorter shrift than he had given me. No cash, no ticket. It was the rule. Discomfited, the officer shrugged his regrets at me and left, possibly to pistolwhip some unoffending orphan.

By now my presence and plight were known among the terminal's hangers-on, and a sharp young fellow, predatory instinct guiding his steps, approached me with words of commiseration. He would help me if he could, he said.

"I need only to purchase bus tickets for me and my *muchacho*," I told him. "Here is a traveler's check worth a hundred and twenty-five pesos. I will sell it for a hundred."

"M-m."

Honorio felt obliged to help, and whispered confidentially to the sharp Poblano, "The señor is honorable—truly. He is my personal friend. . . ."

This testimonial came close to ruining the deal, for Honorio and his machete did not combine to inspire confidence. But I had generated interest, and my additional offer of a calling card to support the protestation of honesty clinched the bargain. The Poblano gained two dollars on the transaction, and I was solvent for the moment.

37

After having taught the Cholulans their grizzly object lesson, the Spaniards stayed on a week or so longer to assure the survivors of the massacre that it had all been for their own good! Incredibly, they succeeded. We have already seen how effectively they had been able to accomplish this in Tlaxcala.

It is provocative to consider how our pioneers to the north succeeded only in leaving enemies in their wake well into the nineteenth century, that enmity persisting, indeed, to this day. In what way did these two civilizing agencies, these disseminators of Christian culture, differ in their approaches to conquest?

The levels of bloodshed, both in Spanish and in "Anglo" America, perhaps stand equal. There was, however, an ingredient in the Spanish attitude toward the Indian missing in the North American's. The redskins who bit the dust in such generous profusion up north were counted as weeds, to be eradicated from God's good earth. Those who bit the dust at Spanish hands— "*comieron la tierra*," to borrow an appropriate phrase out of another context—were considered at least in principle to have souls, thanks to the efforts of the Dominican and Franciscan friars who accompanied the *conquistadores,* or who followed them after the Conquest. Whatever horrors the Indians suffered on earth under the Spaniards—and there were many—they were allowed the solace of believing that heaven was open to them —if they followed the conqueror's rules. Thus, terror was counterbalanced by salvation. While the Spaniards destroyed the Indian's civilization, they left him with the hope of *something.*

The *conquistadores,* even while treasure-hunting, sincerely believed the Almighty was literally, not figuratively, a party to the proceedings. Their brutality was therefore a paradox. On the other hand, the Indian of North America was left utterly bereft even of the subtle comfort of hope. Rather than paradoxical, his conqueror's brutality must be considered to have been absolute.

In either case, if there is in fact justice in the hereafter, heaven help the conqueror!

Cholula having been pacified, then, Cortés "accepted" Moctezuma's invitation to call, and the Spaniards set forth on their final march in an odyssey that, in the end, made the New World European.

Cortés and I had a choice of routes. One of these would take us over the saddle between Popocatépetl and his *mujer durmiente.* This road, when the Spaniards came to it, had been rendered impassible by freshly felled trees, hastily transplanted magueys, and rocky debris. Cortés duly noted that the sap still oozed from the fallen timber.

The other road, which skirted the volcanoes and passed to the north of Ixtaccihuatl was—and is—clear, level, and the obvious choice, as the ambassadors of Moctezuma took pains to point out. Don Hernán of course opted for the blocked road and commanded it be cleared.

Fearing no lurking Aztec warriors waiting to ambush me, I took the route Cortés had spurned, and I am prepared to give numerous and perhaps convincing reasons for making this decision. Instead, I will limit myself to the truth of the matter, which is that by this time I was unable to negotiate the height of my bed without wincing from pain, let alone climb the saddle between the volcanoes. The *Flecha Roja*—the express bus—makes the run from Puebla to Mexico City, speeding through the cool forests of fir, oaks, and pines that cover the undulant plain, with none of those frequent pauses for refreshment that characterized the rural *camiones.* We boarded the bus at Puebla, consuming sixteen of my one hundred pesos to purchase tickets from the inflexible *empleado* and, comforted not by the assumption, but by the fact that Cortés would have done the same had he been in my contemptible shoes, within little more than an hour we arrived at the place where Tenochtitlán had been.

No, Tenochtitlán, the fabled city, is no longer here, shimmering in the sunlight on its island in the broad lake. The lake itself is long gone, of course. Instead, a great metropolis rises from the dried lake bed—a splendid city, in every way deserving its reputation as the Paris of the West. I take nothing away from Mexico City when I say that my Mexico—my Tenochtitlán—is in the sierra, in the dusty villages, in the lush and fragrant jungle. My Tenochtitlán is in the dreaming of it, and in the striving to reach it.

Nor is the capital of the Republic a city to be caught in without funds or documents, so I lost no time in seeking out a taxi driver to speed me to the Buenavista Railroad Station where, it will be recalled, my bag was stored. In that luggage were my "city" clothes; my portfolio of credit cards (they might be useful now, though they could not have purchased me a tamale in the hills); and my airline ticket home. Quetzalcoatl! Suppose I had been carrying these with me on Puebla's street of the funerals. . . .

The cab driver, when I had found one willing to talk with the likes of me and my *compañero,* turned off his taxi meter and announced that he required thirty pesos to take me to the station not ten minutes away. This was far more than I had paid for the unlimited hire of the horse at Ayahualulco, including the boy in bondage to me. The cabby stipulated the price without apology, take it or leave it. Since I needed desperately to reach my luggage, I took it. A wanderer quickly forgets the temper of the cultural centers, but is as quickly brought up to date.

At Buenavista Station, the functionary who faced me across the baggage counter had the power to destroy, but not the authority to reprieve—the very stuff of nightmares. There was my bag, in plain view on a shelf behind him, but he would not relinquish it to me unless I produced the baggage check. But the check was moldering, together with my passport and other documents, among the banana trees and coconut palms of *tierra caliente,* where I dearly wished I could have been at this moment.

It is only fair to acknowledge that, blackened by sun and grime, my beard two weeks untended, my trousers torn and stained with blood and other miscellaneous oozings, I did not present the appearance of one who could credibly claim ownership of a suitcase.

If I could describe the contents of the baggage, I asked, would that not establish the case a priori that the property was mine?

"Puede ser—perhaps, señor. But can you certify who you are?"

"I have a dozen credit cards proclaiming me the cream of a materialistic society. I have licenses to drive automobiles and to fly airplanes, to take books out of the *biblioteca,* and to fish in the reservoirs of North America."

My powers were not as broad as all that, but the situation demanded the most imposing arguments.

"Bueno. Permit me to examine them."

"They are in the suitcase."

"You see my problem, then, señor."

"Yes, and do you see mine?"

"Señor, it is you, not I, who claims without proof."

We jousted in this fashion until I remembered that the suitcase key should be in one of my pockets. I paled to think of my problem if I had lost the key as well and should need to persuade this Cerberus to let me break the lock.

"Mira—look!" I held up the key. "If this will open the lock, will it not prove the bag is mine?"

The *empleado* wanted with all his heart to say "No" to this, but even he had not the obstinacy to deny my logic.

"And furthermore," I said, remembering the sesame that probably would have spared us all this fencing in the first place, ". . . here is my calling card, on which I will sign my name in your very presence."

The key fitted the lock, the portfolio displayed a polychromatic array of cards that must indeed have been dazzling to an *empleado* who could not read what they said—and I had possession of my property at last.

At the cost of all my remaining Mexican currency, another taxi driver agreed to take us to the Hotel Geneve, and a few minutes later Honorio and I stepped into the lobby of that genteel establishment to the mortification of the management.

I had fond memories of the Geneve. During an earlier visit to Mexico the hotel's staff could not do enough for me, and I had spent a relaxing, if sedate week in the company of maiden schoolteachers and librarians "doing" the *Ballet Folklorico,* the pyramids at Teotihuacán, and the like. The Geneve had been my pleasant headquarters in the heart of that area known, because of the concentration there of fine hotels and affluent tourists, as the "Golden Triangle."

It had been a satisfaction to be able to call out to the driver so distinguished an address and know, moreover, that although I had no reservations anywhere in the capital (I could make none, with such an itinerary as I had followed), I would not find myself stranded without accommodations in a great and unforgiving metropolis. This was a presumption of which I was soon disabused.

"We have no rooms available." The room clerk spoke in English, and his tone was final.

"But I had no reservations on my last visit here and you were able to accommodate . . ."

"Please, sir. It is impossible." The clerk looked worriedly at the lady guests who crowded the desk for their messages and room keys.

"Will your cashier change some traveler's checks for me, then?" I asked, forcing him to lay bare in its entirety the hotel's fickle nature. With what unctuous benevolence they had extended this service to me before, at the rate of exchange that made the courtesy worth the while!

"Guests only," he said—as I knew he would.

"What am I to do, then?" I asked, in mixed anger and despair.

"Try the Monte Cassino—around the corner," he said. The Geneve, it seemed, had no great love for the Monte Cassino.

"*Vámonos,*" I said to Honorio, whose machete was, in truth, a strange ornament in this ambient of elderly maidens. Patiently he strapped on the knapsack and we dragged ourselves to the Monte Cassino, my expectations not overly sanguine, for this latter hostelry was a good deal more modern than the prim Geneve and would have even greater delusions of grandeur.

I was mistaken. They granted me superb accommodations, whose splendor impressed me no less than they did my poor Honorio; and their *cajero* readily cashed my checks. The room of course cost more per day than I had spent in the entire previous eight, but at least until the reaction set in I was uncomplaining, and accepted the new scale of disbursement as a fact of my natural world.

We ascended to my room, Honorio and I, to perform a difficult little ceremony. It was farewell to a surly and silent, but unpretentious and faithful *compañero.* If I had seen a latent arrogance in him, it was perhaps an arrogance that hinted at a forgotten pride. In the future, should anyone chance to see me gazing meditatively at an Olmec head on display in some museum, let him know that I see Honorio and all his ancestors in the sculpture.

How does one settle accounts with such a comrade? In the thick-carpeted, plushy, and mirrored hotel room we faced each other. There was no question that if I were continuing on to the Pacific coast—and beyond—he would stay with me. But the journey was now over.

I counted out his hundred pesos. A hundred pesos had been the bargain, to Perote. He showed neither pleasure nor displeasure. I told out a few more to see him home by whatever transportation he chose. The transaction, as far as I could see, still neither elated nor depressed him. I then dug into the knapsack and handed out its contents to him—a few socks and items of linen; toilet articles that—Quetzalcoatl is witness— were scarcely used; a ball of twine; a handful of plastic toys I occasionally gave out to children in the villages; a vial of perfume such as I doled out to the daughters of caciques when the satyr instinct briefly surfaced.

How was he to carry these assorted treasures? I held out to him the knapsack itself, and a small light flickered in his eye at last. I now handed him my jacket—a good sports coat it was, though it did not look it at the moment. If his mother did not flagellate it with the rest of the family laundry at the brook, he should cut quite a figure in Xico, once he had persuaded my old friend the judge that he had not robbed me in the sierra. Having gone so far, I slipped off my trousers and gave them to him also, feeling certain the torn leg would be soon mended. This ecdysial performance over, I dressed in my accustomed city clothes, whereupon our manner seemed to cool toward each other. Honorio became terribly polite. For my part, I gave him some words of advice, perhaps even patronizing him, for he was in my world now. He need not be a *matante de puercos* any longer, I told him, for he, too, now knew the Cortés trail. Let him take my card—I would sign it for him—and present himself at the *Turismo* in Jalapa, where I was well known (an "Act" commemorates my visit there). Perhaps other *extranjeros* might one day wish to make this journey, and I would attest that he, Honorio, would be a trustworthy *compañero*. And he must study the nature guide he had rescued from the *chipi-chipi*. His knowledge of such lore would impress the people of the *Turismo*.

It would surprise me greatly if he followed my advice, but it had all been such a strangely fulfilling experience for me that, in my vanity, I assumed it should have moved him too, and would alter his life in some small way. *Quién sabe?*

I saw him to the hotel lobby where we shook hands somberly and bade each other "Adiós"—and Honorio was swallowed by the honking traffic of the city streets.

The bar of the Hotel Monte Cassino was crowded with American tourists, a young, attractive crowd. It was perhaps to provide them with a touch of exotic color—the "old prospector" sort of thing—that I had been so readily accepted as a guest

251

(under the tacit condition that I bathe). I sat at the bar sipping a margarita and listened to the chatter of my compatriots a little while. One couple spoke of their first *corrida*—the bull-fights. "An abomination," the husband said. His wife, instead, had been thrilled by the spectacle. Psychologists say that a wife sees the bull as her husband and relishes its destruction! Another couple would be leaving for Taxco tomorrow on Tour No. 23. The husband was out of temper because the guide had not been able to guarantee that all restaurants would be air-conditioned. The wife spoke of the silver she would buy. "There is a place you must be sure to look up," advised another. "You can get hamburgers there—almost as good as we have in St. Louis."

I felt terribly lonely. . . .

The following books have helped me find my way through both the geography and history of this story:

The Conquest of New Spain
Bernal Díaz; Penguin Books, Baltimore, Maryland.

5 Letters of Cortés to the Emperor
J. Bayard Morris translation; W. W. Norton & Company, New York, New York.

The Conquest of Mexico
W. H. Prescott; J. M. Dent & Sons Ltd., London, England.

Life In Mexico
Frances Calderón de la Barca; Ediciones LARA, Mexico, D. F.

Historia Antigua de Mexico
F. J. Clavijero; Editorial Porrua, S.A., Mexico, D.F.